Praise for **WHISTLE STOP**

Also by George Galt:

A JOURNEY THROUGH THE AEGEAN ISLANDS

WHISTLE
STOP

A Journey Across Canada

George Galt

FAWCETT CREST • TORONTO

A Fawcett Crest Book
Published by Random House of Canada Limited
Copyright © 1987 by George Galt

ACKNOWLEDGEMENTS

Excerpt from "I've Tasted My Blood." Reprinted from *I've Tasted My Blood* by Milton
Acorn by permission of the literary executor for Milton Acorn, "the People's Poet."

Passage from Harold Horwood copyright © 1987 by Harold Horwood. Reprinted by permission of the author.

Excerpt from "From Colony to Nation." Reprinted from *The Collected Poems of Irving
Layton* copyright © 1971 McClelland & Stewart Limited by permission.

Excerpt for "Three Day Rodeo Planned," May 14, 1985. Maple Creek News. Reprinted
by permission.

Excerpt from "The New Canada," by Bruce McCall. Copyright © 1985 Bruce McCall.
Originally published in the *New Yorker*. Reprinted by permission.

Excerpt from "Watching Trains." Reprinted from *Being Alive* by Al Purdy, copyright ©
1978 McClelland & Stewart Limited, by permission.

Excerpt from "Bridge to Greenville, Mass Valley." Reprinted from *Man at Stellaco River*
by Andrew Wreggitt, copyright © 1985 Thistledown Press, by permission.

Excerpt from "The Circus Animals' Desertion." Reprinted from *The Collected Poems of
W.B. Yeats* with permission of A.P. Watt Ltd. on behalf of Michael B. Yeats and Mac-
millan London Ltd.

ISBN: 0-449-21860-0

Canadian Cataloguing in Publication Data
Galt, George, 1948–
Whistlestop: a journey across Canada

ISBN 0-449-21860-0

1. Galt, George, 1948–   —Journeys—Canada
2. Canada—Description and travel—1981—
I. Title

FC75.G35   1990   917.1′04647   C89-095492-5
F1017.G35   1990

For my mother and father

IN TORONTO ON A CLOUDY MORNING IN MARCH I boarded the train for Montreal. I would stay there a day or two and then move on across the country. Montreal, where in the 1960s my taxi driver pointed to a turbanned Sikh on Ste. Catherine Street and said to me in French: "You see that Jew? More and more are coming here. They have money. They want to own everything." Earlier in my life a mail box near my father's house was blown up with a bomb planted by radical separatists. The priests in the seminary down the road swore violently at me one day when I rang their bell while on a neighbourhood errand. I had spoken in English.

Enjoying an early supper with old friends, I missed the Halifax train and had to stay another day. The next morning I went into Montreal's Musée des Beaux Arts on Sherbrooke Street. A picture came to mind of my mother on the grand staircase inside. She is wearing a long ball gown, a pearl necklace, and long white gloves that cover her forearms. Beside her a Westmount friend has a diamond tiara on her carefully curled hair. My father is standing stiffly by, smiling, and looking a little uncomfortable in white tie and tails. I would have watched by the front door at home as he donned his long black coat and white silk scarf. They all look very young. This is the highlight of their social season, the Museum Ball. It would be about 1959, just before life in Quebec began to

change. In those days the city's Anglo-Scottish elite regarded the Montreal Museum of Fine Arts as their own
heirloom. They sat on its board and its committees, gave
money, bequeathed paintings, took a proprietary interest
in the building and its operations. Their hold began to
slip in the 1960s when Québécois culture was searching
out every possible venue for self-assertion. Now, controlled by the provincial government, the museum has
become an emblem of Quebec's cultural reconquest of
itself. And a *memento mori* of that lost Anglo era which
was ending as my own life began.

Inside, the building looked different, altered by expan-
sion and renewal. Once it had been more tomb-like. The
mummies and Egyptian statuary. The marble Venus. A
collection of religious carvings from old Quebec, dark
and morbid. The heavy, faded tapestries. I used to be
drawn by the people as much as the artifacts. Children
were admitted free, though a sign urged you to drop
money into a round metal well in the lobby. My little-
boys' school was close by. After classes I would sometimes wander through the capacious exhibition rooms
looking at single women with bright red lips and elegant
hats, magnetic yet unattainable. I used to think something should happen in the museum, some encounter,
some revelation. People didn't really come there just to
examine things on the walls, did they? The place seemed
to be concealing its true nature and knowledge. I was
always disappointed as I left.

Now I could see a display of early twentieth-century
posters. The show included several railway images. Four
posters advertised the London and North Eastern Railway. A bright red beach umbrella on a blue sea background stood beside a man and woman in 1925 bathing
costumes that covered them from shoulders to knees.
A second poster pictured The Flying Scotsman locomotive speeding into the night under a full moon. "Dine on
the LNER" said another, with an elegantly set dining table poised right on the rails. Trains have suggested this

kind of romantic escapism for more than a hundred years. Although trains were the harbingers of the electronic age—the first telegraph-line networks in Canada, as in many other countries, were strung by railway companies along their tracks—railways belong to an earlier time. Trains were the premier high-tech products of the Victorian era, and capitalism's love affair with railway development did not last much beyond World War I. The established passenger runs remained profitable for another generation or two, but new technologies began to catch the imagination and money of the twentieth century: first the automobile, then the airplane, then satellites and television transported the sedentary along the scenic routes trains once governed. It may be that more people under the age of fifty have travelled the Orient Express by television or film than have actually bought tickets and stepped onto the train. Railways exist in the mind as much as anywhere now, the fast trains of France and Japan notwithstanding. Slow trains are still the rule in most countries. When I am in a railway coach being overtaken by a bus on a highway parallel to the tracks, I think how time reverses things, the people in stagecoaches a hundred and fifty years ago watching new steam engines passing them by, changing habit to folklore in one generation just as expressways have reduced passenger trains to an anachronism in mine. Trains, even the slow ones, are still too useful, too efficient at hauling certain kinds of heavy freight, and in Canada, too embedded in our sense of nationhood to disappear as folklore in a few decades, yet there must be many like me who feel they are in a mobile museum when they ride a Canadian train. Looking at the posters and thinking of the old railway car I would soon board in Central Station, I knew it would be like stepping into some backward part of the country where custom, food, and architecture had stood still since the 1940s.

The Halifax train would leave Montreal at 6:50. There were still several hours to put in. A friend and I walked down from Sherbrooke Street along Mackay. We peered into the basement where she used to visit me during my last year in Montreal. I remember looking up from my work table and seeing only legs, each pair with a life attached, a life more fully imaginable than if I had seen only faces. Now as we looked down on those student days we saw a pub called Cheers. My rooms had been knocked out and the stone bearing walls exposed. Two young women with long legs were sitting at the bar drinking cocktails.

I walked my friend to her car and said good-bye. Ambling along Ste. Catherine Street, through Dominion Square and into Central Station, memories of this city I had not inhabited for seventeen years made me want to reach back. I called another old acquaintance, one of the few people I knew who had stayed in Montreal, and we arranged to meet for a drink in the pub on Peel Street that sold English beer. A lawyer now with a prosperous commercial practice, he walked into the pub wearing a well-cut, tan suit, a brown silk tie, and a pressed white shirt. He folded his glasses and placed them carefully on the polished wooden table. He wanted to know about my broken marriage. His mother, he said, thought he had married beneath himself. He seemed slightly amused by his mother's social pretensions, yet also troubled. His wife was not a Westmount native. She had grown up in a small town outside Montreal, and her family had no money. As we talked about the privileges and false sense of superiority growing up in Westmount conferred on people, he suddenly said, "It makes it hard for us to get along with almost anyone." I could not remember him exaggerating in this way before. But twenty years ago Westmount boys did not have to accommodate themselves much to the outside world. In a circle more energetic than reflective, people used to speak of my friend as gifted. He was considered an intelligent, athletic, and good-looking young man, confident and full of promise. Now he seemed quiet and compromising, perhaps not chastened, but no longer arrogant. He said he fought with his wife, but would stay married. They had two little girls and a house half-way up the hill in Westmount. On the surface he was repeating the life our parents had led. "I'm glad I didn't leave Montreal," he said as we went out of the bar. "I'm very comfortable. In a way it's still all here for me."

The train to Halifax was called the Ocean. As a child I used to take it in June or July as far as Mont Joli, a town midway between Quebec City and Gaspé. My parents had a summer house near there. The sleeping car I boarded this night in March had probably been in service when I was a boy. I knew most of Via Rail's long-haul passenger equipment was thirty and forty years old, worn and shabby, but I was content to be on it again.

A gaunt man in a rumpled brown suit shuffled by, his paralyzed right hand dangling in front of him. Across the aisle I noticed E. McPhail. He was sitting with shoeless feet propped up in the seat diagonally opposite his own, and his bags and parcels were placed carefully around himself so that he took up all four spaces in his section. I knew his name was E. McPhail because I could see it stamped on one of his bags, and he had written it on the cover of the *Maclean's* magazine he was reading. The proprietary and territorial instincts seemed very strong in McPhail. He was fussing through his things, putting a comb in one bag and pulling out a packet of Kleenex from another, and then adjusting the position of each piece of luggage. Some religious pamphlets spilled out beside him as he kept house. I could see they mentioned faith and the Pope.

McPhail answered my questions tersely. He was a railway man from Prince Edward Island. No, passenger trains were not running there any more. But they still had freights. He imagined they might be gone soon too. "Don't matter to me," he said. "I'll be gone from the railway in another year. Retirement." He looked at me harshly, as if I had made the rules. He spoke with a Maritime accent, pronouncing car as kerr. An uncomfortable man. He pulled at his collar, his sleeves, his socks, trying to make things better, but when he fixed his socks his collar would chafe, so he had to start again. McPhail was in continual motion, like a bird trapped in a room. It was exasperating to watch these Sisyphean squirms and twitches. I went ahead for a drink.

The bar was stuffed into a narrow rectangle occupying less than half a car. People in their twenties filled the four-seat booths on one side. In a two-seat booth on the other side sat a solitary man watching youth glumly while he drank little bottles of vodka. The air was thick with cigarette smoke. I ordered a beer and looked at my black notebook.

The day I left Ontario I had copied a letter printed in the newspaper. "I read on the bottom of page one of *The Globe and Mail*," wrote H. F. MacConnachie of Victoria, British Columbia, "that Foreigners Feel Canada Boring, People Dull. May I bring to your attention my opinion that to be civilized is to be boring and dull? Thank you." An unflattering survey on Canada as a tourist destination had been conducted abroad and made public several weeks earlier. MacConnachie probably represented a significant groundswell of domestic contempt for this poll. I was reminded of Irving Layton's scathing poem "From Colony to Nation" with the stanza "A dull people, without charm/ or ideas,/ settling into the clean empty look/ of a Mountie or dairy farmer/ as into a legacy." Layton wrote those lines years ago, and I knew as I remembered them on the train that the country had many more wrinkles of acknowledged complexity and sophistication than it had possessed in his early days, but the MacConnachies, proud and defiant in their narrowness and mediocrity, still spoke loudly. It was puzzling. In what other country would the ability to bore strangers be considered a national asset?

In the dining car the steward seated George Gunn at my table. I had been looking at the little white stars on the ceiling. They reminded me of the Pinnochio movie I had recently seen with my three-year-old daughter. Here was the carefully constructed fantasy world of trains, just beginning to die as this car had come into service thirty or so years before. You could not see the real stars outside. They were screened by cloud cover. I noted that the lights seen from the train had once possessed a yellower hue, street lights and the lights of hotels, bars and tenements near the tracks and the vertical lines of light marking used-car lots—bare bulbs strung in rows over second-hand vehicles. Now more lights shone white and were strung horizontally, the dot pictures of countless highrises. Around Montreal that was the impression: countless highrises interspersed with flat, lighted rectangles of look-alike shopping plazas.

"What they should have in bars," said George Gunn, "is a big sign that says 'The ego has landed.' " He had irregular yellow teeth, inset eyes, huge biceps, and a gold chain around his neck. There was goofiness to his rambling remarks, but you could see that he was not about to let anyone interfere with his enjoyment of life. "I've travelled in thirty countries," he said, adding nothing about any of them. On his sports shirt he had pinned a button: I LOVE AU. He said he worked in the railway maintenance yards in Halifax.

"I was up in Toronto going to those seminars," he said. I tried to think what he meant. After he spoke more I understood he had the kind of intellect that expected anyone within earshot to see immediately all the preliminaries of the story he was telling. In this way he reminded me of my three-year-old daughter. "You know . . . those mining seminars," he elaborated. "Noranda was serving caviar. I left about 3 A.M. Someone was crawling on his hands and knees to the elevator." There was a pause in which he showed a wide, yellow-toothy grin. "Tell you what: if there are a hundred weirdos in Canada, ninety-seven of them are on Yonge Street." A bumpkin overwhelmed by the big city, I thought. But then he began to speak knowledgeably of his stock market transactions, his broker, and his portfolio of precious metals.

"Where's your free enterprise?" he complained. "That's what I want to know. I'm not against regulations. It's the overkill I'm against." He confided that he had never contributed to the railway pension plan. "It's a rip-off. I manage my own money. What do you do for a living?"

I told him I was writing a book on my trip. "That's why you're listening to me so carefully, isn't it?" Another yellow grin. We finished eating the shrivelled apple turnovers our waiter had brought for dessert. Visually they reminded me of something organic and decomposing. Unless you were like E. McPhail and packed a bag full of food, Via Rail's meals were a necessity, but even the most ardent train buff could not make them into a virtue.

"People I work with aren't into the market," George Gunn went on. "They think it's mysterious. It's not. You just have to know what risks you're going against. Did you ever see Japan?" He spoke for a moment about Japanese trains. Then we were on a boat in the South Seas, which brought us back to Canada, the land of stalled opportunity. He wanted to continue his impassioned critique of statism and bureaucracy. I got up and said goodbye. It was late and the car was almost empty. Passing the last full table of diners lingering under the painted stars, I heard a plump woman in a royal blue pant suit utter these lines: "Did you see *Romance on the Orient Express*? Oooh. It was just like a Harlequin. It was beautiful. Really."

Sexual fantasies on the train. There could be a woman with short black hair, wearing a boa and a feathered hat.

We would talk about Montreal, the rich street life on St. Laurent and St. Denis, how one felt connected to people there. She has a cassette player with some Boccherini tapes. I ask her to play one and . . . and then McPhail began a commotion across the aisle. He coughed and snorted and bumped and zipped. I imagined him making his little house for the day. He had asked the porter to fold away his bed although it was early morning and all the other sections in our car still had the heavy green curtains snapped shut. People were trying to sleep, but McPhail was not making it easy. I had bought a lower berth so I could look out the window. We were in New Brunswick. The train had travelled up the south shore of the St. Lawrence in the night, past Quebec City and through the towns I remembered from summer holidays twenty and thirty years before, weathered riverside settlements with squat frame houses and enormous churches, their silver-clad spires dominating a passive landscape, making the parishes seem resigned and sacrificial. I remember people from English Montreal who were contemptuous of these places, St-Jean-Port-Joli, La Pocatière, St-Phillippe-de-Neri, St-Pascal, Rivière-du-Loup, Trois Pistoles, Bic. Others were merely suspicious, meeting the equal suspicions most natives harboured about the *anglais*. The three-hundred-mile journey by car up that shore, made with my family every year for ten years, was like watching a movie where the characters had all been filmed from the back, so that you could see in rough outline what was happening, but you missed all the subtle gestures and most of the dialogue. The French version was filmed in all its richness from the front. I always wanted to trade places with someone on the other side and see the complete movie, but as a child I could never find a way.

The snow, mostly melted in Montreal, lay deep on the fields of New Brunswick. There were few signs of people; only trees, as I had imagined. No dark-haired women with feathered hats had boarded the train in Quebec during the night. McPhail had hunkered down in the same position as the day before, immured by pieces of luggage planted around himself. We had sat together after dinner while the porter pulled out his bedding, and he had borrowed a magazine in which one of my articles on train travel had appeared. I watched him finish it line by line in the morning, apparently with great effort. When he handed it back to me, he said, "It was very long."

I felt the same way about the morning. How many McPhails would there be on this journey? New Brunswick looked empty from the train window, as if no one had ever lived there. I read and dozed and began to feel doubts about the trip. What if the whole vast country were as vacant and taciturn as it appeared from this window? What could be said about it? I sensed nothing compelling in the landscape. The mean little villages we passed occasionally seemed a poor substitute for civilization, and Moncton, the centre of this part of the world, did nothing to raise my spirits. McPhail looked dully out his window at the drab city, apparently unimpressed too. But March has never been eastern Canada's best time of year, no sign of spring at a time when everyone and everything seems palpably fatigued by winter.

McPhail spread a checked handkerchief across his lap, took out a paring knife, and cut several pieces of cheese. A short, wiry man, he wore rumpled but clean clothes. The baggy black pants and fresh white shirt made me think of a farmer going to a funeral. On my side Dorchester penitentiary came into view, a grim prison in a bleak setting, worthy of any vermilion-stained vampire tale. The old stone walls and towers looked down from the hill onto wet, open fields. Around Dorchester the wind and sun had worn away most of the snow. Everything looked sloppy, brown, bereft. Below the main enclosure were the brick staff houses, built neatly in a row. And below them the barren fields, offering no refuge to the escapee, nor to the passing eye. The day was not even

grey, grey implying a faint sheen. The sky was closer to
a dull, fog white, the lobotomy of hues, a washed-out
neutral shade, as if the land had given up all hope of
spring.

A school house with FROSTY HOLLOW fading on it
darted into view. I made my way up the train, which
looked to be about half full. At lunch, the man opposite
me, wearing a conservative tie and jacket, said the trains
were mismanaged. They should not send them out half-
empty. They should take off cars. We as taxpayers had to
make up the difference. ''They don't care about the trains
out here in Atlantic Canada anyway. They'd like all our
trains to lose as much money as possible, so they could
cut them all out. It's only Ontario and Quebec gets the
upgrading. That's how this country is operated. Been that
way for years.'' He felt disinherited, cheated, born in the
wrong region. Men who feel this sourness can easily
adopt an efficiency-expert pose. They fume that
passenger-train traffic is poorly organized, or the banking
system wastes money and manpower when what they really mean is that life disappoints them or they feel
trapped. I was glad when he left and the steward replaced
him with a grey-haired couple who had boarded at Moncton.

They did not want conversation. It was not out of cold-
ness or maleficence. They were simply expressionless,
even to one another. Canadian quietude, I thought: the
polite containment of the onlooker, the audience. Someone on stage, someone in the parade had just taken the
words out of your mouth. Canadians speak English in a
world dominated by English-speaking foreigners. Why
speak when you are already spoken for? I prodded them
with questions. They answered decorously and went back
to their creamed chicken. I tried again with the same
result, although their answers grew a little more elabo-
rate. This is like edging closer to a frightened animal, I
thought. Would they growl or break and run? Finally the
woman began to talk on her own. She had spent her

childhood on Heron Island in the Baie des Chaleurs, a small community of farmer-fishermen. "I was born in April, a difficult time for crossing. My mother went over a few weeks early, while the ice was still firm, to stay in my grandfather's house. She had me there. You couldn't really leave the island during break-up or freeze-up. There'd be a good chance of going down if you did." Now all the houses had been burned or vandalized. There was nothing left.

"You should record these memories," the husband said. He turned to me. "Not many left who remember." The wife looked at him impassively.

"There came a time when you just couldn't keep people on the island any more," she continued. "It might have been a good life, but very hard. Things changed. They got electric power on the mainland. And the younger people began to leave. It just slowly died away." She spoke of a faraway place she would never see again. She was a kind of immigrant. He wanted her to remember, but she wanted to leave it all in the past. "The government is planning to make a park there. So they say." Her voice made the idea sound preposterous.

We were talking about ice, and he was telling me about driving across the frozen bay when he was young and in the taxi business in Campbellton. The train stopped. After a couple of minutes I realized we were in Truro, unannounced. This was where I planned to catch the evening train to Sydney. I ran back for my bags and jumped off with a few seconds to spare. They had been suspicious people, but not unfriendly. Canadian onlookers who disliked being observed.

Rawf Seas

In Sydney the train station shared a building with Oland's brewery. That is what I noticed first, then the car lot across the street, then the shabby sidewalks. From here, the eastern railhead for mainland Canada, my journey west would begin. I took a room at Paul's Hotel for sixteen dollars, ate some sausages and mashed potatoes at a café counter, and walked the cold, empty streets of downtown Sydney. Neither in the streets nor in myself could I find any reason to stay. There was a train I could catch down Nova Scotia in the morning.

It was snowing just after dawn. The water along Esplanade Street was still frozen. The buildings, the sidewalks, the roads looked even more pocked and broken in the hard, grey light of early morning. A block ahead of me four men stumbled and shoved one another on their way to the station. When we boarded the little train—only two cars—they passed around a mickey of rum. The drinking hour had arrived: 8 A.M. Our car was less than a quarter full. We passed a generating station, a lumber yard, a mall, rows of wooden houses painted pastel colours, and then a pale blue wooden church. The train rolled slowly around a bay and stopped in North Sydney. Two men staggered on board to join the four sitting ahead of me. A fresh mickey was offered around. The two new men had rosy faces and glazed eyes.

"Rough seas, me boy," said one. He pronounced rough as rawf. "Oi needed dis medsin all da way from Port-aux-Basques. Dat's dee only ting fer da rawf seas." He waved the mickey of rum. They were all from Newfoundland, and had arranged to meet on the train. (The

13

ferries from Port-aux-Basques and Argentia touched the
mainland at North Sydney.) Their accents were thick.
Unless I listened carefully to their dialogue, it was a sing-
song of gibberish. Before the conductor and his assistant
had made their way down to our end of the car to collect
tickets, the Newfies had hidden their bottles.

"You know there's no drinking on the train except what
you buy from the bar?" The conductor could smell the
booze fumes. Several of the men nodded gravely.
"Where's da bear?" one asked. The conductor pointed
down to the far end of the car. "Not open yet," he said.

After Sydney Mines the train left the depressed industrial landscape and ran through sparsely settled country
close to St. Andrews Channel. We stopped at Brisdale
with its nominal station, no different from a city bus shelter, and then at Grand Narrows. Pale aqua ice was piled
up along the shore. It was heaving up around the bridge
we used to cross the little strait. To the left was Bras d'Or
Lake, partly clear.

"What do you git when you cross an onion with a
donkey?" shouted one of the Newfoundlanders at his
buddies across the aisle.

"Shut yerself opp," replied one.

"Most of da toime you gits a piece of ass dat brings
tears to yer eyes."

"Holy Sweet Moses," shouted another one, banging
his arm rest.

"If oi don't git anudder drink real quick ois goina put
me foot right troo dis window, boy Jesus."

"Well git yerself one den. Da bear's just open."

I had train schedules and guide books, and a few names
and addresses here and there in Nova Scotia, but I had
made no visiting arrangements ahead of time. It was better to be able to travel where daily circumstances pointed.
Or so I had thought when buying my tickets in Toronto.
But circumstances on this day did not seem to be pointing
anywhere at all. The only energy on the train was coming
from the Newfoundlanders. Soon they would be collaps-

ing drunk and incomprehensible into a cheap Halifax bar; or they might get themselves thrown off the train. I looked at the map and decided on Antigonish, a university town. We would stop there at noon, leaving enough of the day for me to put my little list of names and phone numbers to work.

A red hat on the white ice, growing larger, turning into the man who wore it. He sat on an upside-down pail and held a fishing rod over a hole. Then we came to open water. Rusty boats bobbed near the shore. Farther out you could see white-caps on the brown sea. This was Port Hawkesbury. The trains used to be loaded onto ferries here for Mulgrave across the Strait of Canso. Now they used the causeway. When we reached it, a child behind me asked, "What's the causeway do?"

"It joins Nova Scotia to Cape Breton," answered her mother, apparently believing the mainland had been done a favour. The water closed into ice again, and the tracks took us up the Strait of Canso to Havre Boucher on St. Georges Bay. For a moment the sun broke through the winter greyness. The houses visible from the train were simple and severe, without overhanging eaves, but some had brightly coloured frozen laundry stiff on the line. There were lobster traps, wooden half-cylinders piled against some of the wooden walls. We passed the little station at Monastery where Trappist monks had been established for a hundred and fifty years. The Newfoundlanders rolled back from the bar. Bringing up the rear, as it were, trudged a young man who had developed a very bad case of trouser slippage. He bent over in the aisle to look for a cigarette in his bag and gave the car a late-morning half-moon. They might not have made it to Halifax, but I never knew. Antigonish was the next stop.

Sex and Food and Drink

IT WAS A PLEASURE TO LEAVE ANTIGONISH THE NEXT DAY. I had carried my bags into the station and asked the man behind the ticket counter if he could recommend an inexpensive place to stay. He looked at me suspiciously and said, "I wouldn't know." When I found a motel and telephoned the people on my list, no one was home.

A cold wind blew down hard on the streets. The beverage room with a pool table, the two Chinese restaurants, the town hall, the court house, the jail. The Metropolitan store with its snack counter where a board listed the prices for hamburgers, hot dogs, hot chicken sandwiches. Above it all the Catholic university, a benevolent god-father without which this modest town could easily become a mean one. I bought the local newspaper, the *Casket*, and took it back to my room. Religious pieces were given prominence. One article proclaimed "Pope's New Car Simpler." It was an interview with Daniel Dalvai, head of the Vatican garage. I was grateful for some international news. Were there trains in the Vatican? Not that I could remember. What a travel book that would make: *The Old Vatican Express*, a metaphysical masterwork, red-and-white uniforms, a chapel in the dome car instead of a lounge, and Bingo in the dining car after dinner, just like Via Rail. Dreaming in my motel-room chair, I wished for the old days when there had been more than one daily train out of places like Antigonish. Now if you were on the train outside Ontario and you wanted to stop in smalltown Canada, you had to stay for twenty-four hours. In places where the trains were even less frequent, it could be two or three days. I switched

16

on the television set. A reporter said that in three of the Maritime provinces over 70 percent of incomes were derived from the public purse. Was this a form of socialism or a form of welfare? I knew that few Maritimers would happily admit to either.

In the morning an old acquaintance from Montreal, whom I had finally roused, drove me to the train. He had worked for Devco, the government corporation established to lift Cape Breton out of economic depression. But the lift had stalled. What could save this region, I asked him, from sliding further into poverty and despair? "Nothing," he said. "Drunk to bed. That's all they can do." He wanted to introduce me to the old station master. Instead we found the sour fellow who had given me no help the day before. The old man had gone. "He went down the line," his replacement explained. "Antigonish was too busy for him. He was getting near retirement and wanted to take it easy. That's a quieter station, down where he is." I looked around. The small red-brick building was perfectly still except for our talking. No one else was waiting for the train. I tried to imagine the old man who had wanted to leave this hectic pace. Or perhaps it was more the town, with its university and students, a window on the world beyond, that he had wanted to leave. Perhaps he had wanted to retire to the world of his early days, where trains had been the fastest things on wheels and the principal connector of places.

A single car pulled in at noon. I sat in the crowded bar area for a beer and sandwich. One word rang dependably through the alcoholic rumble. You could hear it in every second sentence on either side of the aisle. The word was fuck. Across the table from me was a bleary-eyed woman with pale, pocked skin. She had attended her son's wedding in Sydney, and was returning to Ontario "where my second husband moved me." She said she had been a cashier all her life, and that her son made fifteen hundred dollars a month in the navy.

"My father was second engineer on the 'Scotia' which

took the trains across the strait to Port Hawkesbury, before they built the causeway.'' She pronounced across as acrass and Hawkesbury as Hacksberry. "I'm from Mulgrave on the Nova Scotia side. We didn't have no use for Cape Bretonners. They wasn't like us.'' When her father died in an accident on the boat, she went to live with her sister, she said, in the station at Monastery. "My brother-in-law worked for the railway there. But a lot of those old stations now, they're tore down. That's the thing about it I don't understand.''

I ordered beers for us. Soon her eyelids began to droop. "My mother was ninety-eight pounds. She beat hell out of my father once after they were married. And he never got drunk after that. He was paid the fifteenth and the thirtieth. You used to buy beer in quarts in those days, six quarts. By the thirtieth he might still have two quarts left.''

She was part of the Ontario underclass, one of thousands who had gone down the road from the Maritimes to Toronto and Hamilton and Ottawa and worked as cashiers, waitresses, hookers, delivery drivers, moving men, warehouse laborers, jobs without much dignity or security, but more than towns like Mulgrave had to offer. Ontario people were cold, she said. "People in Hamilton, when they talk to you, they want something. If you have a beer with someone, y'know? They always want something.''

I left her and watched the dormant March landscape. As we approached Halifax, I went back to talk to the bar steward. The consumption of alcohol on a Canadian train could be a grim business. I wondered if the large thirst of customers on this line had given him any cause for regret. But he seemed to like the work.

"Fringe benefits,'' he deadpanned. His eyes followed a woman's breasts under a tight green blouse as they passed down the aisle. He looked underfed and dry, with cracks at the corners of his mouth. "You wouldn't believe what I've seen. What about your washroom specials? I've seen women go in the washroom, a man goes in two minutes later, they both come out smiling. It's the movement of the train. I've had women tell me this. It does something to them.

"I'll tell you a story. This is a few years ago when I was in the club car, working the main line. We had four circuit dancers on board from Quebec. It was getting late. I told them 'I'm going to bed. Take it easy.' So I went back to my berth, but for some reason I woke up three or four o'clock. I guess I was worried. And sure enough, when I got to the bar, there they were. The two women were stripped to *au naturel,* on top of the tables, and the men were right there with them.

"In the old days on the main line we had two bedrooms in the Club Car. And there were two women who used to book those rooms, back in the days when a lot of businessmen took the train. They made their money, I'll tell you. We had to get them off. We told them there were too many men using the washroom at the end of the car."

Sex and food and drink. He spoke for the rest of the journey about sandwiches and why he always ran out before the train reached Halifax, as he had on this trip. Management was obsessed with not losing money on the snack bar. Leftovers were losses, because they were thrown away. Better to have hungry, irritated customers than to arrive in Halifax carrying unbought food. With beer it was not the same. They always saw to it that there was enough beer.

Sunday

HALIFAX, OLDER THAN THE CITIES OF ONTARIO, AND older still than any in the west. I left the station, which stood at one extremity of the downtown, walked across a slushy park, and turned right onto Barrington Street. I'd been told I would find some cheap hotels there. It was a cold Saturday evening. The first place I saw offered a room for twenty-two dollars. A sign in the lobby said NO VISITORS, NO ALCOHOL. When I looked at others down the street, they were the same—converted Victorian buildings, once the spacious residences of lawyers and doctors and merchants, now run-down rooming houses and hotels. But if I had to have a simply furnished room with peeling paint, I wanted a high ceiling, and these places did provide that. As well, they all had television sets opposite the bed. This was a step forward for low-life accommodation, a mark of the 1980s. Even Paul's Hotel in Sydney had had a television by the sink, albeit a broken one. I went back to the first building, paid my twenty-two dollars, hauled my bags up the wide staircase, and then up a narrower one to the third floor. The bedspread had a brown stain on it. There was one straight-backed chair, a table for the television, and a little sink with a stringy towel and facecloth. I moved the thin gauze curtains at my small window and watched the snow beginning to fall on Barrington Street. I knew no one in Halifax and had no reason to stay long. Wander for a day, and then buy a ticket on the Halifax-Yarmouth run, I thought. A traveller hopes for happenstance and serendipity to divert him from linear schedules and thoughts. A train ticket could be the doorway to adven-

ture, but you still had to find the right train. I wondered
if these dismal Nova Scotia dayliners could lead to any
adventure other than a court appearance for public drunkenness.

Over a plate of Chinese food ("the glue that holds this
country together" a friend once told me after driving
across Canada) I read the Halifax *Chronicle-Herald*.
There were Escape-to-the-Sun ads. An article about the
inept Canadian postal service. A piece complaining about
teenage sex, picked up from an American wire service.
And a serious editorial based on the book *You Will Live
Also* by the Reverend J. Lloyd Brown of Brantford, Ontario. Divine justice and life after death were discussed.
I began to feel that my train had travelled across time as
well as space and dropped me off in the Canada I knew
as a small boy, the simpler world of the 1950s. Another
editorial, inspired by the alleged murder of a Nova Scotia
man by Armenian terrorists outside the Turkish embassy
in Ottawa, was to me a chilling reminder of Canadian
insularity and self-righteous hypocrisy. "Almost all immigrants . . . ," it declaimed, "know better than most
[of us] the value of Canada's heritage, its law, its institutions, its respect for life and liberty. They love this as
their culture, which it is. . . . For those who don't, let
them think of why they came to Canada, and why it is
worth coming to. Let them think of why people flee to
this land, and not from it. If they can think at all clearly,
it will occur to them that one answer is that it is a place
where neither politics, nor ethnic pride, nor ancient
grudges are above the law. It is a land where the individual's right to live in peace is absolute, and where freedom is unsurpassed." The editorial, naive and bigoted,
was a cry of outrage against the fractious world that was
bursting in on quiet Canada. It was also a thinly veiled
attack on unassimilated immigrants. "Take your ancient
grudges and go home," the editor had wanted to say.
"Leave us in absolute peace." He had apparently forgotten all the born-in-Canada thieves, rapists, child-

molesters, and murderers who populated federal prisons. Halifax was an oddity among Canadian regional centres. While hundreds of thousands of immigrants over the last hundred years has passed through the port, most had boarded trains for points west. The ethnic composition of the city had changed only marginally since its founding in 1749. People of British origin still accounted for 80 percent of the population, a proportion far higher than in English-speaking Canada as a whole.

You could not travel very widely by reading the *Chronicle-Herald*, although it did acknowledge major global disasters and political crises. I turned to the book review section, a source of weekend pleasure in most of the newspapers I admire. But the book review section did not exist. Halifax, Canada's oldest seat of learning, where the country's first newspaper was established, and its first university, apparently felt no need to follow the course of contemporary knowledge, or at least the *Chronicle-Herald*'s editors felt no need. I found a list of bestselling books in the Halifax area, and beside it a single book article. This was as close as the Saturday paper came to touching the larger cultural world beyond its circulation area.

It was bright and glinting the next day on Barrington Street. I passed St. Paul's cemetery, closed for burials a century ago. In the brilliant sun each blackened, tablet-thin headstone printed a delicate shadow on the fresh snow. Across the street stood Government House, a stone mansion built in 1807, still occupied by the province's lieutenant-governor. St. Matthew's Church, 1859; St. Mary's Basilica, 1829—this was an old street with rich layers, unusual for Canada. I walked up towards the Citadel and then looped around into the more modern part of the downtown, past the new World Trade Centre and back down to St. Paul's Church, which stood in front of an ample yard called the Grand Parade, where the militia used to drill. People had been praying in St. Paul's since the time of the French-English wars in the mid-eighteenth century. As I looked at the church, I realized my appreciation of religious architecture had never been compromised by a distaste for what goes on inside it. From the exterior, St. Paul's was a felicitous wooden structure, erected by pioneers who were probably strapped for cash but who nevertheless managed to raise a handsome spire.

I was late and took a seat in the back pews. They were singing the second hymn. "Jesus is the man who cares for others/ Jesus is the man for me!" A worried-looking man handed me a folded program, moving his lips and raising his eyebrows at the same time. Purple grapes and green grape leaves decorated the first page. "We are the branches," it said. I learned this was the fourth week of Lent. At the bottom of the page the congregation was urged to "Pray continually for peace in the world, remembering particularly the troubled areas." The hymn ended. "Death transcended, fate is ended/ Now he makes man's destiny:/ Jesus is the man for me!" I heard my little daughter's voice chirping inside me, "It rhymes, Pappa." The room rumbled as everyone sat. People nearby turned discreetly to look me over. They were all dressed according to the code I remembered from my Anglican boys' schools, dark suits or blazers for the men, conservative dresses or skirts and jackets for the women, though the hats women wore in abundance twenty-five years ago were rare on younger heads now.

Communion with the holy spirit: the minister was consecrating the bread and wine. "He broke it and gave it to his disciples saying, 'Take, eat; this is my body which is given for you. Do this in remembrance of me. . . . ' " It was a part of the service that had always disturbed me when I was at school. I sensed an element of the occult that I disliked, and also an element of crowd control. I had never taken communion. "He gave it to them, saying, 'Drink this all of you. This is my blood of the new covenant which is shed for you and for many for the forgiveness of sins. Do this as often as you drink it, in remembrance of me.' '' They were standing up, out of faith and habit, and moving up the centre aisle to take the sacrament, the flesh and the blood. There were many silent bows and after-you gestures as the line lengthened pew by pew. It was a disciplined procession, played out against the cool colours of the organ pipes behind the altar: white and a pale grey-blue. The theatre of the dead, I thought, as I slipped out into the sunshine on the Grand Parade.

Serendipity

THERE WAS AN EVENING TRAIN DOWN TO YARMOUTH. People would be going back after the weekend in Halifax. I put my bags in a locker at the station and made a long-distance call to a woman in Yarmouth whose name I'd been given by a friend. The male voice that answered said she was out of town. Below the station along Lower Water Street the wind off the harbour was cold and damp. Remembering a reading advertised in Saturday's paper, I doubled back and walked up Spring Garden Road to the public art gallery. Dorothy Livesay, the Winnipeg poet, was making an appearance.

In the reading room at the gallery I saw a man who looked familiar. At first I could not identify the face with its bushy beard. Then I remembered it belonged to a poet with whom I had appeared in an anthology of young poets nine years earlier, a writer whose work I admired but whom I had never met. His picture had been included in the book. I walked over to say hello.

"You're Don Domanski, aren't you?"

"No," said the man, looking puzzled. "My name is

Greg Cook." I hovered for a moment, pondering the news. "I work," he added, filling the silence, "for the Nova Scotia Writers Federation." A friend in Toronto had mentioned this group and had told me to call a Greg Cook if I wanted to contact any Halifax writers.

"You look like Don Domanski's photograph," I said.

"Don Domanski has red hair," replied Greg Cook. "You must have seen a black-and-white. We don't really look alike at all."

A harpist dressed in a white bridal gown acted out her dramatic monologue, and then Dorothy Livesay read her poems. It was an occasion like the morning church service: placid and genteel. Again I had the sense of being in an earlier time. After the question period I talked again with Greg Cook and his wife Miriam.

"Come home with us for supper," he said. "You can pick up the train when it stops in Wolfville." On the way to their car I wondered aloud if the real Don Domanski, author of *The Cape Breton Book of the Dead*, would have been this hospitable.

"You can meet him if you want," said Greg. "He lives with a woman in Wolfville. But he's a recluse. It's hard to get him out." In the parking lot my host stood in front of me and opened his smart beige trench coat. Like a flasher. Then he opened the jacket to show me his vest. With a wide-brimmed hat, black beard, and long hair, he had a 1960s look. "All second hand," he grinned. "There's a place called Frenchy's that has excellent stuff. You can afford to be a writer here. Harold Horwood had to go somewhere for an award once and he bought a tuxedo at Frenchy's for three-seventy-five." Harold Horwood, I knew, was a Newfoundland novelist.

We headed west. You can cross this long, thin province by train or car in about an hour going directly from Halifax to the Minas Basin, on which Wolfville sits. Along the way, at Grand Pré, they showed me the headland that broods in Alex Colville's paintings. This was Acadian country. We passed dykes built centuries ago to reclaim the rich marshes from the sea. "The Acadians came first and took the best land," Greg said. "When the English arrived, they wanted it. That's the long and short of the story, and that's really why the Acadians were expelled." History lay heavily on the land here, history and religion. Watching the contentious marshland out the back-seat windows, I could hear Greg's voice in front speaking of an eighteenth-century evangelist he had been researching, Henry Alline. He described Alline as a charismatic figure who altered the tenor of faith in Nova Scotia and New Brunswick between 1776 and 1783.

"He may also have been quite a ladies' man. There are suggestions of that, but we don't know. He wrote hymns and pamphlets and was the driving force behind what was called the 'New Light' movement. The traditional churches disliked him and the loyalty he inspired, but he was an early Nova Scotia democratizer, a predecessor of Joseph Howe." The voice in the front seat was speaking of this saddlebag preacher and pamphleteer— dead for ten generations—as a heroic figure whose legacy was still felt. Alline had been a major influence in the establishment of the Baptist Church in Nova Scotia. Greg Cook had been a Baptist preacher for three summers, starting at the age of seventeen. Wolfville's Acadia University, where he had studied, had originally been a Baptist college. So there was a personal link to Alline as well as an intellectual fascination with him. The possibilities for this kind of century-straddling affinity seemed much richer on the back roads of rural Nova Scotia than in the central-Canadian cities I knew. Those cities had all but obliterated their past. Who but the most unworldly eccentric could claim to feel in the electronic circuitry of Toronto the living presence of Egerton Ryerson, Ontario's rough equivalent to Alline? Ryerson's name lived on in the polytechnical institute that commemorated his energetic support of public education, but the man on a horse, reins in one hand and bible in the other, presented a comical image if it came to you on the subway, the girl with orange hair and pins in her nose on one side of you, and the young businessman, his face buried in *Eat to Win*, on the other. Ontarians had been too preoccupied with prosperity and progress to invest much energy in protecting their roots. (By 1980 a soul-destroying amount of Ontario's finest nineteenth-century architecture had been razed in the name of economic development. It was a paradox of Ontario culture that an essentially conservative populace had shown so little interest in conserving its own material history.)

The Cooks lived in a small frame house beyond the town on the Wolfville Ridge, with a view of the Minas Basin. I had caught them without much food. Miriam stretched some leftover stew with extra vegetables, and we sat and ate and talked about the literary personalities who had passed through their kitchen. A gentle, pretty woman, Miriam told me she had once thrown the western-Canadian poet, John Newlove, out of her house for drunken misbehaviour. Al Purdy, a better poet, and usually a more decorous drinker than Newlove, arrived later the same night. His competitive instincts aroused, Purdy demanded to know what outrageous conduct was required of him so that he might enjoy the same fate as his fellow scribbler. I knew my good friend Al was a large presence in Canadian literary culture, but I had not expected to cross his shadow here in Wolfville; for a moment the country seemed small and closely knit. The Cooks asked me how far I was going on the train later that night. I said all the way to Yarmouth.

My host looked doubtful. "You don't want to go to Yarmouth. Although I guess I'm biased. Yarmouth to me is where people die. I only go back for funerals, and to see my mother." He talked more about his home town, how it had only a few interesting people; how the train arrived late when everything, maybe even the hotel, had closed for the night; how it was the wrong time of year. Suddenly I lost interest in Yarmouth.

"What you ought to do," my host said, "is stop at

Annapolis and see Harold Horwood.'' He left the table and made a call. Harold Horwood, he reported, would pick me up at the Annapolis station. I was surprised, also slightly embarrassed. I knew Horwood by reputation and had read some of his magazine pieces, but I was about to pay a visit to Newfoundland's best-known novelist without having read his books.

When the Cooks dropped me at the Wolfville station the air was heavy with rain. A sign on the door to the darkened waiting room said it would be open thirty minutes before the train stopped. I walked around the block: down the main street where puddles reflected the overhead lights, down a dark side street, and back along the tracks. A yellow light shone now from the station, making yellow panels on the platform. The door had been unlocked. A man was wiping the floor.

"Is there a ticket agent?" I asked.

"There hasn't been a ticket agent for years." He was the custodian. He said he drove a truck for a living, and spent an hour a day maintaining the station. "I keep the place up pretty good. Paint the walls, put back up whatever's falling down." A calendar with a picture of two skiers hung on the wall. Every day, including this one, St. Patrick's day, had two notations scribbled on it. "I put down what time the train comes," he explained, "so we have it in writing." It was a way for him to hold onto something that never stayed in the station more than a minute or two. "The morning train to Halifax is always late," he said. We were alone in the room. No one else was waiting. He was fastidious about the floor, which gleamed with several coats of varathane. He wiped it slowly, square metre by square metre, though there was no visible dirt. When he heard the train he stopped and walked down to the wall calendar.

This was the old Dominion Atlantic Railway, as the sign still indicated on the station. The ride to Annapolis would take about an hour and a half. We stopped at Kentville, scene of the incest trials a few months before, then at Middleton, though I could not see either place. Heavy sleet blocked the view. "They want to take the train off after Middleton," the conductor told me. "We've got poor trackage beyond here. Needs a lot of money. But they tell me this is the most travelled passenger line in the whole country. Figure that one out." No one I had met working on the road for Via Rail was willing to promise the railway would survive past next month. There was often a resigned air to the operation, and a feeling of fatigue. Yet the old-timers still took great pride in railway traditions, in their occupational skills, and in the long-established hierarchy. "When I get off," a conductor later said to me, "there's no more train."

At the Annapolis Royal station I saw a thin man with long grey hair standing on the platform. He looked like Greg Cook's description of Harold Horwood. I would approach this man and say, "You're Harold Horwood," and he might reply, "No, I'm Wilbur Trounce. What business is it of yours? Writing a book? Izzat so? I happen to grow the largest buttercup squash in Nova Scotia and I'd like to show them to you. My son-in-law can put you up." But when I spoke to the strange man he said, "Yes. The car's over here," and we hurried through wet gobs of snow to the parking lot.

"You can go to a bed-and-breakfast or you can take your chances with us," he said abruptly. I decided to take my chances, and tried to remember quickly what I knew about him. He had written novels and had a reputation as a Newfoundland folklorist. I had read a magazine article of his not long before on one of the Newfoundland outports. In the car he looked fifty-five, maybe sixty. I regretted not having read his books. It struck me as perverse, visiting an established writer without knowing his work. Even more perverse, I decided not to admit my oversight. He talked about himself as we drove to his house, and I bluffed my way through all references to what he had written. It was not difficult to feign familiarity with this title and that. Authors on the subject of their own books are easily encouraged.

It would have been better if I had known more about him. When we arrived at the house and went upstairs to his living room I sensed a suspicious note to the questions. Why was I here? He did not put it to me directly, but that is what he wanted to know. I wondered why myself. A warm room on a cold night, an older writer with stories to tell, a chance encounter at the Halifax art gallery, a house that happened to be not far from a railway station, altogether it smacked of opportunism on my part. But travelling, among other things, is opportunism, no matter where you go. It means taking your own currency to countries with favourable exchange rates, or putting yourself at the disposal of other people's hospitable impulses, or simply bringing a lot of money to a comfortable place where other people are willing to feed and shelter you. Travellers go where the going is good, and when things turn sour most of them go elsewhere or go home.

The talk turned to money, a conversational subject I have found most writers favour over literature. I described my publisher's contract, the terms and the modest advance I hoped would take me across Canada. Horwood said he had always supplemented his book royalty income with fees from freelance journalism. He told me how much money he had earned the year before, a good income for a writer. And then he explained how they lived, growing much of their own food, digging clams in the mud flats that ran out from their backyard, and constructing their own house. Corkie, his wife, was standing in front of the fire, saying how dull fresh clams could be if you ate enough of them. We were upstairs where they had built the living room and kitchen. Their two small children were asleep below. Plants crowded a small sun room at the top of the stairway and spilled out the door into the living room, hanging from the ceiling and standing in pots. The feathery green and the natural hemlock walls gave the room a soft, cushiony feel.

"It's time for a glass of mead," Horwood said, as if we had earned it by discussing money. I had been offered mead before, but it had always turned out to be pompous nomenclature for beer. Perhaps from reading Virgil in Latin class, I had always associated real mead with spears and shields, roughly sewn garments, bad teeth, battlefield filth, and epic decisions. My host ducked into the kitchen and carried out a large jug of golden liquid. "I make this myself," he said. His honey wine had the colour of a low sun reflected off water, a silky golden sheen. It tasted sweet and smooth. "We get the honey from a local beekeeper. You can find just about everything you need to survive here. I make my own beer and wine too. The climate is very mild. Corkie was still picking broccoli from the garden in December."

When I woke after the first light in my corner room downstairs, I could see the Annapolis Basin. It evoked memories of an earnest history master at my boarding school who spoke of the Basin with the same reverence he accorded the Tigris and Euphrates. In Canadian terms it was comparable, but I could never interest myself much in what sounded like a large pail of salt water. The story of Samuel de Champlain's 1606 settlement, which some historians say was the first in Canada, may have been heroic, but it was also chastening. As a school boy you learned that in the central courtyard of the common habitation built by Champlain's settlers North America's first experimental seed bed was planted, and that Champlain started Canada's first social club there—the Order of Good Cheer, and that the first Canadian play was written and performed in the little fort. But what most impressed me was that even here, on one of Canada's mildest and most fertile shores, the settlers lasted less than a year. The site was abandoned after the first winter. For school children the message was ambiguous. You had to conclude the country had been almost impossible to settle.

Nevertheless the land had somehow acquired a population. That could mean we all possessed the fortitude of
seventeenth-century peasants. Or might it mean we were
merely here on sufferance, until seven years of bad luck
forced us to abandon our homes?

"That's a lot of nonsense about Annapolis being Canada's first settlement," fumed Horwood at breakfast.
"They hang onto that story for the tourists. You see it
printed everywhere around here, in spite of documented
evidence of much earlier settlements in Newfoundland."

"Yes," said his wife. "The chicken thing." She was
given to cryptic comments which Horwood would then
explain.

"Whitbourne talks about buying eggs and chickens at
Trinity in the late sixteenth century. Well, obviously
someone had to be settled there if they were raising
chickens."

He offered to drive me around town on his way to pick
up the mail. Snow was blowing down again. Under a
thick grey sky the town looked scrappy and beleaguered.
Here and there on the main street a Victorian building
survived. Some had been restored. We went into one
frame structure with a plaque outside. It was called the
Adams Ritchie House, built in 1712. A young man in one
of the offices showed us a cupboard where we could see
the composition of the exterior wall—mud and marsh
grass.

"This is supposed to be the oldest wooden structure
in Canada," he said.

"I think that's very questionable," Horwood interjected. "We know the Mallard House in Quidi Vidi, for
example, was used as a dressing station when Amherst
took St. John's." The young man looked doubtful, but
Horwood had momentum. He insisted again that historical claims were exaggerated in Annapolis for the sake
of tourism. And he seemed to enjoy this debunking pos-
ture. There was a hard-edged, hectoring side to him that

took satisfaction from the exposure of other people's flabby-mindedness.

In the local health-food store Horwood purchased bags of engevita yeast and buttermilk powder. I remembered reading somewhere that he had been regarded as an eccentric in Newfoundland because he had adopted some of the practices of the counter culture in the 1960s. "I mix the yeast in a glass of water," he said. "I like the taste of it." We walked along to the Mad Hatter, the local bookstore. He introduced me to the owners. "This is George Galt, who has been visited upon me by Greg Cook." I bought a paperback copy of one of his novels, *Tomorrow Will Be Sunday*. The author assured me it was an excellent book.

"I was never popular with the critics. My novels came out when it was fashionable to write about the anti-hero. That wasn't what I wanted to do." Later, outside the post office, he opened a letter from his publisher. "Ach," he croaked, "reviews of my latest book." He scrunched up the photocopies and threw them on the car floor without reading them. "Just shit."

I accepted his invitation to stay another night. The train back to Halifax would leave at nine in the morning. The tracks of the old Dominion Atlantic ran across Horwood's driveway and through his front yard, about a hundred metres from the house. I asked if I could flag down the train and board it there. No, they would stop and let you off in the driveway, but you had to board at the station.

Another storm. Wind yowled and screeched around the writer's homemade house. Snow scratched at the windows. Looking down from Horwood's big living room window, I could see brown water churning in the Basin. He had given me a typescript to read, a piece he had written on this Annapolis micro-world where they had lived for seven years.

"Especially in the light of evening," I read, "before or after sunset, the Basin from our vantage point suggests harmony and peace, symmetry and the repetition of pleasant rhythms. Unless you've been born here, you can never get used to the tides. Twice a day they come creeping up to cover the rocks that tower far overhead for a few hours, then the Basin seems to empty itself, the beaches are exposed, and the water disappears over the clam flats until what's left truly looks more like a river than an arm of the sea . . .

"Here I am less impressed by the power of nature than by its fecundity—aspens that put on seven feet of growth in a single summer, an alder shoot that rises from the ground at the end of April and grows at the rate of an *inch a day* so that it towers twelve feet high in autumn, a bank of soil, piled by a bulldozer, that clothes itself in a single season in ferns and rushes and the lovely flowers of jewel weed hanging higher than your head. You feel here that nature will not be put down, that the ugliness, the scars, the devastation, are only temporary blemishes that this great surging tide of life will cover and soften and make beautiful almost at the moment the would-be destroyer turns away to light a cigarette or open a bottle of beer."

Out in the storm there was no sign of the lush hothouse Horwood had eloquently evoked, no sign of life except one crow hovering level with the living room window. The bird was fixed on an invisible pole, aloft but rendered motionless by the wind. For a moment I wished I had begun the trip when the alder shoots were beginning to rise.

Horwood had also handed me a historical pamphlet entitled *A Brief History of Acadie* by Réné Babineau. "It was at Port la Tour, in 1620, that an Indian maid gave birth to a son. The father was Louis Lasnier, originally from Dieppe. André Lasnier was probably the first child of European extraction to be born on the North American continent." Horwood's pen had thundered in the margin: "European fishermen and traders by the *tens of thousands* had been consorting with Indians for *more than a century*. Not to mention Norse children born in Vinland 500 years earlier.'' His Newfoundland background had given him a longer and more common-sense view of history, and an impatience with historians who brushed his island off the North American map.

I asked him at dinner why they had left Newfoundland. ''My family pushed me out,'' he said with a mischievous smile. Various relatives, according to the story, had installed themselves in the house he had built at Beachy Cove. ''It didn't look like they were going to leave. So we did.'' I watched his pale blue eyes in the long, thin face, the red-yellow grey strands of long hair, the salt-and-pepper beard. The eyes were restive and curious. Even now, they suggested, he could move, build another house, find fresh enthusiasm for a new place. He had been a journalist, a politician (sitting in the Newfoundland legislature for two years after the province joined Canada), a labour organizer, and an essayist and novelist, but the list seemed less a summation than an interim report.

We drank a bottle of brandy I had bought in town. At nine o'clock you could hear the train's whistle and a faint rumble as it rolled past the house, muffled by the wind and snow. I asked Horwood how long he had known he wanted to be a writer.

''I certainly knew by the age of twelve, maybe before that. I was filling notebooks with stories then. When I was very young, four or five, I wanted to be a flyer. The Lindbergh flight over St. John's was a very big event. I tried it later. Took lessons in Trinidad for six dollars an hour. But I didn't like it.

By morning several inches of snow had fallen. It had drifted into ridges across the driveway. ''I can't stand going early to trains and planes,'' Horwood told me over breakfast. He said it in the clipped, definitive way he said everything. I fretted silently, thinking of the snow drifts. ''If we leave before the train crosses the property, we're all right,'' he insisted. Fifteen minutes ahead of station

time we hurried into the car, he took a run at the driveway, plowed through the drifts, and sped down the winding road to Annapolis. We were on the platform about a
minute before I heard the train hoot.

"Thanks for taking in a stranger," I said.

"Not the first time," he replied. "Someone got me up
in the middle of the night once at Beachy Cove. You must
have heard of him even if you haven't read his dreadful
novels." He said the name of a gay Canadian writer
whose first novel had been a *succès de scandale*. "He
arrived late one night saying he was lost and posing as
someone other than he was. Next day he confessed he
was a writer and had really come to meet me. Of course,
he tried to make love to my cousin John. But John was
old enough then to know all about these things." Horwood had already scurried off the platform and into his
car when I turned from inside the coach a moment later
for a last look.

Halifax

EAST OF HALIFAX, UP THE ANNAPOLIS VALLEY. PAST
empty fruit storage buildings with faded lettering. UNITED
FRUIT COMPANIES OF NOVA SCOTIA I made out on one.
Obsolete warehouses, a few around each settlement, well
built but abandoned, left over from the railway age.
"They used to be strung up and down the valley, but a
lot have been torn down," said the middle-aged man opposite me. "The ones remaining are really a rarity." He
had grown up near Berwick on a fruit farm. "Those days
the only transportation company you ever heard tell of
was a farmer with a couple of trucks. It was all on the
train then. Now it's all done by the trucking companies."

From the train window we could see the little loading doors high on the warehouse walls where the apple crates used to be hoisted onto freight cars. "I moved to Halifax twenty years ago," he said, "but I got caught in the downturn. Worked for an oil company. Got laid off. Then I went broke in the car business." He seemed edgy and downcast. Most of the men I met or overheard on Nova Scotia trains were unemployed. I felt prosperous by comparison, though I was concerned about the cost of four months on the road.

I had decided to stay this time at the Halifax YMCA, the cheapest rooms I knew of. "The YMCA has the right to inspect rooms without notice. Any damage to the rooms and/or contents while rented will be the responsibility of the tenant," read the piece of paper I was handed at the desk. In my room two flights up, the yellow walls were bare except for a mirror with splotches of black and a notice: PLEASE DO NOT STICK POSTERS ON THE WALLS. As I unlocked my door after Chinese food, a man down the hall poked his forehead and eyes out of his room and stared at me. I looked at the eyes. They stared. I went into my room and heard the other door close. When I crossed the hall to the bathroom later, the eyes appeared again. All night doors slammed up and down the hallway. In the morning outside my little window the first day of spring showed an inch of snow, fallen through the night. I looked at the chrome chair upholstered in green vinyl, plastic tape holding together the rips. And the dirty cream-coloured curtains with cigarette burns in them. And I packed my bags and carried them down to Barrington Street where, for ten dollars more, the rooms had cigarette burns but harder beds and quieter guests.

I walked, and then rode a bus around its route. People appeared to be moving in slow motion. I could see them lifting up their legs and slowly putting them down, like mime artists, as they made their way along the sidewalks. In Toronto did people run, or here did people slowly float? Motorists stopped, I saw, for pedestrians who wanted to cross the street in the middle of a block. We passed streets of handsome old frame houses with finely crafted wooden bays by the front doors. The bus cost two-thirds what it would in other cities I knew. The phone booths still took dimes. Again I felt sent back to an earlier decade.

Province House, the provincial legislature, built in the early 1800s: according to my guide book, Charles Dickens called it "a gem of Georgian architecture." Some things had remained unchanged since his visit a hundred and fifty years before. The Speaker of the Assembly, for example. From the visitors' gallery I could see him, a small man at the centre of a small amphitheatrical chamber, fitting architecture for lilliputian theatre. He was wearing a black stove-pipe hat and a black robe. The thought crossed my mind that an amateur drama group might have rented the room. When I listened carefully I could hear that a government member was making a speech, blustering about fish. He said the word "opposition" the way Cape Bretonners did, with a sibilant *s* instead of a *z*. The premier, dressed in a dark blue suit, with a roll of stomach sagging over his belt, was laughing at private asides from his seat-mates on the front benches.

From Province House I walked up Prince Street and rang at the press club under the Carleton Hotel. A young man opened the locked door and asked me to sign a book. "The reason this is such a good press club," said someone at the bar, "is that members from the working press are a minority." The beer, I noted, was cheaper than on the train. "You have to go out of Halifax to find good country music," a woman said. "I hear it's quite popular in Toronto. People in Halifax don't want it any more. They grew up with it." She had been raised on a farm in New Brunswick. Farther down the bar was a copy of the day's *Chronicle-Herald*. "Blueberries," the front page shouted. There had been questions in the legislature. Local blueberry production was threatened by European tariff proposals. I nodded to the silent drinker beside me, and said I was from Toronto. Oh? He had a brother in Toronto who worked for a magazine. He gave the name, which belonged to someone I knew, one of my editors. We shook hands and ordered another drink. He too had grown up on a farm, but was now a prosperous lawyer. "Farming was just work; that's what I remember. You put the hay in one end, shovelled the shit from the other, and drew milk from the middle. I hated it. Now they've got all these bells and buzzers which must make it better." In the press club the people had good jobs and dressed well, but when you asked where they came from, it was often from a farm or a fishing community. Many were not very far from hard labour on tractors and boats, at most a generation or two. Halifax was the Saturday night in town stretched into a lifetime, which meant, perhaps, that no matter how sophisticated you became, you were more grounded in basic necessity than people in the larger inland cities.

A man called Harry Flemming sat at the bar. I remembered the name from his occasional commentary on national radio. Harry was a lawyer who did not practice law. The consensus of opinion at the bar was that he was a man of superior intelligence. "Harry could have made a lot of money," I was told, "but he wanted to take it easy." Harry was bald, with intelligent eyes that would not be hurried. He looked sixtyish, and contented. I asked him about the easy-going atmosphere.

"People in Halifax would like to have the money," he said, "but they don't really want to work all that hard." We talked about the newspaper, known in the club as the Comical-Herald. He said it was second-rate. "There's no excuse. It's a rich operation."

I left the press club and walked back down Prince Street and along Barrington, past St. Paul's cemetery. Fresh snow glistened on the sidewalk under the lights. Wandering through the soot-blackened headstones, I looked at the names. The women were Amelia, Abigail, Rebekah, Lucy, Charlotte. The men were John, Richard, Benjamin, Thomas. The thin slabs teetered over the snowy graves, black on white, a field of precarious tablets that in another short span of stellar time would be lying flat on the earth or under it. And I too would be laid out flat. But for a moment there was this undeniable frame of human time, the headstones pitched halfway over, I lifting a foot to make another print in the snow, as mourners had done when these bodies were buried, and as someone would one day put a foot beside me. On such nights in St. Paul's, I thought, ghosts take shape.

Walking farther down Barrington to my hotel, close to midnight. A hotdog vendor wheeling his bicycle cart through snow past old brick buildings. Empty sidewalks. Standing on a corner, a shapely black hooker with a striking face. Her black coat, black skin, against the white snow. A single car purred on the pavement. The hooker returned my stare for a moment. Then we both looked away.

In the morning cable television printed the time on the screen, 7:45, and the temperature, -5°C. It also printed the temperatures for dozens of other places. It was + 18°C in Casablanca. I switched the channel. The soft-porn exercise program was on for breakfast, three well-built women in leotards and leg warmers shimmying and thrusting to a popular song: "Let's get physical. Lemme hear your body talk." I left the room and walked down to the water. In an otherwise clean slip beside the restored wharf buildings a condom floated. Commuters were arriving on the ferry from Dartmouth. I boarded it and rode out into the windy harbour which offered a full view of the downtown. An artificial heritage monument had been erected beside the old wharf warehouses. Recently constructed, it was crowned with rows of dormers on the top floor; small windows were widely spaced lower down, echoing the rhythm of the old frame buildings nearby. Halifax was a good-looking city, even in March.

A magazine writer whom I had not met but whose work

I admired had invited me for lunch at the university faculty club. As Harold Horwood had, Harry Bruce talked freely about money. He told me his accountant had just instructed him to mortgage his house a second time to pay his income taxes. Harry wore a sweater and slacks and running shoes, and drank gin with lemon. "I must have made a lot of money last year," he said. "I don't know where it went." We drove around the city after lunch, up Citadel Hill, then to the north end where the ramshackle houses crowded against each other, past the area devastated by the 1917 munitions explosion, along the water and up the Arm—a long inlet with expensive properties backing onto it. He told me he would be moving to Guysborough County in a couple of years, back to the farm his grandfather had worked. "It's been in the family since 1840," he said. The land was never far away.

I wanted to leave the city and start west. The train to Moncton did not depart until the next afternoon. Halifax was an easy place to linger in. One could be lulled for days, have lunch with someone, drink at the press club in the evening, meet the local characters, sink into paralytic oblivion as a permanent observer. I remembered other travels where the foreign language and unfamiliar images jarred and sharpened perception. Seeing one's own country differed from that. It would be easy to fall into the local rhythm of a place like Halifax. No one pretended that this was the centre of things. You were accepted easily, it seemed, whoever you were. At the press club that night I looked in the newspaper at apartment ads, an idle fantasy. It was time to move on.

To Prince Edward Island

"YOU KNOW WHY PEOPLE READ DALE CARNEGIE? BE-
cause he tells you you're good. I read him a lot. Everyone
wants to be told they're good once in a while. I like
people. I make friends wherever I go." The man opposite me in the dining car felt I wanted to talk about books.
Dale Carnegie was his favourite author. Another leap
backwards—I had not met anyone since the 1960s who
lavished such praise on Carnegie. Bill the man's name
was, a master mechanic for Via Rail, twenty-eight years
old. He wore a suit, and a tie around his thick neck. He
was square-faced, without any worry lines, barrel-
chested, and had large hands, though the hands were
smooth and clean. The company had promoted him into
a supervisory job. He told me about his house, his wife
and children in Moncton. "I'm bilingual," he said, "so
I don't care about these fights over language." But he did
care. He went on to say he thought the crusade for French
rights in New Brunswick was going too far. We had
moved up the Arm, through a rock-cut adjacent to the
manicured yards of expensive waterfront houses. Harry
Bruce had said this was the only upscale neighbourhood
in Canada built along railway tracks. But I remembered
renting a room once in Toronto's fashionable Rosedale
district in a house that shook when trains passed. The
back yard abutted on a freight line. A meal would be on
the table and the cups would rattle, as if on board. For a
moment you wished you were a passenger going somewhere, and then the room was still, a moment of post-
viatic depression, and then you forgot the train and went

on with what you were doing, until the next one pulled you away.

We skirted the Bedford Basin with its little islands, patches of snow on the mud. Birds fluttered up as the train passed. I walked back to my seat in the coach. Across the aisle a man about twenty-five, dressed neatly in jeans and boots and sports shirt, was talking about the Ontario beer strike. He was out of work. "I don't understand those companies. They should be hiring more people, not less. Don't they know it's working people like us who buy the beer? If we don't have jobs, who's going to buy the beer?" His travelling companions were unemployed too. They were all young, spending their days on trains, on street corners, in bars. They had unemployment insurance, or savings, or money borrowed from people with jobs. But there was frustration and resentment in what they were saying.

A different sort of young man boarded at Truro, wearing a pack on his back. He unloaded into the empty seat beside me. He had saved money in the boom years in Alberta and toured Europe. "Athabasca country," he said he was from. "A place called Boyle." Back in Canada only a few days, with a three-week rail pass, he was going to look at his own country on the way west. But he had already made up his mind. "Canada is so dull. Everyone has a car, everyone has it easy. You take life for granted here." He was disappointed, but he added, gazing out the window, "I love all this space." He was eager to hunt and trap when he returned home. "That wall," he ventured several times, "I don't really get it." From East and West Berlin the week before he had seen the wall. "I had to get a visa to go through. But then if you live on the communist side, I heard you can't leave. How far does that wall go? How do people get out of there?"

I left him and went back to the dome observation car, one of the "park cars" as the CPR used to call them. This had the name Evangeline Park. At one end was a bad painting of the church and the statue of Longfellow's Evangeline at Grand Pré. Up in the dome a man was saying, "Since I lost my wife I've bought everything on TV you can get. They're going to have a hundred ball games on this season. The only thing that sickens me is the tennis." He looked old enough to be retired, as did everyone in the dome except for a young woman with an infant sleeping in her arms. We stopped at Springhill Junction where for years, according to my little book, a coal train with one coach met the main line passenger train. Today there was no one on the platform. The tatty stucco building with its faded green trim and the grey shed alongside stood apparently unused. We continued on through more trees and snow to Amherst, with narrow frame houses painted pale colours, and a red sandstone station, and then into New Brunswick, along the flat plain by the Cumberland Basin, past enormous frozen boulders of tidal mud in hobgoblin shapes, and then to Sackville: a stone station, a few shanties, some small houses; little more could be seen from the tracks. Dorchester Penitentiary again, sunny on this late afternoon, making the walls and the four towers look even darker.

At Moncton I used my rail pass to board a bus to Cape Tormentine. There were no passenger trains on Prince Edward Island, but a rail pass would take you on a bus to the ferry, across the channel, and on to Charlottetown. It was dark when we drove into the mouth of the big boat. Rails were sunk into the floor of the bottom deck so freight trains could be ferried across—room for thirty cars, a stevedore said. The bus passengers trooped upstairs to the cafeteria, where the food was even less palatable than on the trains. I ate a hot turkey sandwich, amorphous brown sludge for five dollars. A question began to formulate itself. Could anyone survive several months eating only Via Rail food? I doubted it. Maybe this was the hidden, demonic side of Canadian travel: anorexia trainosa. Long-distance passengers had not really deserted the trains for planes and buses. They had

died of malnutrition. But in truth there was no reason to
complain. I remembered railway food in Peru, tasty roast
chicken which had later induced severe vomiting. It was
easy to forget that Canada was such an unperilous place,
safe and comfortable as long as you had a little money.
The demonic side was far under the surface, much less
obvious than the bad food, dangerous vehicles, and bad-
tempered officials who bothered travellers in poorer
countries.

As we came into Borden on the southern shore of
P.E.I., a pharmacist from Moncton stood near me looking at the Island map in the ferry lounge. "I was born in
O'Leary," he said, pointing to a dot in the remote northwest of the province. "When I was a boy the Indians
from Lennox Island used to come into town to sell their
baskets. Everyone was afraid of them. Would have been
thirty years ago or more. They didn't do much but drink
and sell baskets. Then their chief, he married a brilliant
white person. That changed the tribe." People were
drifting down to the cars and buses. "I'd like you all back
here well before we dock," the bus driver had said. Every
passenger dutifully sat in the same seat she or he had
occupied on the ride from Moncton. There were no late-
comers.

It was almost midnight by the time I had walked from
the Charlottetown bus terminal to a downtown motel.
Reddish mud had oozed up through cracks in the streets
and sidewalks and frozen stiff. The houses were all dark.
My motel room, with two double beds, chairs, a desk
and table, half a dozen clean towels, and a colour television, was the same price as the grungy rooms in Halifax.
The man behind the desk explained it was the off-season.
I had roused him from bed. He spoke with a British accent
and treated me formally. What was my occupation? His
hand was poised over the space for occupation on the reg-
istration form. A what? I told him again. "A rider?" He
looked perplexed and suspicious. "I write," I said loudly,
scribbling in the air with an invisible pen. The perplexity

left his face, but the suspicion remained. He asked for a key deposit.

In the motel coffee shop at breakfast, I recognized the poet Milton Acorn. In my twenties I had read his book *I've Tasted My Blood* and admired the poems as much as any I'd seen by a Canadian. I stood by his table and introduced myself. He looked at me carefully. After a long pause he said I could sit down. "Sorry to hesitate," he began, "but I sometimes get accosted by people who pretend to be interested and are nice to me for a couple of minutes and then start shouting and denouncing me." He wore a rumpled black leather jacket, a pair of old pants, and blue running shoes. His face was unshaven, greasy silver hair hanging down one side, and eyebrows poking out like little wings about to fly off in different directions, carrying his rheumy distended eyes. Shovelling down eggs and toast, coughing badly, he looked very ill.

"Just out," he said cryptically.

"Hospital?" I guessed.

He nodded faintly, using his eyelids more than his neck. "Cut-budget hospitals. Get out just as soon as I've backed away from death one step." He spoke in phrases and half-sentences. "The killer-goon-anti-lifers," he mumbled several times. And then he let loose, his mind leaping about like a man with his shirt on fire: international monopoly capitalism, the greenhouse effect, dying trees, the rebirth of fascism, Halley's Comet, the Treaty of Versailles, the Communist Manifesto, the Second International, William Lyon Mackenzie and the Upper Canada rebellion of 1837, the ill treatment of the Maoris in New Zealand, the Ulster border as a reflection of the Maine-Nova Scotia border and vice versa, the forty-ninth parallel ("the most pathetic object on earth"), the fact that Marx "never said a word against Robert Owen," the fact that "socialists now are all Nazis," the flu epidemic in the Great War "which killed five times as many people as the fighting," land in the United States—all controlled by the big corporations, the Dieppe raid—a foreseen massacre, and the abortion issue again. "The killer-goon-anti-lifers don't understand. No working-class babies, no revolution." All this made connections in his mind, but he offered none to the listener. It was an exhausting encyclopedic wash of his obsessions with the corruption of the powerful and the plundering of the weak. When I asked him if he planned to remain on the Island, where he grew up, or if he might return to Toronto, he shouted at me angrily.

"I can't go back! The anti-lifers and the Zionists! I'm in exile. Rusticated exile." His face relaxed and then came the bump, bump, bump of his disconcerting laugh. "Huh, huh, huh," like Art Carney on the old Jackie Gleason show, but without the joy. "The RCMP started following me around and getting me thrown out of hotels. They set traps for me. Invited me to readings. Some expert scoundrel would stand up and denounce me and distort my words. Mulroney," he continued, without missing a beat, "looks young, but acts like an old prime minister. He has antique ideas. Hitler was for choice. The killer-anti-lifers. . . ." And then he said darkly, "There's a conspiracy to block my books."

"Where do you live?" I asked, thinking I might call.

"In Parkdale." He said the street name. "They should call it Ravendale. Huh, huh. Young ravens down from the north. Old ones never come. I know. They say they keep growing. Long as they live. But they can fool you. They have a way of making themselves look bigger than they are."

"Like people," I said. He nodded faintly, again with his eyelids. Ill, possibly dying, he proffered the kind of honesty that comes with wearing your unconscious mind as well as your heart on your lapel. That made him an easy target for ridicule, though I did not find him ridiculous. He seemed to me untouchable, immured with his ravens and perceived conspiracies. I went back to my room and tried to capture exactly what he had said over the previous hour. I wanted to pin down the way his mind had bobbed and weaved—a contradiction. It was like trying to remember in sequence every headline of a large newspaper you've just read, all the articles unrelated except that they originated on the same planet. I could see a globe spinning wildly in Milton Acorn's mind.

Peter drove into Charlottetown from the country and took me to lunch. We had met one morning in the Chinese restaurant on Barrington Street in Halifax. He was "from away" as the expression goes on Prince Edward Island, not a native. He had come in the early 1970s when P.E.I. had been a haven for disaffected children of the Canadian middle class, young people with grand social theories and low personal ambitions. "We used to sit around getting wrecked until one o'clock, go out to the barn, lift four boards, and then sit around and smoke more dope until supper time. There were all kinds of fiddlers and singers. People would go out to see each other, and for the music, in the church basement on a Saturday night. Television has ruined all that." He looked back nostalgically to the days when he had belonged to a social movement. "People used to come and take pictures of us." A superannuated hippie, he called himself. Like the movement, his life was in disarray, two marriages with a child each time, and both wives had left him. Of the people I knew who had thrown themselves into the rebellion of the 1960s most had found ways to lead productive lives. But some, like Peter, were stuck, waiting for the old promises to come true.

I wandered through Charlottetown that afternoon, thinking of my maternal grandparents. Like many Maritimers born in the late nineteenth century, they had emigrated to New England, my grandmother from a farm near Summerside on the south shore of P.E.I., my grandfather from a farm on the north shore at St. Peter's Bay. They met in Boston, married, and lived in Massachusetts for the rest of their lives, becoming staunchly loyal American citizens. My grandfather rarely spoke of his early life. But in the year before he died, at the age of ninety-two, he rose from his bed several times and said desperately to his wife, "I've got to get to the Island." He was ill and weak, and she was able to restrain him. In his place I had come, as I had promised I would many years before. It was too late to send the card. She too had died. I carried her memories with me, stories of wandering down to the water's edge at her father's farm and scooping fresh lobster out of the sea, the horse and carriage into Summerside on weekends, the butter making, the embroidery, the deep cuts of snow along the roads in winter. And I could hear her voice in the house they built on a piece of old apple orchard outside Boston. Sitting at the sky-blue kitchen table on the dark blue linoleum floor. "I just decided that whatever happened, I wasn't going to live on a farm. That's all my poor mother ever did: work without end."

There was a cousin on my grandfather's side whom I'd been told to look up. That had been ten years earlier, when I'd been planning a holiday on the island. The trip had fallen through; I supposed the cousin had since died. But when I rang F. W. Hyndman from my motel room a gravelly voice answered and invited me for a drink. "I'm eighty-two," he told me in the living room of his house on Water Street. We looked at a family tree. He was my mother's second cousin. "During the First World War all the people around here were looking for traitors. We had a funny name, so a lot of the kids decided we must be the spies. I went home one day and asked my father who we were and where we came from. He told me my great-grandfather, Robert Hyndman, got very sick when he was studying at Trinity University in Dublin and was told he needed a northern voyage. So he took a passage across the Atlantic and was found sitting on a rum keg on the north shore of Prince Edward Island by Anne MacNutt, whom he married. That was my father's story. Robert Hyndman had actually been sent out to settle his father's estate in Antigua. This was about 1823. On the way the ship was careened in Halifax. He went over to P.E.I. to have a look, and he fell in love and got married. They sent out the money for his passage home three times, according to a great-aunt of mine, but he never went back. He lived in great splendour for a while out on the north shore. Built a house and built a number of ships too, and I guess blew all his money.''

F. W. Hyndman, my second cousin once removed, was given to unequivocal opinions. In this way he reminded me of my grandfather (who once told me that ''all niggers should be put into one or two of the southern states and told they can't leave''). F. W. had my grandfather's dark mottled skin, the same ears, and the same build. I listened to his provincial views on Pierre Trudeau, French self-assertion in Quebec, Roman Catholics and political power, the rise of black people, and government handouts. At his farm outside Charlottetown, he said, he still flew the old Red Ensign, ''not that ridiculous red-and-white sheet the Liberals brought in,'' a reference to the Canadian flag adopted by Parliament in 1965. ''I get angry,'' his wife said, ''when I hear it said that the British exploited all these people in Africa and the West Indies. They treated them very well, really. When you think that five servants used to do the work that one does now. It wasn't a hard life.'' They were both loyal monarchists. A picture of him bowing to the Queen on a royal visit hung in their study, a memento of his time as the province's lieutenant-governor.

We argued about public broadcasting. ''Canada doesn't need the CBC,'' he fulminated. ''I remember when it came to Charlottetown. It put two private stations out of business. Took all the good national shows away from them, shows with advertising.'' Then we argued about government aid to artists and writers. ''What you do is not essential. You don't produce food. People can live without culture, and right now the country is going broke. We've got to tighten our belts.'' Even more than my grandfather, he espoused a draconian and punitive view of the world, and more than my grandfather, he was voluble and impatient to express himself. I disliked his narrowness, yet also felt a reluctant affinity. This was where part of me came from. Whether I wanted to claim it or not, it was mine.

Fixed to the outside of the building where my cousin lived was a plaque that said, "The Robert Longworth House 1858." The walls were shiplap, a fanlight spread itself delicately over the front entrance, and a pentagonal dormer decorated the third storey. It was one of many houses built by the Victorian gentry in Charlottetown's waterfront area and recently restored. We had eaten and the sun had set. I prowled along Water Street and Great George Street, back and forth along the downtown grid, thinking of F. W. Hyndman in his tweed jacket and Milton Acorn in black leather. "If this brain's over-tempered," Acorn had written, "consider that the fire was want/ and the hammers were fists./ I've tasted my blood too much/ to love what I was born to." My cousin had said that racial mixing was making cities like Toronto "powder kegs ready to explode." I saw little evidence of racial mixing in Charlottetown. Only the Chinese restaurant, whose owner told me he had come to P.E.I. twenty years before from Hong Kong: "Charlottetown very nice place. Very clean. Very quiet. Very friendly." True. The little city had been largely excused from the onslaught of modernist architecture, air pollution, traffic jams, bums, muggers, and run-away adolescents with green hair. The lead headline in the *Journal-Pioneer* that day was "Refusal to Install Street Light Almost Leads to Resignation." On the main thoroughfare stood quaint old storefronts dressed in wooden window frames. The long sheets of plate glass were free of mullions, in the style of the last century. A shoe repair shop, the kind of enterprise that elsewhere would be relegated to a cramped cupboard on a sidestreet, occupied one of these emporia. Other businesses, lively in larger Canadian ports, were non-existent here. A hooker would have been hard to find.

I stopped for a drink before bed at the Charlottetown Hotel, attracted by the bulk and age of the building. It was the kind of gracious old hostel, with a high airy lobby, that had been abandoned or even demolished in other Canadian cities of this size. In the bar, which must once have been the ballroom, a band played hybrid jazz and what sounded like high-school dance tunes from the 1940s: clarinet, trumpet, electric guitar, drums, and piano. The horn players wore golf shirts. On the floor, tables of young men were drinking beer. One customer, wearing a baseball cap, sat by himself, his table filled with empty glasses. High above, the ceiling was divided into nine squares with plaster borders; embedded in the moulding were grapes, oak leaves, and portcullises. An attractive woman about forty, wearing a grey felt hat with a wide brim and a red feather, sat down beside me at the bar. She was the woman I had imagined meeting on the train.

"Do you mind telling me what you're doing," she asked.

I put away my little black notebook.

"I'm writing something myself," she said. It was a book about politics. She wanted "to impeach the prime minister." She told me these things flirtatiously. We all have our Saturday-night lies, she seemed to be saying. "I moved to Toronto in my early twenties with three girlfriends. They all did well. One became a travel agent, one a department-store clothing buyer. The other one, she had a tough time at the beginning." There was a pause. "She became a hooker. She had lots of rich clothes and a high-class apartment. Then she came back here and married a very wealthy man." My train lady immediately regretted having told me this. The flinty sophisticate gave way to the cautious Island girl. "Don't ever tell anyone I said that. Don't use my name. People in Charlottetown don't know about her past. You don't share your secrets here. The Island is very tight." She moved onto the floor then to join a table of friends, perhaps because my black book made her uneasy.

Back at the motel, I saw my shoes were smeared with ochre from the red street mud, loosened by the midday sun. I had tried to enter Province House, where plans for a Canadian federation were first discussed formally in 1864, but the doors of this national shrine were barred because the P.E.I. legislature was not in session. I had wanted to see where my paternal great-great-uncle, a Father of Confederation, had sat and deliberated. But practical considerations—the cost of hiring a custodian?—had locked the building. There were few tourists in March. The sleepiness and absence of pretension were attractive, though I imagined if you stayed long enough they could cloy.

Just after dawn, on the bus out of Charlottetown to the ferry, we drove through the ubiquitous commercial strip, with its A & W, Burger King, car lots, and shopping centres. It would be easy to obliterate the Island past if people ceased to care. For now this was still more or less the P.E.I. my grandparents would have recognized. The driver was playing a country-and-western tape, The Kendals: "Put it off until tomorrow." Outside, russet snow clung to the ditches, and the dirt roads from a distance looked like red ribbons pulled over the hills.

The ferry was the John Hamilton Gray, which meant it could have been named after a nineteenth-century premier of P.E.I., or after a New Brunswick Father of Confederation. They were contemporaries with the same name; people on both shores could claim the boat, a neat solution to internecine quarrels. It was a clear Sunday morning, zero degrees centigrade, but the air felt colder on the water. Broken ice stretched as far as you could see. From the deck it looked to be about twelve inches thick. Some pieces went much deeper. You could hear them grind and crunch as the ship furrowed through. The frozen chunks looked pure white, arrowing the sun back up in needles that hurt the eyes. The pharmacist had said he could remember being stuck on this boat for seven hours once in thick ice. March was the worst month. "Big cubes blow into the channel," he had said. "And this year spring is late." I thought of my grandfather, insular, ice-bound, sometimes melting for a moment in summer. He was good with his hands, and he made things for me. What he could not give in words he gave in kind. He had brought the potato-growing habit with him to Massachusetts. "Come down for a treasure hunt," he would say when I was four or five. And we would go down to the garden and dig for potatoes, underground magic, pulling any number of white bulbs out of the dark sleeve of his soil. Year by year a little more of the garden was sodded over. Until the year I looked out the back window and saw only a small patch of coloured blooms. "We'll just have the flowers now," he said, his eyes closed, rocking back and forth on the glider seat in his glassed-in porch, thinking what, I never knew.

Are You Jewish?

At Moncton I caught the afternoon dayliner to Saint John. It was a more genteel crowd than rode the Nova Scotia trains. There were briefcase men wearing jackets and ties, women wearing dresses and raised heels, and adolescent girls in school uniforms. We followed the twisting Petitcodiac River for thirty miles, passing through villages with watery names like Anagance (from an Indian word meaning "little portage stream") and Penobsquis ("stone brook") to Sussex, with its brick station, and to Hampton, with its frame station converted into a country store. "In Vancouver," said a tweedy man beside me called Alec, "people would often turn their minds to business and money on the golf course. I've never heard the go-ahead types talk that way in Saint John." He lived in Quispamsis, outside the city, and worked for the federal government. "I'm an engineer four. Fire codes. That's good money. I'll have a pension in a few years amounting to about thirty thousand from all sources. Indexed for inflation." He had come over from Scotland as a young man, and had kept his accent. Life around Saint John was unhurried after the west coast. Change, if it came at all, came slowly, he said. "I can walk down the streets of Saint John and from looking at the faces I could be in England or Scotland. You rarely see any other types." He left the two-car train at Rothesay, along with a line of others, mostly well dressed. I had meant to stop and see this enclave of elegant old houses, once a summer place for well-heeled residents of Saint John, but I suddenly felt warm and very weak, the beginning of a fever. In any case, the station at Rothesay had been converted to a photographer's studio—nowhere to stow luggage. When we arrived in the city, twenty minutes later, I called the Y and the cheaper hotels. They were all booked, though the Y could give me a room the next day. Dizzy, I lay down on a bench in the empty waiting room. I was losing track, I thought to myself. Of why I was here. Losing track, tracking down, were these old hunting expressions, or railway coinage? One track mind—that was probably of railway derivation. And going off the rails, as in "they bought a case of gin and went off the rails on the weekend," that was definitely a railway legacy. "Engine, engine, number nine, going down Chicago line," I heard my little daughter's voice chanting. Time to find a bed. I loaded myself into a cab and was driven up the hill to an expensive motel.

"You'll want a room with two double beds," the clerk informed me.

"Why would I want two double beds?" I thought out loud.

"I'll give you two anyway," she insisted. My mind

was foggy. I went upstairs to the enormous room and fell asleep on one of the purple bedspreads. When I awoke it was dark. I consulted my list of phone numbers, which included one name for Saint John. The number was good; a faint female voice whispered, "Hello." I asked to speak with Mary Palmer. The voice sounded affronted. "Mary Palmer is dead."

"I think I'm looking for a woman about thirty-five."

"Oh no. My sister was much older than that." The list of phone numbers had not been much help. People were either busy or away from home or dead. I dozed again, dreaming of clicketty-clack. And then morning: behind the purple curtains, another cold, grey sky. I took a cab to the Y, seventeen dollars a night, then walked down Hazen Avenue to the bluffs above the valley where the tracks lay. Dropped in the middle of this baleful hollow, the station was an ugly contemporary structure with a flat roof and two flat wings, surrounded by muddy yards. The street at the edge of the bluffs was Carleton. I followed it to Wellington, then to Dorchester Street. Carleton and Dorchester may have been commemorating the same colonial official, Guy Carleton, later Lord Dorchester, a strong-minded early governor of Quebec, but more likely the Carleton was Dorchester's brother, Thomas Carleton, first lieutenant-governor of New Brunswick. I walked on to Waterloo, down it and onto Charlotte (George III's consort), and stopped at the edge of King Square which crowned King Street. How many King Streets in Canada? It would be like guessing the number of beans in a jar. In the square, which was a small park, I looked at a map of the city: Crown Street, Duke Street, Canterbury Street, Prince William Street, Queen Street (and Queen Square), Orange Street, and Princess Street. Saint John was founded by Loyalists who fled the American Revolution. The street names emphasized that history. But they were not peculiar to Saint John. They were repeated everywhere in English Canada. Queen Streets in Ottawa and Toronto and in countless

Ontario towns; and King Streets in Regina, in Vancouver, and all the Prince Streets, the Edwards and Elizabeths and Georges. The names on the map were reassuring, but they also left a feeling of containment and predictability. This was little England reincarnated, and the same colonial deference was echoed in city plans across the country. If naming were conscious possessing, Canada had been slow to make up its mind and possess itself. Better to be a tenant of the Crown, the old names said, than a self-proclaimed owner of untested title. I had read an essay by the novelist Hugh MacLennan about the Saint John River. ''The Saint John River people along the lower reaches are such staunch retainers of the past that 'conservative' is too weak a word to apply to them. There is something endearing in their stubborn dislike of change.'' But endearing perhaps in the same way an old family servant might be endearing: service and duty bought in the currency of self-denial.

MacLennan had also written that the 1877 fire, which gutted downtown Saint John, ''was a tragedy. Old Saint John must have been beautiful, for all of its principal buildings and dwelling houses were in the splendid style of the first Loyalists. Rebuilt in one of the ugliest periods of architecture known to man, and rebuilt in a hurry, Saint John today is angular red brick and salt-stained clapboard.'' That was twenty-five years ago. Now an even uglier period of architecture had crusted over the face of modern cities, and the angular red brick of a century ago survived as a testament to craftsmanship and imagination. Down the steep hill of King Street and along Prince William, I walked several blocks of elegant old commercial buildings, brick and stone, some with mansard roofs, others pillared and porticoed, leftovers from a lost age of adornment when the city was a wealthy seaport. At Prince William and Princess, date stones anchored all four corners, three bearing the year 1878, just after the great fire, and one cut a year later. Farther on, a Second

Empire bank building showed the face of a man among carved flowers and fruit. He was spitting coins.

"Look for an incredibly gross bright blue coat," Mary Palmer had said when I had finally reached her through the phone directory. She was standing by the market entrance with someone called Tommy. "Beshya dono whermfrm," he mumbled gleefully, and leered at me. "Eh?" he challenged. The he shouted drunkenly, "Halifax!", spit flying in a wide fan from his missing teeth. He let go of her arm, swore lifelong allegiance to us, and Mary and I walked to Reggie's, a crowded sandwich shop where you paid on the honour system, ordering from the counter, carrying your lunch to one of the tables, and then reporting what you had eaten at the cash register on the way out. It was a pre-war eatery with a wooden storefront, the same long panels of glass I had seen in Charlottetown, and a tin ceiling. Mary wore a red blouse with sheep printed on it, one black and the rest white. Over soup she said she had run as an NDP candidate in the last federal election. "I was able to talk about some of the social issues I'd had to deal with as an unemployed single parent. It was my way of saying look goddamit, something can be done!" She had performed quite well, scoring 6800 votes against the Liberals' 8000. The Tories had won the seat with a majority. Even here in the heartland of conservatism, the socialist party could take almost a quarter of the votes. It was the Canadian solution to the tensions of pluralism: institutionalized dissent. There had always been a Canadian suspicion of firebrands and loud-mouthed malcontents. Mackenzie King, prime minister for twenty-one years, a brilliant schemer who kept his schemes concealed, a secret crackpot dressed up as Mr. Conventional Wisdom, wrapped his people in the grey cloth of quietude and dispassionate ambiguity that remained the uniform of the cautious Canadian soul. If you played by the rules and spoke temperately, you would receive a polite audience, and you might even be able to steal some ground. But no shouting please.

After lunch I walked the market, built in 1876, a year before the fire, and untouched by it. The timbers supporting the roof looked like the skeleton of an enormous hull, Noah's Ark upside down, built by local shipwrights. Two stuffed heads, a moose and a caribou, watched the array of produce on the floor. And a large zebra and dromedary, perhaps papier-maché, were fixed above the entrance to an antique dealer's stall. The smell of fish and flowers. An oriental food shop, a bakery, two butchers. Apples, oranges, bananas, nuts, vegetables, spices, all along the main and two side aisles. Paint peeling off the brick inside the long, tall building. And faded flags hanging from wooden braces by the semi-circular windows set high in the side walls.

There was a fruit stall called Pete's Frootique. The owner had a thick Nottingham accent. He wanted to talk. "When I first came over I went to Texas, then to Alberta. Then I was a partner on a farm in northern New Brunswick. I found New Brunswick a very homey place. The first thing I saw was clothes hanging from the line." He asked if I had seen him on television. A national show had given him a weekly spot, he said. "They like the way I caress the fruit."

Up the aisle stood a sandwich bar owned by a genial man in his mid-thirties. We climbed an open stairway into his office-loft above. Hockey sweaters hung from a rafter. He was part owner of a team in the intermediate league. I ate some of his smoked meat—from Montreal, he said—and listened to him talk about his business ("Nineteen eighty-one super, just great; '82 to '83, even better") and about the market building that had just been reinforced to satisfy fears that the roof might fall in. "I used to have fifty dollars in my pocket, and the next day I'd have six, and I'd think, where'd it go? Well, lessee, the wife stole twenty . . . y'know? But I can sell! I'm a great salesman! This is a good little business!" He had owned the shop only a few years. He talked about the smoked meat and the ham and the roast beef downstairs as if he were holding it in his palm and cutting pieces for me. You could taste the pieces in his words. There was a pleasant aroma of wood smoke drifting from the stove. "They won't allow any more wood-burning stoves in the building, but if you have one already, you can keep it." We stood and looked out the window onto the market aisle below. He pointed out his pile of split logs. "It was a cold winter, really bitter. I jot down the temperatures, just like an old guy." He reached for his diary, and read: " 'January. -18, -18, -15, -12, -20, -20. Overcast. Very cold. Overcast. Cold.' I just write a couple of words, so that next year if business is up 36 percent I can look back and say, 'Well, geez, it snowed every day this week a year ago and it was minus twenty. No wonder I'm up.' " He knew his customers. He could pick people out in the crowd below and tell stories about them. "There's Stanley, smart as a whip. He must be eighty-something. The guy's got lots of money, thousands. See that garbage can? Stanley picks through that and whether it be a bottle or an old piece of copper, he'll find it and sell it. It's old-age day today. They've all gone to the banks to cash their pension cheques and come here to buy a few potatoes, maybe a piece of meat, European style. They don't have much storage space. They live in small rooms."

I descended into the market again. It was true; mostly old people were shopping. I stopped to watch a small, officious man in conspicuous garb. He spoke sternly to a lank-haired young woman in jeans and a sweat shirt. There was an air of comic criminality to the proceedings.

"I might have to ticket you if this keeps up," he said.

"Why don't you ticket *them*?"

"I could ticket them. I got the right. But I got the right to be lenient too. I don't have to nail you neither. But if it keeps up I got to ticket someone. That's my job."

He jangled a heavy ring of keys menacingly. Several people had described this man to me. He thought himself the market sheriff. He had accomplices, so that as long as he stayed within the precincts of the market, his mock-authority was not undermined. It was a piece of posturing that had become a way of life, a permanent excursion into make-believe. Listening to his spiel—like a long and senseless courtroom preamble, the by-laws, the penalties, the importance of policing, the threat of anarchy—I thought of my daughter and her distorted recitation of the absurd litany of my rules. "If you don't finish your milk, Pappa, your teeth will turn yellow and your mouth will fall out. And anybody can *not* have a cookie."

Down to the water. A row of wharfside warehouses had recently been redeveloped into a huge shopping centre called Market Square. It was late afternoon. In the expensively refinished basements of the warehouses, bars were filling with young men and women who talked loudly through the aggressive music. The decor was nautical. Two men wearing pressed shirts and business suits were walking through the low basement passageway. I heard a scrap of their conversation: ". . . up against the wall with a paring knife. . . ." At one of the bars I sat and drank a beer.

"Can you tell me," asked the customer on the next stool, as if he were finishing a long speech, "why a man has to live in one house, with one wife, holding down one job, going to one church?" I said I couldn't. "Maybe that's why some people have two cars," he added. Then he said loudly, "Two beers!" gripping a bottle in each fist. "Let me explain," he went on. "I'm a shirt salesman. Get the picture? I'm on the road a lot." His own shirt, thick blue stripes on white, was open at the collar, and his navy blue tie hung loose like a pendant. "I'm a success," he said sadly. "I could sell a shirt without buttons and sleeves. Say now, that would be an undershirt, wouldn't it? Guess I do sell those. Wanna hear a tongue-twister? I'm a shit-hot sure-fit short-sleeve shirt salesman. Say it fast."

A fever seemed to be creeping over me again. I walked

up Dock Street to the Y. In the halls of the residence old
men clustered by the windows, smoking. My room was
near the end of one corridor. Outside the last door sat a
man in a chipped chrome armchair. He had been talking
to himself when I had left my bags earlier in the day, and
he was still talking to himself now in the early evening.
"No one be kind, heh, heh," I heard him cackle that
morning. Now he was wearing a Via Rail cap and suck-
ing on a cigarette wedged delicately between two rigidly
straight fingers. His nails were obscenely long, as in a
vampire film. "I've lived here for 974 years," he was
saying to the empty hallway. "And I've never been, I've
never been . . ." The voice dropped to an unintelligible
mumble. "Should go into business, ha, ha," I heard as
I closed my door. His laugh sounded fake, like a bad
parody, as if he could dimly remember something called
laughter, but could not recall the feeling that went with
it. His hollow cackle penetrated my walls. I took a glass
to the bathroom for water, and an old man, his hands
shaking, brushed past me in the hall.

"Those damn pills," he mumbled. A distinct and ugly
smell trailed after him. I was with the sick and the senile,
hidden away on the top floor of the YMCA where no one
could see them, lonely men who had lost their connections to the world. Had they ever had any real connections? I wondered if any of them dreamed of escape. It
looked a sour fate, to die ailing or demented in a lonely
cell at the Y. I swallowed some of my own pills for the
fever, and slept.

In the morning I had an appointment. On Carleton
Street I had passed the Jewish Community Centre, which
looked like an abandoned church. A woman lived in the
city, I was told, who knew the history of the Jews of Saint
John. When I had called, she had been wary, but at the
same time gracious. We would meet at her office, on the
top floor of one of the nineteenth-century commercial
buildings I had passed. Over the front entrance was a
stone archway with 1891 carved into it. Up three flights

of dark stairs I found her working in a sparsely furnished studio. She was an attractive, middle-aged woman. Her papers were spread in the sun on a big table.

"Are you Jewish?" she asked, after taking my coat. She did not understand why I had come. I tried to explain my curiosity. "I'll tell you a little," she conceded, not quite sure of me. The first Saint John Jew had been Solomon Hart, who had come in 1858 from England, a cigar maker who set up a cigar factory. I asked if he had been related to Aaron Hart, an early settler in Three Rivers, Quebec, whose son Ezekiel had been denied his seat in the colony's legislative assembly in 1807 (because an elected member's oath had to be taken "on the true faith of a Christian"). I thought I might ingratiate myself with this question, but it further aroused her suspicion. "How do you know about the Quebec Harts?" she asked nervously. I said I was interested in the history of minority rights in Canada. This seemed to satisfy her. By the 1920s, she continued, the community numbered a thousand. "We still have a Mr. Isaccs. His family came in 1878. My own grandfather came at the turn of the century, sent for his wife and children, and then saved and sent for his parents. My grandchildren would have been sixth generation here. But the golden age is over. There used to be between two hundred and fifty and three hundred families. Now we have fifty-one. We haven't had a rabbi for two years. We like our children to get educated, and with an education there's not much you can do here. The children have to leave."

Was there anti-semitism, I asked? "It's always been covert. But I'll tell you: I was invited to only one non-Jewish birthday party when I was growing up. The service clubs have been open for decades. But the Union Club only opened up in the late 1970s." I had read about the 1889 Union Club in a brochure published by the city. The pamphlet said it "continues today as the city's exclusive club. Until recently, ladies were not allowed on the gentlemen's side." Her contention about Jewish exclusion was easy to believe. Canadians had had a bad habit of attaching a waiver to their tolerance and compassion. It said in small print on a back wall of the psyche: "Except for certain groups under certain circumstances."

"But in most ways we're accepted here," she went on. "We've had a Jewish mayor, for instance. Sam Davis."

"Really? I met him once at a conference. It didn't occur to me that he was Jewish."

"What do you mean?"

"He didn't look Jewish. Not that I remember."

"I don't know what people are getting at when they say about *looking* Jewish? Do I look Jewish? I don't have a turned-down nose."

"If I keep my eyes and ears open," I continued uneasily, "I can sometimes tell what a person's background is."

"How can you tell?" She was offended. "What makes a person look Jewish? I don't think those stereotypes apply any more." Had we been talking about stereotypes? I said Toronto was a multi-ethnic city in which some awareness of racial variety was inevitable. She stared hard at me.

"Listen," I began again, "I had a Jewish girlfriend . . ."

"Everyone has a Jewish girlfriend," she cut in flatly. We changed the subject and talked more about her family. Later she said, "They were smart to let Jews into the service clubs. Jewish men are very good at raising money. Don't quote me on that."

"Why not?"

"Because it's not a nice thing to say."

"But it's true," I objected.

"It's true," she nodded.

I collected my bags at the Y and walked down the hill to the station, past the yellow-shingled shed of John Beal & Co., THE MARITIMES LARGEST DEALER IN NEW AND USED GOODS. SCRAP METALS. BATTERIES. BOTTLES, and across the vast unpaved parking lot. A grey-haired woman with a cane was waiting on one of the benches for the train from Moncton. She pointed to the three wall panels, blown-up photographs of Saint John's old Union Station with its neo-classical front entrance.

"We used to eat dinner in that station sometimes," she said to me. "The restaurant was very good. It was open every day. And the station was open all night." Her father had been a Canadian Pacific conductor. "I think he made five dollars a day. While I was still at school I had a train pass. But he wouldn't let us on the train unless we really had to go. We just didn't run for fun." She could not remember when the old station had been demolished. I asked the clerk at the ticket counter. Seven or eight years ago, he thought. Why had it been torn down, I asked?

"Some people didn't know what they were doing," he said. "Many a happy day spent in that place."

"How'd you like to pay the heating?" snapped the taller man beside him. He wore a Via Rail insignia on his jacket and appeared to be an inspector. He waved at the pictures on the wall. "We got one like that in Halifax costs seventy-five thousand dollars just to heat." The inspector went out the door onto the platform.

"Wouldn't know a station if he lived in one," the clerk grumbled.

Two self-propelled cars from Moncton rolled in punctually and were disconnected. Eight people boarded the single car that was going on to Fredericton. Every passenger had at least two seats. Some had swivelled around the next pair of chairs to give themselves space for four. It was pleasant to be able to stretch and lounge. The dayliner cars in the Maritimes had been crowded and noisy. This one felt more like a limousine on rails than a mobile tavern. In a few minutes we were crossing the Reversing Falls Bridge at the mouth of the Saint John River. This afternoon the "falls" were indeed in reverse, tidewater sluicing back up over the rapids, bringing with it the sludge and scum washed down by the river a few hours before. A dubious tourist attraction, it reminded me of a backed-up toilet. But the image to retain was of the city, not the falls. Looking back you could see the downtown, all red brick, stone, and steeples. If you cropped out the recently built Brunswick Square complex on King Street, the view resembled a Victorian engraving. It was small enough to be all of a piece. I thought of Mary Palmer, who had said she never walked a block without seeing someone she knew. She had acted with local drama groups and done some radio work. "I'm not famous, but I'm known," she had said. "Being what I am to everybody here is part of me."

Saint John combined some of the comforts of a small town with the larger possibilities of a maritime commercial centre. In a relatively poor province it enjoyed a measure of prosperity. But the unemployed were there too, if anyone cared to acknowledge them. They were in the streets and taverns around the market, and they appeared as statistics in newspaper reports on the idle shipbuilding industry. It was impossible in the Maritimes, if you kept your eyes open, to ignore the poverty. I had seen it from the train between Moncton and Saint John, the poor villages, clusters of old wooden dwellings in hollows, their frames shifted and sitting on angles, the paint faded and peeling, the hope of new houses nowhere in sight.

About fifteen miles out of the city we left the cobalt blue water of the curving Saint John River and made a straight line to Fredericton, through Enniskillen, Hoyt, Rusagonis, and the indefinite sounding Waasis. The scruffy spruce and birch that I had seen everywhere the train passed in New Brunswick made room for some pine stands, but the dominant impression remained the same: a land of trees, not people.

The woman seated in front of me was talking across the aisle. "My parents are gettin' up in age too, eh?" she said. "Eh?" You heard it everywhere in the country, just as the joke books suggested. It went together with the disconcerting habit many Canadians had acquired of turning assertions into questions, as in "I called because I thought we should talk?" This verbal tic acted as a kind of insurance, Canadians being enthusiastic avoiders of risk. You wanted to say something, but you did not want to face the odds of being challenged or denied. So you bought coverage at the last moment with an interrogative. "Eh?" was not so ambiguous, but it did suggest a similar nervous uncertainty. "Eh?" was a way of asking whether anyone was listening, perhaps not a surprising tactic of discourse in a country with one of the lowest population densities on earth.

Canadians have always been ambivalent about themselves. Neither American nor British but indebted to both, neither internationally powerful nor diplomatically inconsequential, not confident landlords of the vast land mass we purport to own, but not furtive squatters either, we have been a fence-sitting people, figuratively and even literally, the majority of us living within a hundred miles of the world's longest undefended fenceline, our southern border. It is sometimes not bad positioning to sit up on the perimeter. At the very least you get a bifocal, bipartisan view of the world. A sideline perch confers the ability to see beyond all the maniacal dogmas that propel less reserved peoples to reach through fences and strangle one another. But a dispassionate perch on the edge of things may also erode one's ability to take a stand.

Fredericton: arrive 16:10 the timetable said, and we did. Inside the old brick station I sat on a wooden bench with carved scrolls at the end of its arms and read my *Budget Guide to Canada*. The author had had the uncanny prescience a year ago to recommend all the cheap inns in the Maritimes that were about to fail and close their doors, or so it seemed. Invariably the first number I had called at each stop was that of a hotel or motel in the book that had just gone out of business. I called Mary's Bed and Breakfast from the pay phone by the bench with the same results. Mary's phone had been disconnected. A clerk at the ticket window told me of an inexpensive place "just along the station road and up the hill."

Twenty minutes later I was still climbing the hill with my bags. It had begun to snow. I wondered if I might be lost. "You gotta walk all the way up this sucker of a hill," a gas station attendant said when I stopped to check my directions. It occurred to me then, and was confirmed many times later, that a long walk from station to bed had become a typical feature of modern railway travel in Canada. The hotels that once had clustered around stations were now sleazy watering holes, or they had been demolished, or, in the big cities, they were priced for people on expense accounts. Overland travel now was designed for the automobile. Motels were out on the highways, miles from where the train stopped. The local station, only a generation ago a commercial hub, had become a municipal reject, run-down, badly placed, inconvenient. Even the ticket clerk had seen me as a man on four wheels, although I had just stepped off his daily train. He had certainly sent me into automobile country. At the crest of the hill I turned right on Prospect Street and walked past Wendy's Hamburger drive-in, Speedy Muffler King, the Esso car wash, a Renault dealer, the Little Rock Beverage Room, a fitness centre (to which no one walked), and a Lada dealer. At the end of the strip, with its franchise outlets for Anytown, I found what I wanted. It was the last lot—uncut bush stood on the other side—a motel called Journey's End. The sign showed white letters on shiny black. It had a red sun setting in the bottom left hand corner. If I had been designing a chain of cut-rate funeral homes for the heavy-metal generation, this name and sign would have been perfect, with the added motto: Death Goes Better With Video Rock. As the pay-off for my long, cold hike, however, the sign was insinuating. I did not wish to die in Fredericton, more particularly not in a motel room. I was having a rush of fever again, and the thought crossed my overheated mind that if the journey were going to end, I would like more than a television set for company.

After a sleep, the decision to leave the Maritimes was easy. I wanted to board a train and stay on it. The Ocean, which travelled west, left Moncton at six every night, and there was a noon connection from Fredericton. I knew this part of the country could be salubrious in more clement weather. It would be pleasant to return aimlessly some summer, but not again in the cold and wet of March.

Budget Guide to Canada recommended the Carleton restaurant. Down the hill I wobbled, heavy with codeine. Here were the British street names again: George, York, King, Queen, Churchill, Aberdeen, Argyle. On Charlotte Street three-month-old Christmas wreaths, brittle and faded, hung on several doors. The little houses were neatly painted, some with enclosed porches, and some with gingerbread fantasies. Each looked as if someone's grandmother lived in it. Most were dark, or showed one room with light. It was not yet nine o'clock. When I reached the Carleton restaurant at five to the hour, a woman was sweeping the floor and a CLOSED sign hung in the window.

After eating in the local Chinese restaurant, I went into the Lord Beaverbrook. My guidebook said this hotel had a bar where you could get a quiet drink. Possibly the author suffered from a serious hearing impairment. From well outside the bar, you could hear a raucous country-and-western band. A board in the lobby advertised "Music by Drifter." The drinking room was crowded. I ordered a beer beside a man who introduced himself as Phil and his girlfriend as Suzanne. She was French-Canadian, an accountant from Grand Falls.

"All this fucken shit," she kept saying. Phil was married to someone else. He wore a heavy gold wedding band, and said he owned fifteen apartment buildings.

"You know what it's like, George. Once you've gone black, you can't go back. It's the same with these French-

Canadian girls here." Suzanne, a very pretty young woman with a frightening appetite for Scotch, seemed not to comprehend these remarks.

"I don't know Phil very well." She put her hand on my arm. "I'm getting a divorce. I didn't want to stay home and have a family. All this fucken shit."

"I read a lot of that psychology and sociology stuff," said Phil. "If you really look at them, they all go back to Freud. But mostly I read Robert Ludlum."

"I don't read any of that fucken shit," said Suzanne.

On the way back to Journey's End, I asked my cab driver, a woman from Newfoundland, what she thought of the premier of New Brunswick. The police had found marijuana in his suitcase as it was being transferred onto the Queen's plane during a royal visit. With the precision of physicists looking for ever smaller particles of matter, the press had been analyzing for months Mr. Hatfield's denials and explanations. The electorate was weary of this little scandal, and my driver answered bluntly: "People are sticking their noses up someone else's asshole." The language problem again: these earthy comments were making me feel overcivilized. In my large motel room, on the enormous bed, with the colour television switched on, I realized that most of us knew the Maritimes better through television reporting than any other way; much of the dialogue I had listened to over the last few weeks would have been censored from any newscast. This was one of the pleasures of being on the road—seeing past the pinched vision of videotape, discovering in a known place the unknown range of sights and sounds.

A Dream About
the Queen Mother

At Moncton I caught the Ocean for the overnight trip into Quebec. Two images from the Maritimes lingered in my mind. The first was an old black-and-white photograph a woman in New Brunswick had shown me. It was a picture of her alcoholic father as a boy, standing with his family in front of their unpainted wooden house. They were proud-looking, tight-faced, poorly dressed. She repeated a story her father had told her. The night the family next door had finished wiring their house for electricity, the neighbourhood gathered to watch all the lights go on. But her father's mother, ashamed of her own poor candlelight, locked her doors and allowed none of her children to see the miracle. The other image was one I had seen from the train window in Nova Scotia. Maritimers often stopped on a rise by the tracks and watched the train roll by. Somewhere between Annapolis and Halifax we had passed an old country couple standing by the line with their arms raised. They had the look of people who were not only acknowledging the daily train, but waving good-bye to an era.

Just after midnight the Ocean stopped at Mont Joli. It was here we used to detrain en route to the town where my family kept a summer house. Metis Beach was half an hour from Mont Joli by car. One of several communities on the lower St. Lawrence where well-heeled English Montrealers retreated for the hot months, Metis was served by steamboat in the mid-nineteenth century, and then when the railway age reached down the river, by train. The town had a small wooden station, and a special weekend train that ran all summer from Montreal. When the train made its last run one August in the 1960s, I knew the world was changing, not my own unstable adolescent world, but the larger one which I had assumed could make some valid claim on permanence. Then the hotels, which had continued to populate Metis with widows and spinsters from the railway age, were abandoned one by one and torn down. Twenty years later I could see them all clearly, the white Cascade Hotel by the stream; the Seaside with its high hedge, rocking-chair verandah, and small sandy beach set into an otherwise rocky shore; the Hillside, on top of a steep little rise; and the rambling Boule Rock Hotel, named after the bare-faced bird island that sat in the water offshore. Built for the railway age, the hotels failed soon after the weekly train was withdrawn. The house I had stayed in as a child, an implausible fantasy perched on the edge of a cliff at the river, was gone too, but remained perfectly intact in my mind's eye. I could still see the comical World War I recruiting posters that a previous owner had framed on the walls, and the old ice house full of sawdust; the maze of corridors and stairways that led to seven bedrooms on six levels; the faded tongue-and-groove pine walls; and the fire extinguishers, like lightbulbs full of water, that hung in racks by each chimney. The fog horn—long since fallen silent—would boom across the broad bay from the point, and the lighthouse would flash through the thin summer curtains after dark, so that there were moments when the house seemed seaworthy, self-contained, ready to float you anywhere your imagination could travel. It had all burned to the ground one fall, and no one would dare to build again on that impossible precipice.

We pulled slowly out of Mont Joli, past the old station hotel that years ago invariably had half a dozen rusty pickup trucks parked in front of its tavern entrance. The ground floor was now an electrical repair shop. Along the same street was the grim new Hotel de la Gare made

of concrete blocks. I settled into my upper berth and
flipped through the *Time* magazine dated March 18.
Someone had left it in the dining car. "I do not understand those who go to tanning parlours," one letter began, "and I find it bizarre that Caucasians want to change
the colour of their skin. . . . It is time white people
learned that the natural color of their skin does not need
to be changed to be considered attractive." The letter
was signed by a Stephen Canada. It rained often in the
summers at Metis, and the fog sometimes moved in for
days. In Canada we more easily accepted the land for
what it offered. Americans were harder to please. They
wanted suntans even on rainy days.

The upper berth felt claustrophobic, though familiar. I
remembered my childhood fear of being folded into the
ceiling when the beds were made. Everything in my space
looked the same as it had thirty years before: the dull,
buff-coloured paint; the porthole-shaped mirror; the
chains at either end attached to wheels for rolling the
berth up; the blue curtains that snapped shut, sown
around a bar for half the bed's length (a safety net to
catch tossing passengers); the little hammock along the
outside wall for clothes; and the leather pouches for your
watch and money.

The memory train. My childhood had been contained
in the four hundred miles between Mont Joli and Montreal. At 6 A.M. the porter shook me awake. We were
nearing Drummondville in the Eastern Townships, not
far from where I attended a boys' boarding school between the ages of thirteen and seventeen. After the summer holidays, after Christmas and Easter, we boarded a
train in Montreal for the ride back out to the British-style
academy. School ties had to be worn on the train, and
school rules observed. Like all railway journeys, those
partook of being neither here nor there, no longer on
holiday but not yet in class, no longer leaving but not yet
arrived, like a decision slowly and deliciously reached.

The train postponed committment, prolonged doubt, heightened anticipation, and sometimes nurtured regret.

I decided to stop and look at my old school. Passenger trains no longer ran through the nearby town. I would have to catch a bus from Drummondville. The early-morning air pinched my face as I walked from station to station. LA CHOSE LA PLUS PRECIEUSE QUE TU POSSEDES EST AUJORD'HUI, said a sign in the bus depot. A crudely painted picture of Christ hung on the wall. I ordered toast and eggs and listened to three men argue beside me in French. Another man shuffled into the room, delicately but stiffly, like an atrophied ballet dancer. He took a seat at the long counter. He was so emaciated that his frame seemed to exist only as a vehicle for his amazing handle-bar mustache, thick and black.

"Bonjour, Joseph," the waitress said. He moaned something to her, his fingers tight on the counter. The nails were animal-like, curled and caked with dirt. The waitress put a glass of water in front of him; he gripped it with both hands, placed it on his mouth, and drained it in one go. Then he lit a cigarette with insane panache, like a mime artist making smoke from nothing. He sucked at it greedily—this could be his last breath—stood, bowed to the counter, and began his odd shuffle and strut across the floor, wheezing histrionically, huff-step-huff-step-huff. Choo-choo man, I thought. People like him used to populate railway station lobbies and washrooms. I had wondered where they sought refuge now that so many railway terminals had been closed or emptied. Empty lobbies were not what this type wanted. He sought anonymity, but not solitude. The crowded concourse had been ideal for him, a high turnover of strange faces onto which he could project his own high turnover of inner demons. Now he had nowhere to go. No bus terminal could ever satisfy delusions of grandeur in the same way the old railway stations did. Airports were miles from the street, and the street was choo-choo man's work-place. The sidewalks were his world, and the train station his omphalos. Shunted off to the scuzzy bus terminal, he probably saw the civilization of which he was a reluctant part going swiftly all to hell.

Looking around this particular bus depot I would have agreed. It was a relief when the driver collected tickets and we pulled away. Not far down the road we passed through the town of L'Avenir, which means future but would probably translate as hope, the quintessential New World town. Such names conveyed a sense of infinite promise without any obligation. Who could say when the future might arrive? The deadbeat drinking establishment, the sad houses, the big church, the Caisse Populaire, these were the makeshift facilities of today. But tomorrow. . . .

Later we rolled through Ulverton, a charming, preserved village, and then we met the muddy St. Francis, with large chunks of spring ice afloat. The same river had rushed below my bedroom for three years at school. It looked tame now; I had listened to many strict injunctions about the river during those years. The school authorities were more frightened of the fast water than we students were. Expelling boys was one thing, expelling water from their corpses another. "Mrs. Jackson, I have the worst possible news. Your son Fred was washed away this morning just before chapel. He was scheduled to read the daily lesson, and that's when I realized we were short a boy. I confess his housemaster may have erred in sending him down for five pails of river mud in which to anchor our new goal posts." The old school: a hard-hearted institution that could still elicit in me draconian fantasies and depression dreams, but I had also made friends there and learned strategies for coping with some of life's inevitable misfortunes—stupid people in authority, for example. That, I saw later, was one of the advantages we have over day schools. At day school you might have to put up with the occasional insufferable autocrat, but you knew that after four o'clock your suffering was over. At boarding school you could be under the nose of some mean oaf for all your waking hours, which meant you had to devise survival techniques that now seem remarkably adult to me: flattery; eloquent prevarication; blackmail; and the opposite of blackmail, moral suasion. Some boys simply said to hell with it and ran to Montreal. The school would save face by hauling them back so they could be expelled. But as these boys had already judged residence at the school the worst punishment imaginable, expulsion was a hollow sanction.

I reached Lennoxville on a local bus from Sherbrooke, and registered at a motel. A few months later train service would be restored to Sherbrooke, but Lennoxville had, years before, been permanently eliminated from passenger train schedules. The little town had some new stores and the streets appeared to have fewer potholes, but I recognized it as the place we were allowed to visit one afternoon a week to buy junk food. I proceeded over the tracks, past the buildings of Bishop's University, across the bridge spanning the St. Francis, and onto my old campus. The effect was shadow-like, an echo of an echo. It was twenty years since I had left this little world, and though it looked the same—a couple of inconspicuous new buildings had gone up—the reality paled beside the memory. It was disconcerting to go back after many years to a place once known so intimately. One could pretend to be reassured. One could claim a share in the continuity. But in truth when I turned my back and cut my ties I had become inconsequential to the community. Whether I were dead or alive no longer mattered.

Feeling like my own ghost, I walked up the road by the playing fields and past my old residence above the river bank. It was Easter break and the grounds were empty. Several figures loitered in my mind: the bouncy, squat senior master, his hairless nose fitted with filters (which fell into our soup once); the dry-voiced English teacher who wore a red wig (I did not win his favour with my negative critique of a short story he read us from a magazine—at the end of the class he announced he had written it himself); the homosexual chaplain, a charismatic pedagogue who would beat you black and blue with his large hairbrush and then surreptitiously cuddle you a few days later (I heard that he died on a train); the maniacal chemistry teacher who was given to explosive rages and bull's-eye chalk throwing; and the slow-witted militia major who inspired both his football team and cadet corps with fierce discipline.

The school, I had heard, was co-educational now, having amalgamated with its equivalent girls' institution ten miles away. That would make it a gentler, saner place. Spring flowers had been planted in front of the main building, a soft adornment that would have been dismissed as effete in my day. This building was called, in a failure of imagination that baffled me at first but then seemed typical, School House. It was a three-story brick structure with stone trim. Off the masters' common room at one end of the second floor was perched a balcony with a stone railing, and under it, the seat of authority, the headmaster's office. The front entrance bore the dates 1842 and 1917 on either side, the year of the school's founding and, I presumed, the year School House was built. Over the entrance a carved lion's head roared the words Per Aspera Virtus, and below this the school crest appeared in stained glass: the bishop's mitre, the shield, and the motto, *Recti Cultus Pectora Roborant* (Correct Training Strengthens the Heart), which triggered in me a recitation of the two Latin graces, one before the meal and one after, that we heard in the dark dining room three times a day.

Above the entrance and to the right were the windows of what used to be the prefects' room. The prefects were the school police. They had what were called "caning privileges," and the fact that it was deemed a privilege to inflict humiliation and pain on fellow students was a clue to the moral tenor of the place. A prefect who once used his privileges on me became a senior official in the prime minister's office in Ottawa, highly respected for his disciplinary techniques. It was expected that many of us would reach positions of power and authority, as had previous generations of little boys in purple blazers. But by the 1960s the school had become in some ways a grotesque parody of itself. Young people across North America were stepping into a world shaken loose by television, rock music, dope, easy money, and easy sex. Meanwhile we were being prepared for life in pre-war Canada. Which war? Sometimes you couldn't tell. The rifle I learned to dismantle and clean in my first year of cadet training was the Lee Enfield 101, last used in battle by Canadian troops in 1918. In my final year I carried and saluted with a ceremonial sword. We learned all the rules of gentlemanly self-presentation—you could be beaten with a stick for not having a clean handkerchief folded to a point in your blazer pocket—but the inculcation of this arcana did not strike me as timely. I did not know then that it was remarkable piece of good fortune for a writer born after the war to have in some tangible and powerful ways experienced life before it.

There was only one master who had taught me and still lived near the school grounds. He had retired, but kept his property at the edge of the campus. He had kindled my interest in history, perhaps because he took himself lightly, and because I was attracted to his gentle and cultivated personality in what often seemed a brutish environment. When I arrived at his door, having called from the village, I saw he had grown old and was drinking too much. He had always displayed an aristocratic insouciance. I remembered him on weekends, relaxed and glassy-eyed, watching the school team at football or cricket. After the war he had left his law practice in Montreal for school life in the country.

"I'd a dream about the Queen Mother," he said as we sipped beer in the kitchen. "Someone asked her if she'd like a cup of tea. 'Actually I'd like a little drink,' she said. Then someone invited her to sit down. 'Oooh,' she groaned. 'Is something wrong with your leg?' she was asked. 'No' she said. 'I think it's my liver.' ''

I nodded. The dream explained a great deal. He and I talked of the school twenty years ago while his wife cooked dinner. ''About that time we began to take boys whose last names ended in -ov and -ski,'' he said. I asked him about the railway his family had owned. He seemed to enjoy the memories.

''It was the Canada and Gulf Terminal, which went from Mont Joli up to Matane. I sold our 49 percent share to Mr. Briand—the fellow who owned Quebec Telephone—in about 1947. I was the oldest brother, you see. He gave us a good price.'' Here was one of the last people still alive in Canada who had sold his family railway. Once there had been many such independent rail companies. For forty years around the turn of the century laying new track had been the great capitalist gamble. If you won the game, your tracks were a prolific money maker. The next generation raised money by selling off the assets.

It was unusual for a man working at the school to have come from the same Montreal establishment as most of the boys. If the masters were characterized by any one quality, it was not a common social background and not academic excellence, but strongly held views or eccentric personalities unsuited to the public school system. The fact that many of the students came from enormously rich families had to be disguised, perhaps as much for the sake of the impoverished masters as for the other boys. An egalitarian regime governed behaviour in everyday life at school, but everyone knew this was temporary. After their last year the rich boys would go back to their money, and the others would have to work hard to maintain the social pretensions such schools encourage. The Anglo-Scottish plutocracy of Montreal had possessed more wealth for much longer than any other group in Canada, including the Toronto establishment, and boys who were going to inherit these old Montreal fortunes enjoyed a subtle arrogance and embedded confidence that owed more to European upperclass assumptions than to whatever pioneer energy their forebears had exhibited.

Some of us took away from the school a heavy load of social baggage that had little use in the outside world. Like suitcases packed for the wrong climate, these bags had to be discarded if the traveller wanted to enjoy himself and stay healthy. Unless he were one of those who knew he would soon be enjoying a comfortable investment income. Then any notion, however archaic or cockeyed, was admissible. I learned at school that enough money could have the odd effect of insulating its inheritors from everything that mattered, even their own intelligence.

Omer Lavallée and Jean-Louis Lamarche

APRIL FIRST. GREAT DOLLOPS OF SNOW WERE HEAPED ON the hills of the Eastern Townships; it was still falling at 5 A.M. as we drove into Montreal. The mild weather of the past few days, the spring flowers, the reprieve from the longest winter in years, all buried. I had spent the weekend with old friends. Outside the front door of the brick farmhouse, the children's tricycles stood cloaked in drifts; around the end of the long driveway six snow-dusted horses pawed the ground, upset by the world's abrupt change from sloppy brown to cloudy white.

"Are the horses from the urine farm?" I asked, remembering how my friends' neighbour had been making a living the last time I had visited.

"There's no more money in that," said Joel. A healthy

fox with a thick coat bounded across the road and plunged into a deep snowbank. We switched on the radio. A male voice was singing "O Canada" to begin the broadcasting day.

In the city the snow had already turned to slush. I put my bags in the house off St. Laurent Boulevard where another friend, Simon, had offered me a room, then walked to Central Station where I bought a train ticket to Quebec City for later in the week. Next to the station stood the basilica, a reduced replica of St. Peter's in Rome. I used to look down at it from the window of my father's office when I visited him in the Sun Life Building opposite. There seemed to be an unbridgeable gulf between these two monumental structures, one the seat of Catholic power in the city, darkly Latin and ornamental, the other a symbol of Anglo commercial hegemony in Quebec, a massive pile of receding stone tiers which spoke of opulence muted by Protestant restraint. There was a French-Canadian farmer who drove his cart into the city to see the cathedral. "Not bad," he said, and then, looking across Dorchester Boulevard at the Sun Life Building, he added, *"mais quel presbytère!"* (But what a manse!) I had heard the joke years before. It revealed English Montreal's contempt for French-Canadian church-fostered ignorance. It also alluded to the convenient *modus vivendi* operating between the English business elite and the Catholic clergy. The English restricted their cultural influence to their own small communities, but exercised controlling power in finance and commerce. The church, which supervised French-speaking schools in the province until the 1960s, imposed its rearguard world view through religious instruction and a classical education. The winners were the English elite (awarded Caesar's realm by default), and Quebec's conservative priesthood. Some Quebec historians have argued that the English powerbrokers arranged to keep French Quebec out of business and permanently dispossessed, but the fact of history remains that the balance of material power in Quebec began to shift only when French-Canadian politicians wrested the antiquated educational system away from the French-Canadian clergy and modernized the schools. An anti-clerical act by and for French Canadians, it could have been achieved fifty years earlier had any Quebec government so willed.

Down sloping Peel Street I walked to Windsor Station, the Canadian Pacific terminal. Always I could see my father's mother when I came to the doors of this russet Romanesque building. The station, like my grandmother, was made in another century. As a boy I knew its age and dependability, like hers, went back as far as anyone could remember, which was tantamount to forever in my mind. I did not know that just before my grandmother was born many people thought the transcontinental railway was an idiotic and ill-fated experiment, nor that just after she died the passenger train business would enter a steep decline. Trains were part of the world we received from her, as predictable as the snow piled high in the churchyard across the street from the station's heavy doors. Dressed in a fur coat and elegant black hat she would be standing by the entrance waiting for a ''red cap'' to trundle her bags in from the platform. It might be Christmas. She would have taken a parlour-car seat on the train from Ottawa, one of those roomy swivel chairs with a footrest and a little table for your drink, though she never drank. The railway system, with its dogma of timetables and fare schedules, seemed to me to fit naturally into her complex code of interlocking rules—the rules of religion, gentility, and family tradition. When she stepped off the train she stepped out of a world both ordered and powerful, and brought some of those qualities with her. But my grandmother's generation could see that the power of the railways had peaked, and with it, perhaps, their own. She spoke wistfully of the 1920s when she had sometimes travelled with her first husband by private rail car. The lavish comfort of first-class railway accommodation in the early part of the century, the building of stations and the laying of track, the apparently endless dreams of railway promoters, in my childhood she knew all this was firmly in the past.

I went upstairs to the CPR offices above Windsor Station. At the northeast corner in a little tower with a view of Dominion Square worked the CPR archivist. Five hundred years ago the cramped rooms in towers like this were equipped with racks of arrows. Train tracks covered the world in an age when history was still venerated. Railway companies made their stations to look like ancient temples and castles, giving the impression that trains had existed for centuries and would survive for centuries more. Every small child who walked through a large train terminal in the railway age must have believed this fiction, as I did.

The archivist, Omer Lavallée, an amiable, moon-faced man, told me he was a fourth-generation railway worker. "My great-grandfather worked as a stone mason contractor for the oldest section of Canadian Pacific, a small railway up near Joliette, Quebec that was opened in 1850." Lavallée himself had joined the railway at seventeen, and had worked in the paymaster's office for twenty-two years. "It was a pleasant job; since we knew what salary everyone was getting, they always paid us well." His duties included a regular run with the last railway pay car in North America along the CPR line through northern Maine. "Until 1960 we were still going there once a week—a paymaster, a clerk, a policeman and a cook. We paid cash, out a wicket at the back, payrolls of forty or fifty thousand dollars a week." He said he had passed the exam for conductors and enginemen, and ever since had carried a standard-time railway pocket watch. I knew he had written several books on early railways and railway construction. He was deeply embedded in railway culture, with the allegiances and peculiar enthusiasms that long-time railway employees often adopt. He was not, however, a merciless railway bore with a one-track mind. I listened to him speak of his own life, fused from the city's two opposing language groups.

"My mother lived up on the Plateau Mont Royal. Grandpa was an upholsterer. He was thoroughly bilingual—Montreal Irish. My father came from a French-Canadian family in Joliette. They seemed higher intellectually. But the Irish side were not fools. They were very frank with one another. The smallest thing could start a terrible argument, yet in a crisis they would all stick together like glue.

"My father's family always seemed to be slightly artificial. Because they were too polite with one another. There was a table rule that you never discussed anything unseemly when the sisters were around. Perish the thought you should discuss any type of crime or violence. But politics too was considered very unseemly." I thought of the false clichés about cultural differences in Montreal that I had absorbed at a young age. Anglophones were supposed to be cool, calculating, repressed, humourless, and materialistic. French Canadians were supposed to be the opposite, emotive and spirited. Lavallée's background defied all generalizations except one he made himself, that Montrealers were a breed apart, more tolerant and sophisticated than people in the rest of the province. "This is a cosmopolitan city, and it wears the cloak imposed on it by the rest of Quebec very unhappily." He was referring to the language law passed by the Parti Québécois government which had made French mandatory as the language of work throughout the province. I did not agree with him entirely. Parts of the law had been salutary. If the French language were to survive in North America, it probably required legal protection. But I was not eager to discuss the subject. Anyone who had lived or taken an interest in Quebec during the 1960s and 1970s had already spent too much of his life arguing the issue, which usually began on a lofty plane—human rights, the advantages of language instruction, cultural co-existence—and often ended with a sour comment like, "They were rude to me at the bank when I tried to cash my cheque in English."

Down from Omer Lavallée's tower, I went onto the cavernous concourse of Windsor Station, largely empty now. The two brass clocks were still hanging from arched girders high over the floor, still keeping time, but where most of the tracks once ran up to the station the ground had been paved for parking. The schedule boards that once were changed by men with long sticks were gone. Remaining were the immoveables: the spearhead prongs in rows—inspired by the same fantasy as the tower?—crowning the black iron fence between the lobby and the platforms; and below the spearheads, the sliding doors, once imbued with magic, because through them you entered the infinitely mobile world of railwaydom; and above it all, the long translucent roof, four rows of glass panels running the length of the concourse, giving an unusual, light-headed effect to a building otherwise preoccupied with iron and steel.

Outside on the sidewalk you could still see the big Guaranteed Pure Milk bottle on the roof of the dairy company building, and a tall chimney marked GPMCO. (Thirty years ago I used to wish the giant for whom that bottle had been made would appear and pour himself a glass of milk.) The carillon was spilling notes over Dominion Square and down the hill. Commuters, whose local trains had taken over the few tracks that remained at Windsor Station, began walking briskly through the front doors. It was after four o'clock. The term "rat race" was thought to have been coined in the gallery of New York's Grand Central Station when observers looked down at the first commuters scurrying in every direction to their trains. Railways were then the pre-eminent symbol of modernization and the machine age. But they prefigured the development of faster and more flexible carriers that overtook them and left stations like Windsor hollow and bereft.

I went back to Simon's flat and opened the refrigerator.

In it I found a roll of polaroid polachrome film, a roll of Kodachrome 64, a shrivelled half lemon, a tin of moldy tomato paste, a bag of onions, and three cans of beer. I took a beer.

"My culinary needs are limited," said Simon. His toes were sticking out of the old pair of shoes he wore around the flat. I drank and listened to him talk about his four years in Canada. He had come from England without money, and had found a job in Winnipeg selling frozen meat over the telephone. He excelled at this job. The owner had made him sales manager. "A very nasty place with very nasty people," said Simon. "I soon discovered the meat was not terribly good, and was often not delivered. But I made a lot of money out there." A small man, he was about five foot five, but built like a barrel. He had mastered a credible rendition of the Canadian accent, and retained a streak of British arrogance which suited his own educated British inflections. When I asked if he had read Evelyn Waugh, he exclaimed, "Wah? But it's Woaw, surely."

Simon led me to the neighbourhood tavern where we were meeting our friend Joel and a French-Canadian artist they sometimes drank with, Jean-Louis. *Bienvenue aux femmes*, said a sign, but there were mostly old men inside, sad and beery-eyed, many of them sitting alone in the dimness. We found Jean-Louis at a table in the back. He had the frame and face of a man in his seventies or eighties, thin and wizened, with a wispy beard and eyes pulled into slits, like the pictures of Ho Chi Minh just before he died. "My body is finished," he told me later. He was not yet fifty.

It came out that Jean-Louis had been active in Quebec's separatist underground when he was younger. "Quebec is not the same no more. There have been too many lies. Politics is not honest. It's an illusion, because power is an illusion." He was not at all bitter. He said he had escaped the bounds of politics, and that culture should be universal. "The English had the money. We had nothing. I don't forget that. But why should we talk about things that happened two hundred years ago?"

The group at our little table was growing, and the noise level was up. I pulled out a fifty-dollar bill when the time came for me to pay for a round. "Put that away," murmured Joel, a practiced tavern drinker. "Orange bills draw flies in here. Never pull above a purple."

The young man beside Jean-Louis had been listening quietly. Down from the Saguenay region in central Quebec, he spoke no English. "Look, he said suddenly to Jean-Louis in French. "They're fascinated by us. But we don't care about them. It's not important, Toronto. New York yes, London, Paris, Italy, yes, but not Toronto."

"I know lots of artistic people who went to Toronto," continued Jean-Louis. "They went for the money!" He was shouting. "Art has nutting to do with money."

"I'm a cultural worker," the young man said.

"He's a sculptor," hollered Jean-Louis. "Enough bullshit." His voice was giving out.

"I am not just making sculptures. I am working for the cultural collectivity of Quebec."

"Words!" shouted the older man. "You work with your hands. Like me."

A sign on the wall in French said "Social Adjustment Hour—16:30–20:00." At one glass of draft beer every fifteen minutes, the group was becoming very well adjusted. Doubting a beer-sodden memory, I went into the washroom to write in my notebook. When I came back Simon remarked he could "move among them much more easily than local anglophones whom they fundamentally distrust."

Jean-Louis greeted the owner's son. In French he said, "How's it going? You have a lot of mistresses?"

The man, bulky, with a dark bushy mustache drawn across his long face, replied, *"Moi? Non. Ça fait . . . une semaine."*

"Va shiez," said the artist. He suggested we all go back to his house on de Bullion Street and talk more

quietly. "Come to my house, yes. But don't ask too many questions. My body don't let me go, go, go no more."

In the house on de Bullion, a street where Montreal's prostitutes used to prowl, bottles of wine were opened. There were five of us, all from the tavern. While Jean-Louis was in the kitchen preparing food, the sculptor told me his old friend was a *personage*, but not an influential artist. I must meet so-and-so and see such-and-such to get a proper picture of artistic vision and energy in Quebec. In particular I must meet some people from the Saguenay who he believed had shaped the arts in Montreal. The idea of a "proper picture" struck me as tyrannical. I said I was thinking of riding the train up to Chicoutimi. Jean-Louis came into the room.

"Don't go to Chicoutimi! If you go there all alone, you'll have only misery. They'll take you for an RCMP. They're very suspicious."

A photographer who was selling funeral plots for a living arrived with a case of beer. At mid-life he looked sad and alcoholic. He told me he had sold more than two thousand dollars worth of burial property that day, all on the telephone. "I have to make a certain number of calls. Like a quota. It sounds funny, but it's not." He said he was desperate for money.

Pleased to have an audience, Jean-Louis began talking about himself, in English. "The judge said to me, either you stop drinking or you stop driving. So I said, 'thanks for the advice,' and I quit the car." He had gone to art school against the wishes of his family. " 'Don't go there,' my father told me. 'It's for rich people.' He was a very uptight person. But he used to say again and again, 'To have a bus is to be a slave,' because he drove a bus for a while. He wanted something better for me.

"My father had no money. My grandfather worked on the freight trains. Out in the cold. The pay was very little. My grandmother had twenty-one children. Seventeen lived. Because the priest used to tell them, when they touch their wives, it's only to make babies. Ridiculous! They were not even farmers who could grow their food." He had scratched out a living after art school by selling his drawings in taverns and restaurants. Amphetamines and alcohol had wasted his body. Two marriages had collapsed. He was settled now with a third woman, a professor. It was her house we were in on de Bullion.

I went upstairs to look at his work. He was shy, and pretended to be showing me his work table, his tools, the big window that gave him light. He talked about the arthritis in his hands that made it difficult to execute the fine details that filled his panels. He did not speak of the panels themselves. Hundreds of them lay stacked around the room against the walls and on the furniture. "It's my work that has saved me. No matter what else I've done, I've always worked on my pictures." The images were powerful, more compelling than most canvasses one saw displayed in commercial galleries. He was a creature of the 1950s and 1960s, and his panels retained the concentrated energy and daring of that period. Almost all were collages, mind-spinning arrays of images that suddenly settled on the brain with a meaning and then darted off again to lead you into something new. The panels had no established worth in the art market. Jean-Louis explained he did not exhibit in galleries, and sold only a few pictures a year to friends.

"The selling part, I'm no good at that. I live completely out of the system." He held a grudge against gallery owners. He said he had been cheated by them when he was younger. Instead of marketing his work he had sold drugs, driven a tractor, worked as a handyman, and shovelled snow. Now he was living on welfare. "For a while I was painting landscapes for a Hungarian. Three dollars each. He had guys with vans, and they took them all over Quebec to sell. He was happy. He thought he was screwing me up. But it was no problem for me. I painted two or three days a week for him, fifteen or twenty landscapes a day, and then the rest of the time I did my own crazy stuff."

We went downstairs. Simon was playing a lugubrious Glenn Gould record. The funeral plot man looked exceedingly drunk. He said he wanted to gamble—fifty-dollar stakes. Jean-Louis talked him down to one. It was a simple matter of cutting cards. When the photographer-salesman lost three times, his face sagged. He confessed that he had no more cash. He had been hoping to win money for beer. Someone suggested we all join hands. "To feel the temperature," Jean-Louis explained. We sat in a tactile circle, five men and a woman. "That's good," said Jean-Louis. "Everybody's warm. We know how we are."

I saw Jean-Louis again the next day. He said he had fallen asleep on his kitchen table after the party. He was coughing and his back was sore. "Sometimes I put wet tea bags on my eyes," he said. The man with seven ears, someone had called him the night before, because of his ability to hear conversations across a crowded room while engaged in one nearby.

"I used to paint nature," he said, looking out into the rain. "Now I trip on it. I can trip on a turtle as well as a jet plane. Wait a minute." He left and returned with one of his panels. "Keep this. If you ever sell it I'll kill you."

He had given me a small collage that contained a revolving universe of images, a visual diatribe on technology from the wheel to the space shuttle. On the back he wrote several lines, beginning with "Fraternity and tenderness" and then rocketing off into the "cosmic universe" and "understanding of an amicable unity," apt words for the oblong infinitude he had constructed on the other side.

I collected my clothes and went into a laundromat, hoping the rain would stop. "Moonlight Feminism" had been scratched on a building up the street. There was whimsical graffiti all over the neighbourhood. St. Laurent Boulevard and the adjacent street had been an immigrant district for two generations, and then people like

Jean-Louis had moved in and started to change the flavour of the area in the 1950s. Now it was a mix of students, artists, professionals, and the old immigrant families who had chosen to stay. A few buildings had been fashionably renovated, but most remained as before. It was still possible to live in the quarter without much money. The rents were relatively cheap; so were the taverns and restaurants. The penalty for being poor seemed less severe here, though there was evidence of miserable poverty on St. Laurent—old people struggling home with a few tins of food, ill-clothed, canvas bags strapped around their feet, hopeless. In the Lavoir St. Laurent, where I was washing my clothes and waiting out the rain, were a young couple living on unemployment insurance, a pensioner, and two students. The laundromat was typical of the neighbourhood, occupied by hard-up people, but not in itself demoralizing. It had the feel of a trendy delicatessen, with light beige walls, potted plants on the divider between rows of washing machines, art deco prints on the walls, propeller fans in the ceiling, chairs and magazines, and a powder room. The laundromats I remembered were dirty and desolate by comparison. Here you were not punished for having no money.

The clouds broke. It was a good day for walking. The rain had washed away most of the snow, and there was little traffic. I walked west of St. Laurent, towards the mountain, looking at Montreal but thinking of a house in Toronto and the little girl in it, my daughter. It was Easter Sunday, and she would be searching for the eggs hidden in her mother's living room. The Montreal streets were quiet. Inside the houses I imagined people lazily eating pieces of Easter chocolate; and some of them yearning for the pleasure of walking alone in another city, away from home.

From the mountain lookout I could see St. James Street, no longer the nation's banking centre, and beyond it Old Montreal and the river. I wandered down the mountain and into the historic district. "No more heroes," someone had scrawled on a building on St. Denis Street. Painted across the first storey of a venerable old pile on St. James Street were the words "Ignorance is strength." The same building had a grand entrance guarded by the heads of Roman soldiers, but any fear or respect they might have inspired had dissipated with the decline of the street. Other buildings displayed Greek heads and roaring lions, but the trumpets no longer sounded from these neo-classical and Second Empire façades. You could tell the money had been drained away. The rich old buildings were beginning to crack and chip. In another generation, if nothing changed, they would be derelict. Perhaps when the galling memory of Anglo domination had grown dim, they would be reclaimed and restored, though so much of English Montreal's fine architecture had fallen to the wrecking ball that the illusion of permanence once conveyed by this street was gone.

Below St. James Street on Place Jacques Cartier were grouped several horse-drawn calèches. Jean-Louis had said his father managed two fish stores in succession down here in the 1940s. A man and two women trundled past me in one of the little black carriages, clip-clop, clip-clop. They grinned awkwardly, the man squeezed between his two friends. I remembered Jean-Louis saying, "All my male friends are *mysogènes*. They don't understand I'd rather spend an afternoon talking to three women than a night in the tavern with guys I've known twenty years."

Old Montreal, deserted on a damp Sunday, looked from some angles like my favourite French city, Bordeaux, block after block of vintage architecture and the smell of water nearby. I passed an enormous billboard promoting the pleasurable ambience of the city. It pictured a row of mansard roofs, like the tops of the houses I walked by on my way down into the old quarter, but on the billboard the roofs were painted a medley of pastels. On them danced a ballerina. *"Montréal Poésie,"* read the caption, *"la fierté a une ville,"* which was not fully translatable, because it captured the difference between Montreal and the cities of English-speaking Canada, a profound divergence in outlook and sensibility. The rough equivalent would be a sign proclaiming "Toronto is poetic: pride hath found its place," which would be ironic and only half true—in Toronto the pride would be hubris.

Going to the train the next day, I walked down St. Laurent Boulevard one last time, past Anaarkali Herbes et Aliments Naturels, the Hoffner Boucherie, and the Marché Imperial (a Vietnamese store); it was a polyglot street supposedly reduced to unilingual signage by the language law, but it would probably continue to have holdouts like the Slovenia Meat Market. In any case, the street would have polyglot undertones as far ahead as anyone could see. Boucherie Slovenia might appear superficially "francized" (a nasty bureaulogism introduced by Quebec officials to denote the rewriting of public signs in French), but the law could not put the butcher himself through its culture grinder. If the language police expected everyone in Montreal to act like a tenth-generation French-Canadian, they would have to cut out tongues.

Quebec City

THE DAY WAS COOL. PATCHES OF SUN FLASHED THROUGH the grey sky. For three miles the train tunnelled, emerging on the other side of Mount Royal and stopping at the suburb named after it. When I was a small boy we lived in a house in this suburb; my father walked to the little station every week-day to catch the train downtown. I remember it as a flat place with look-alike houses and no stores or offices. Property lines were important. Some homeowners did not like you to walk on their grass, or slide down the snow in their yard. To make excitement one day I threw my shoe through the bedroom window and insisted that someone had tossed a rock into my room from outside. In the back yard one summer, a tall Hungarian whistled love songs to my mother's maid, whose room was next to mine. At night as I went to sleep I would listen to his European ballads. Twice a week the milk wagon rolled slowly down our street. In the 1950s it was still pulled by a horse. The animals were sensuous intruders, with their big yellow teeth and frothy lips, their odour of horse sweat and droppings and feed, transported briefly into my sanitized suburban world, becoming a dot at the far end of the street, and then disappearing into the larger realm of milk vats and hay bales and huge rolls of milk tickets.

St. Joseph's Oratory came into view, its breast-like dome presiding over the north slope of Westmount's little mountain. A gigantic monument, the Oratory announced Montreal from thirty miles away on a clear day. From the train you could also see the shrine's male counterpart, the art deco tower that marked the University of Montreal campus. Past the long view of these landmarks the train ran alongside acres of repetitive apartments, highrises and fourplexes and sixplexes in a treeless landscape, mean and dull. "People have to live somewhere," shrugged the older man in a well-tailored suit beside me. "These neighbourhoods are much better than the slums in the east end. Oh yes." A lawyer, he had business in Quebec City. He said he lived in Maisonneuve, once a town and now a ward of Montreal, an area he assured me had "some very good streets with good houses."

I watched the countryside and read the paper. *The Gazette* reported the results of a recent poll indicating that "about one in five Canadians would move to another country if they were free to do so." This was said to be double the proportion who showed an interest in emigrating a quarter of a century earlier. Had Canada deteriorated or the rest of the world improved?

We followed the north shore of the lower St. Lawrence, passing towns reminiscent of de Maupassant stories— L'Epiphanie, La Pérade, and La Chevrotière. At Trois Rivières, anglicized as Three Rivers by everyone I knew as a child, several families with small children boarded. The car began to fill with the sweet aroma of Easter chocolate. The children were being fed their treats to keep them quiet, a gesture as hollow as the chocolate rabbits, because the sugar intake soon had them rollicking loudly up and down the aisles. The countryside was punctuated by the silver spires that dominated every town and village. Behind me a woman said earnestly in French, "Good Friday always makes me sad. The day our Lord died. A very sad day. But Easter Sunday gives you a lift."

I had good memories of Quebec City. Francophones there used to tolerate less than perfect French in situations where, before the language law, Montrealers would easily bristle. The English-speaking population of Quebec City had dwindled to a rump by the 1960s when I first visited. Few of the natives had had much exposure to English. For the most part they were pleased to have a conversation with anyone in their own language, however limited.

We stopped at Ste-Foy, the end-of-the-line suburb. Below it on the timetable was the silhouette of a little bus. Everyone detrained. The lawyer and some of the mothers with children were met by people with cars. The rest of us waited. The bus was on its own schedule, independent of the train. There was a long delay, time to stamp in the cold, stare at the wasteland around the tracks, and contemplate the one building in view, a shack clad in yeast-coloured aluminum siding. It looked like standard-issue bunkhouse architecture, but was meant to be taken for a railway station. On the bus we rode along a commercial strip into the city passing the motels and gas stations and fast food outlets that crusted the rim of every Canadian city now, a consumer belt that took you in tired and hungry at one end and rolled you out fed and fuelled at the other.

But inside the old city walls, little had changed. The big hotel, the Chateau Frontenac, a gigantic red pile built by the CPR on a cliff overlooking the St. Lawrence, retained it pseudo-medieval look, with an arched entrance to an enclosed courtyard, a massive central tower, and a turreted profile. Better than any other structure, the Chateau Frontenac symbolized Canadian Pacific's immense economic and political power. Construction was begun in 1893, which made it one of the younger buildings in the historic district. Yet from the river it dominated the skyline of old Quebec, a monument to English-speaking capitalism emblazoned on the family arms of French Canada. The CPR had been clever with this building. They had designed for grandeur and opulence in an architectural style acceptable to local tradition. The politicians and businessmen of Quebec City had adopted the hotel as their own. It was easy to imagine the government taking steps to save this building if the CPR ever decided to demolish it. The Chateau Frontenac had insinuated itself into French Canada's heritage in a way that most Anglo-built structures had not. The nineteenth-century Montreal mansion of CPR president William Van Horne, for example, a Sherbrooke Street landmark with unique historical associations, was destroyed by a developer in 1973 when the government refused to impose protective measures. Some Quebec nationalists thought the house an odious reminder of Anglo domination, implying that its loss would be a gain for Quebec's self-respect.

I carried my bags up the rue St-Louis where *chambre à louer* signs hung in the windows twenty years ago. Now the houses with rooms to rent placed painted wooden signs outside their front doors and called themselves hotels. The street was beginning to have the look of a well-worn tourist hangout, with a number of boutiques advertising "authentic Quebec handicrafts." I found a cheap room at the top of one of the narrow stone terrace houses. The Ursuline convent was visible from my tiny window, a view that suggested Handel, perhaps because he was composing his music when some of the roofs below me were being built. Other things came to mind: the mystical Marie de l'Incarnation (founder of the convent in 1639); Kateri Tekakwitha, the Quebec Indian saint credited with miracles; Leonard Cohen, the poet who used her in his demonic novel *Beautiful Losers*; Norman Levine, who said in his book on Canada that Quebec City reminded him of a well-kept cemetery; and my ex-wife, who came here with me when we were young and in love, and looked over these old houses with me from a little window like this, the eaves heavy with January icicles, and our lives light with all the amorphous anticipations of early marriage.

A Frenchman talked to me in the downstairs hall as I waited to use the pay phone. He had come to Canada for three weeks to visit his son, who had emigrated from France several years before. The son had bought this hotel and lived with his family in the basement. The father was telling me that Canadian hospitals were outrageous. "I cut my hand while I was helping my son repair a window. I wanted only a dressing, to make sure it wouldn't get infected. They charged me fifty dollars! I wanted only a bandage. I didn't ask for Peru!" He talked on about his misfortune. It would never happen in France. Was this any way to treat foreigners? What sort of country were we living in here? He was raising his voice, making an appeal, as if I ought to give him a refund. I was not sympathetic. My own experience with doctors in France made me skeptical of his comparisons. To cure what turned out to be a minor ailment, a urologist in Aix-en-Provence once recommended cutting off my right testicle, for which dubious cure he planned to charge a substantial fee. I told the Frenchman, who said he was an engineer, that Canadian medicare worked fairly well if you were a resident.

"But I only asked for a bandage!" he complained again. What was I doing in Quebec? Researching a book about Canada, I said. "Canada has no culture," he told me earnestly. "You are all pioneers and hockey players. If I were you I would write about history. About the Indians."

I called Dr. Schwarz, and accepted an invitation to dinner the next night, then walked back down rue St.-Louis towards the river, past the Chateau Frontenac, and down the steep winding street which my guide book said was cut into the cliff by Champlain in 1623. Really? He must have had help. It would be interesting to know exactly whose hands chipped away the rock to flatten what is probably Canada's most travelled walkway. We remember only the man with the idea, Champlain, our country's first real estate developer.

The twisting street led into Quebec's lower town, known as Place Royale. All the buildings had been restored or reconstructed since my last visit. What had been a scruffy but authentic historic neighbourhood had been remade into a sanitized tourist attraction. Immense sums of government money had been poured into the project. Original buildings from the English period—beginning with the Conquest in 1759—had been razed and replaced by copies of structures that were thought to have stood on the same lots during the earlier French regime. In this folly were exhibited the worst instincts of Quebec nationalism: the impulse to rewrite history and turn back the clock to a simpler, more racially pure time; and the vindictive impulse to steal ground, in this case literally, from the anglophone community's cultural garrison. It was a petty kind of feuding: if you kick over my sand castle, I'll kick over yours. *"Je me souviens."* Quebec's motto rang through these restored streets. "I remember." But for the extremists there was a subtext: certain historical realities should be expunged.

Wet snow was falling lightly again. Not many people were out in the streets. I wandered into a restaurant in one of the old stone buildings and ordered some food at the bar. On the stool next to mine sat a middle-aged man making occasional utterances to no one in particular. His accent was heavy—more like Gaspé inflections than Montreal *joual*, but different from both. He said he was from the Saguenay region, and had grown up in Arvida, the aluminum company town. If I listened carefully I could understand him. After the accent, I noticed his eyes, wounded, but bright and defiant, and then the untrimmed beard, and the cheap shirt and pants under an expensive jacket, the attire of a man who was not quite sure where he was going. Léon had had two wives, children with each, several businesses, several houses, and had filed for bankruptcy three years before, escaping to a farm in the country with enough assets for a frugal but independent rustic life—or so he claimed. In his monologue (once launched he was unstoppable) he kept reverting to "la crise," by which he meant the rapid rise in interest rates around 1981 that had scuttled his businesses. He was bitter, but had a plan to redeem himself.

"My novel will cover the fifties, sixties, and seventies," he explained. "It's never been done. It will be a little like Dallas or Dynasty, but set in Quebec." He also wanted to establish a think-tank on his farm. "The truth. That's what is lacking. Let me tell you about the cars I used to own. I had debts," he said proudly. "You know what I call those years when my generation was building this world that people are running all to hell now? La Belle Epoque. We're making paupers of our children. I feel betrayed. My generation, born around 1935, we made the world you see around you. Take a look at downtown Montreal. It was all built in the 1960s. We did that. The ones that followed, born in the forties, they've turned on us, put us out in the street."

Léon wove back and forth between pomposity and confession. "I have been a mercenary in the service of internationalism. Before I went into business, I worked for several large American companies. They used me.'' At bottom he was desperate—and baffled. ''The state now, it wants to steal children from their parents. This could make men impotent. Excuse me, but it's true.''

He had conspiratorial theories, all tied into an interlocking zeitgeist, and fuelled by a large inventory of felt injustices. ''Now I'm in exile, with my sheep. The big families control everything anyway. Out there on my mountain, I live with thieves and fugitives. I could tell you things about the mafia, for example. It's like this. When I see a criminal, I think politician. And when I see a politician, I think criminal.'' Auditing his tirade required all my foreign language skills. The pace was exhausting, and the supply of paranoia endless. I said good-bye, and he gave me his address and phone number in a place called St. Gabriel de Brendon. ''Come for a weekend. Continue your research.'' He invoked an image he had used earlier. ''Like the Felix Leclerc song. We are all trained seals, balancing balls on our noses, without respite.''

The next morning was sunny and cold. I walked along the wooden promenade at the edge of the cliff overlooking the river, but found it blocked with snow. Passing the church where we had sung hymns on a school choir trip, I remembered the blind lady descended from an old Protestant family in Quebec, Mrs. Dobell, with whom I had been billeted. Twenty years ago she had been in her eighties and frail. There was a walnut knee-hole desk in her apartment, and pieces of porcelain bric-a-brac she cautioned me not to touch. Her rooms contained a dried-flower and dried-orange-peel scent that seemed to me to have died away in Canada with her generation of genteel Protestant widows.

At noon I stopped to talk to Parks Canada's district manager. I had expected an architect, but found an amicable accountant, overweight, with pale eyes, soft and guileless. He led me out of his office in the restored fortifications and down the street to an Italian restaurant for spaghetti and red wine. We spoke in French.

"I don't think I could enjoy life as much anywhere else. I like to wander into the old town on a summer night, sit in a café and take a glass, just watch the world go by. It's very small here." He was of the new adult generation in Quebec, a member of the expanded professional class. "Religion counts for nothing with us," he said. His wife had a job, and his two-year-old went to a daycare centre. He said he relaxed by watching television. "Mostly in English. The programs are better."

Parks Canada had opened a new maritime museum, he said, down by the port. After lunch I went to have a look. The displays illustrated the part played by maritime trade in Quebec history. In the lobby a life-sized tableau showed an artificial horse in a cargo net being lifted onto a ship's deck. When the tableau was in motion the mock horse rose helplessly in the net, then sank down again. It was the vertical equivalent of the water-wheel animal walking around and around the well. Our word museum is derived from the Greek *mouseion*, temple of the Muses, a place of mystery and enlightenment. I thought of Léon's last words to me. "We are all trained seals." A group of school children raised and lowered their heads as the mock horse went up and down.

Upstairs I sat through a movie in French, a cartoon depiction of Quebec history. The bad guys were the English, ruthless and manipulative. They had one thing on their minds—money. Insensitive and amoral, they also spoke in execrable French accents. (They all sounded like Goofy in the Walt Disney films.) Morally superior were the Québécois peasants, victims of a terrible holocaust—British commerce. *Je me souviens*. Old habits were hard to relinquish. Even now, with Quebec society obviously altered, it was comforting for some people to make and watch this kind of obsolete propaganda.

At dinner time, just after dark, I walked back down Côte de la Montagne, the street carved in 1623, and joined Dr. Schwarz in a restaurant. We had corresponded but never met. I knew him by reputation as a collector of French-Canadian fine art and a literary dabbler. A Jew born in Poland, he had emigrated first to England, where he had attended medical school, and then to Canada. He looked about sixty, married to a much younger woman, the elegant Québécoise who sat beside him. There was another man at the table; an adult son from an earlier marriage had stopped in Quebec City for the night on his way back to England. He had not seen his father for years. The situation felt delicate, as if I had stepped into a private funeral or a family birthday party. Whichever this was, I had shifted its tone. I wondered if I was meant to serve as a buffer.

The son was English. He referred to his circle in London as "dispossessed, a bit shabby, young, leftish." He was searching for some piece of missing knowledge on this North American trip. He knew little about Canada and his father's Canadian life.

"Space and cold winters," said the doctor. "That's what made this country."

"When Canadians try to explain Canada to me," said his son, "it's always as against the States. Is that your only measure?"

The young wife interjected: "English Canadians are more worried about—how do you say it?—about being *gobbler* by the Americans." You could see she felt untouched by any such annexationist anxieties. She was self-assured, a thirteenth generation French Canadian who still owned her original family seat on the Ile d'Orléans a few miles outside the city.

"What's the difference?" asked the young Englishman. He had just finished a holiday in California. Quebec City was all he had seen of Canada.

"Canadians set limits. Americans take risks. They're more likely to be back-slapping optimists."

"I crawl into the drains when I meet someone like that," he replied.

We drove back to the luxury apartment where Dr. Schwarz and his wife lived. He poured us snifters of cognac and they both talked about meeting Picasso's widow in France. They had taken the first steps to arrange the vast exhibition of the artist's work in Montreal. He felt hurt that government officials had elbowed him out of the planning. His wife was indignant. Listening to them, I saw that Dr. Schwarz bore an uncanny resemblance to Picasso—the bald pate with a thin fringe of grey, the short stocky build, and something in the lines of the strong handsome face. When you looked at it, the doppelganger doubled. His wife had features in common with Jacqueline, the painter's widow: the same long neck, the same oval head, the same facial structure. She reminded me of Picasso's well-known painting of his wife. I had stepped into a fable, two people wearing masks from another country, the stranger taken in and fed, the rediscovered son, the odd visual echoes.

An Orson Welles film came to mind. It was called *Fake*, a slippery movie that left the audience feeling duped. *Fake*, in which Picasso made a cameo appearance, unwittingly showed how difficult it was to make sense of this cunning little Proteus. The highly regarded artist was also famous for being famous. He had painted himself a public personality, which expanded as the reproductions of his work multiplied. Picasso, as the French say, was in the air. A great artist, a comic hustler, revered by curators, but envied by con men, who saw him running a kind of legal counterfeit operation—not printing money, but painting it. Picasso. The name had become an incantation. It meant what you wanted it to mean.

Dr. Schwarz brought out a copy of the large and expensive book he had recently put together in honour of Picasso. The colour plates in it were from paintings by a Quebec man, the poems by Dr. Schwarz. We drank another glass of cognac. The book's brooding images were strongly influenced by the dead artist. Sunk into feather cushions on a cream-coloured sofa, watching Picasso's look-alike turn the over-size pages of these Picassoesque paintings, I felt that I too, passing briefly through this room, was living in a borrowed skin.

The Ottawa Train

UP TO QUEBEC CITY I HAD TAKEN THE SLOW RIDE. Going back I booked a seat on the express, which allowed a quick connection in Montreal with the Ottawa train. It was a private journey. Food came to us at our seats, as on a plane. The new LRC cars ("light, rapid, and comfortable" being the claim made for them) offered no public lounge areas, a change which reduced the opportunities for meeting people and talking. I watched the landscape pass. Winter was beginning to feel less like an inconvenience and more like a terrible Biblical prophecy. Last year's bleached corn stalks were visible, poking up out of the dead fields. Snow still lay in the furrows.

At Central Station in Montreal I sat by the Ottawa track and waited for boarding time. I had taken the New York train from here to meet a woman once. Railway terminals, unlike other downtown buildings, were loaded with hopes for and memories of change. This was the end of the pier, where you put things behind you or gratefully ended a journey. Here you were reminded of possibilities and lost causes, a mixture of suspense and regret.

My seat on the train was identical to the one I'd had from Quebec City, with an attached fold-in tray for the potted meal. In my notes there was a quote about the Ottawa train from Bruce Hutchison's 1943 book on Canada, *The Unknown Country*.

"Everyone will be on it, and it is your perfect chance to study the Canadian ruling class. It is the only place in Canada where you will be sure of seeing every lady in fashion, every man well tailored, for as a people we don't know much about clothes. We have invented none of our own and have been content to imitate the Americans, who don't know anything about them either. But at least on the Ottawa train everyone will be strictly in style: sleek Montreal bankers who have generally managed to run Canada; corporation lawyers; perhaps one of those witty French-Canadian advocates who can make our courts sound like a trial in a good stage play; a few of the abler French-Canadian politicians, plump, pink, healthy, with ties a trifle too vivid; and transplanted London businessmen in short black coats and striped grey trousers."

I walked up and down the train and saw none of the people described in Hutchison's popular book. If any of them were travelling today, they would be in the air above us. Trains were no longer fashionable. They were used now by people with lower incomes, and by those with a fear of flying. In any case, most of the sleek bankers had moved to Toronto. I had not seen London businessmen in black coats and striped trousers since I had last been in London. Why were French-Canadian politicians in 1943 distinguished by their pink plumpness? The most famous of them in my lifetime, Pierre Trudeau, was neither pink nor overweight. His right-hand man, Marc Lalonde, looked like a Gallic Ichabod Crane. Perhaps eating habits in Quebec had changed. The comment about ties a trifle too vivid was a remark I recognized from my old Westmount days. *I like French Canadians, they're splendid people, but as my wife always says, they have the most dreadful taste. I've been in some of their houses. You need a pair of dark glasses to soften the blow.* But the disdain was mutual, as depicted in the animated cartoon I had seen in Quebec City. If they were jolly peasants with red tuques—or plump lawyers with loud ties—, we were stuffed corpses bent over our ledgers.

The train left Central Station, rolled past the financial district and the industrial buildings south of Dorchester Boulevard, past the Farine Five Roses sign blinking in red on the ten-storey flour warehouse, the grain elevators below Old Montreal. The Lachine Canal was free of ice. Past the rail yards we came to the intersection at Sebastapol and Wellington. This was the hard-up neighbourhood described by Gabriel Roy in *The Tin Flute*—the crowded tenement housing with open outside stairways to the second-floor apartments, the yellow brick Atwater farmer's market with its art deco clock tower, the twin domes with copper turrets on a local church, and juxtaposed in the distance, high on the hill, the Gleneagles apartment building, constructed in the last year of another era, 1929, the *édifice l'âge d'or* of upper Westmount, where wealthy old folks could rent comfort with a view. It seemed to me that no other Canadian city could have the same lasting magnetism. But I was not a casual observer. My affiliation was irrevocable, the kind that forms only once, when you are young and the perceptions of particular shapes and textures and smells and sounds leave an indelible imprint.

Ten minutes out of the city, at Dorval, thick snow began to blow down, enlarging the shrunken heaps of plowed sludge at the edges of the parking areas. A blinking sign said the air temperature was two degrees centigrade. My intention had been to start this trip at the tail-end of winter, but the trip was almost a third done and winter's cold tail was still wagging the late spring. By March—or April in a bad year—Canada east of the mountains could feel like endless winter, with a vague memory of some hot green days, just enough time to grow food, and then the crackle of dead leaves, the brittle blue sky, and the land would be frozen again. All you could see from the train window was weather—a white-out. After an hour the storm let up. Then you could make out in the twilight dark areas of bush, old tree lines marking empty fields, and infrequent clusters of farm buildings showing a few dim lights. I did not see any people through the window until we reached the outskirts of the capital.

Bureaucracy

THE OTTAWA I KNEW WELL WAS COMFORTABLE AND MIDdle-class. It had come into being in the 1960s and 1970s when salaries in the federal public service, which for decades had been low, caught up with and in many cases exceeded those paid people in comparable jobs elsewhere. The National Capital Commission had spent federal money on parks and bicycle paths and the restoration of heritage buildings. The Rideau Canal, a few decades ago mouldering in desuetude, had been saved and remade into a long winding water-park. Ottawa was a wellgroomed, insulated city. I thought of it now as an enormous daycare centre for adults.

The YMCA residence was like a hotel, with telephones in the rooms, and private baths. In the morning I called people on my list, bureaucrats I had met on magazine assignments in Ottawa, and people I had known from my years living there. I called my member of parliament. They were out of town, or in day-long meetings (another distinguishing feature of Ottawa); one was at a funeral; another was recovering from a nervous breakdown. Only my oldest Ottawa friend could see me on short notice. He had just been fired, a rare occurrence for a bureaucrat, and had received a handsome settlement. We arranged to meet for a drink. I searched my memory for other names, and remembered a man in the public service who wrote entertaining plays. The director of the

National Arts Centre also came to mind. A year earlier
he had sent me a letter about a piece of literary criticism
I had written. His secretary said he would see me the
next day. The man who wrote plays was more elusive.
After making my way through a battery of telephone re-
ceptionists, I found him working at home.

The playwright was an economist who had risen
quickly through the public service and had last served as
a senior policy advisor. In the bar across the street from
his squash club he wore an old sweater and a pair of
baggy grey flannel pants, not the careful attire of an ambitious public servant. When the policy unit he had
worked for had been disbanded, he had taken a year's
leave of absence to write scripts. No one had listened to
his unit anyway, he said. "We were right on so many
issues. The government just couldn't stomach the political consequences."

He had a sallow-skinned face from which sardonic
cackles erupted. He was disillusioned with Ottawa. There
had been a change over the past fifteen years, he said,
from vocational public servants, those who believed
serving their government was a high calling, to career
bureaucrats, who simply considered it a decent job with
a good income. He criticized the forecasters inside Ottawa who were saying the Canadian economy could soon
shift onto a new plane. "The truth about high-tech products is that the competition is cut-throat. With a few exceptions, Canadians can't survive out there in the mean
world markets.

"Trees and rocks," he concluded, "and prairie grain.
They're our staples, and it's going to continue that way
for a long time to come. People in Ottawa don't understand that. They're making nice salaries working in the
office towers you see all round you here, with video
screens and computer terminals on every floor. They
think the whole country lives like this."

On the way to see my old friend I walked along the
canal. In another month tulips would be sprouting in the

flower beds. It was a comfortable little city. If you had a university degree and you waited around Ottawa long enough, you would almost certainly find a job in some government department. Money stuck to the middle class here. Life was not effortless for everyone. At the highest levels of bureaucracy I knew people who worked as hard as anyone in the country. But I had also noticed that further down in the heap it was possible to coast with impunity.

I met my friend in a restaurant on Elgin Street. He was enjoying his large severance settlement. He had bought a house, and now he bought me drinks. He was free-lancing, he said. He had enough money to do nothing at all for six months. An inconstant friend but good companion, he would always land on his feet. He was too private and self-reliant to call and keep a friendship alive, but was always happy if he heard from you. A reflective man with an easy smile. For six years he had lived in an Oblate seminary, under a rule of silence much of the time, and I assumed this had given him an emotional independence most people never have. He was contained but not cold, and with those he knew well he was frank about himself. A few years earlier he had told me his life's savings had disappeared in the volatile silver market. He had always wanted to be rich so he could join the smart set in some larger city. We used to spend evenings drinking and dreaming up ideas for new magazines, new books, new board games that would make a fortune. And he had ideas of his own. First he was going to import jewellery, then fur coats. He would start a new Hollywood gossip sheet, fabricating every story himself in his little room in Ottawa. Then it was a suspense novel he was writing. There was always some great project afoot that was going to make him a pile. "I think I've really got it with this one," he would say. Losing twenty thousand dollars in the silver market did not chasten him much. It was just a slippery step on the intricate path to millionairedom. His women did not find these fantasies attractive. One wife had left him, and the next woman had thrown him out. Now he had remarried. ''She's very busy, at work and at her dancing club,'' he told me. ''We meet in bed at night.''

We drank several beers. He spoke of a recurring dream he had been having since the age of four or five. He would find himself on a desert island, the only male; all around were sleeping females, dreaming of him. The first fantasy of possessing riches, I thought. And his first rule of silence. We talked about the senior bureaucrat who had worked with us a full year without producing anything more than a letter or two a week. ''Let's brainstorm,'' he would say, and there would be a brief tempest, strategies would be rejigged and hopes raised, and then the tempest would pass, and you would be left with another senseless report to write while he gathered his energies for the next storm.

''What about a board game,'' I said to my friend, ''called Bureaucracy? The winner would be the first one to discover the rules of the game.''

The Entertainer

THE DIRECTOR OF THE NATIONAL ARTS CENTRE, DONALD MacSween, worked out of a roomy office on the east side of the building overlooking the Rideau Canal. His secretary showed me in, and the director motioned for me to sit in one of the comfortable arm chairs.

''I'm one scotch ahead of you, and I had a long lunch,'' MacSween said, opening a cabinet that held bottles of liquor and a little tub of ice. He poured me a full glass of whiskey. ''This is the best job in the arts in North America—if you're not an artist.''

MacSween began to explain what a worthwhile institution the Arts Centre was, "part of the national cultural overlay in a country that has such strong regional characteristics." I remembered the centre's budget had been under attack in the press. The director was looking for allies. It was pleasant to be courted in this way. MacSween reminded me of educated people I had known in France and Greece who thought that writers were socially useful, and that they placed quite high on the social scale, about where, in Toronto, a respected lawyer or professor might sit.

My host said we could attend the French play that was premiering in a few minutes. Was I free? He would also give me tickets to an English performance the next night. Everything would be arranged. Why didn't I stay until Sunday and meet the novelist Mordecai Richler? MacSween could see that I was invited to the right party.

"There's someone else I should introduce you to," he said, grabbing the telephone. I wandered around the office while he talked. In the private bathroom, across from the shower with a cake of soap on a rope, was a framed letter from Italy's ambassador applauding the director's managerial talents. Beside the door into the bathroom a bizarre wooden sculpture decorated the wall. Apparently a protest against environmental pollution, it explained itself cryptically. "And Man Flourished . . . Then There Became an Increasing Awareness of the lack of Nature and the City Conservationist was born. . . ." I could hear MacSween on the phone.

"What are you doing?" he asked. "Carving a wave? Oh. Good." He hung up. "Alex Wyse, the artist," he explained. "That wooden sculpture on my wall is his. If you're still here tomorrow, you can meet him." MacSween refilled our glasses. "About 80 percent of the complaints I get here are about the food, the seats, and the washrooms. You know, art is all very well, but are you comfortable?"

We hurried down a series of windowless corridors to

the theatre. The play was by Genet, and featured two lesbian housemaids. "If I were God," MacSween confided as the houselights dimmed, "I'd have put breasts on the back. You want something to hang onto. And genitals. Genitals should be more accessible for manual manipulation, somewhere around the knees." I instinctively shifted my knees away from him, though a moment's reflection told me he did not have designs on my legs. MacSween was simply enjoying his own ribaldry, a kind of freedom that most officials in Ottawa—where caution and self-censorship were the rule—would not have allowed themselves.

At the reception after the play I found myself standing with the star Monique Mercure, an actress I admired. She had stolen the evening and I told her so. "But it seems no one liked my performance," she sniffed. "They're not coming to talk to me." Dismissed as a critic, I spoke instead with an impoverished French-Canadian fiddler from rural New Brunswick who had a bit part in the English play.

"Isn't this great?" he bubbled. "They puts us up in a hotel for the whole run. Then it's back home to bread and beans."

MacSween paused in his calculated circuit of the gathering to point out the director of the French theatre, André Brassard. "When I made that appointment, it sent a *frisson* through the upper levels of the cultural bureaucracy. André had been involved in a court case, accused of running a ring of young male prostitutes. His sexual proclivities were known, as was his brush with the law. Some people were very upset. But he's extraordinarily talented. It's the best thing I've done here."

In the early hours of the morning, MacSween and I ordered smoked meat sandwiches and beer in a delicatessen on Rideau Street. He was still exuding energy. "In Montreal I joined the only law firm whose name was a perfect iambic pentameter," he was saying when we heard a call for Mr. Turmoil on the restaurant's P.A.

system. ''That must be for me,'' he grinned. Behind the half glasses, the beaky nose, the small eyes in the long face, a manic agitation was at work. ''I practised law in Montreal with Brian,'' he went on, referring to the prime minister. ''One time, I remember, he came back to the house. We talked politics, always his favourite subject. He held forth for an hour or so, laying out the plans in minute detail for his climb to power. But never any mention of what he wanted to do with political power once he got there, no vision of what he felt the country needed.''

MacSween allowed there had been rumours the new Tory government might want him sacked. But since he was appointed by the Arts Centre board, the board would have to be replaced first. He thought that unlikely. ''I've become something of a national capital booster,'' he said, as if anticipating the sadness of having to leave, ''a municipal bigamist, married to Montreal but having an affair with Ottawa.'' He liked ''the quality of the people'' in the capital. He repeated a notion I had heard before, that those who moved in higher circles in Ottawa were distinguished by their ''brains and caring.'' They had given up lucrative opportunities elsewhere, the argument ran, to apply themselves to shaping the national destiny. I had observed that they generally thought highly of one another, and were all agreed on the desirability of a strong federal presence in the rest of the country. This preoccupation with the national dimension of every issue in a regionally structured country seemed thin and remote to me unless I was actually in the capital. From inside Ottawa all the brains and caring busy in all the office towers looked like a powerful beam shining across the land, but if you went a few hundred miles away from Parliament Hill, Ottawa's luminaries cast a much dimmer glow, like a flashlight under a blanket.

At lunch time the next day MacSween was having another party. There were actors—a man from Toronto with an elegant D'Artagnan mustache, and his wife; the female director of the English play; and Ted Johns, the playwright. I sat beside Alex Wyse, a punctilious middle-aged man wearing a navy-blue pinstripe suit. He sat across from the playwright, whose rustic wit was not equal to Wyse's slick gobbledygook about stock market manipulation delivered in an imperious British accent.

"The thing that amazes me about myself," said Wyse, "is that a chap like me can have such a strong influence. A word here, a word there, to the right people mind you, and I can send millions this way or that. It's a strange talent I have. Don't you think it's odd?"

Ted Johns, who sounded like a left-leaning populist with a quick, anecdotal sense of humour, appeared to be both mildly offended and intimidated. "Are you really very rich then?" he asked glumly. He had just mentioned his own grievously low income for the year before.

"I do very well," the sculptor replied. Then to me he murmured, "Reverse psychology. That's how I like to operate. You get so much more out of people."

MacSween drove the three of us to the sculptor's house after lunch. He said he had seen Jean Boggs, the former director of the National Gallery, walk by in the restaurant. "She's always a sun surrounded by satellites. Never without them. Young, good-looking, well-groomed, gay, male curators. The kind that if they're wearing a jacket, they forgot to put the arms in. Like an archdeacon."

"I saw them looking at me," said Wyse.

"Alex, you may get there yet. You may have to make some sacrifices, mind you. But art for art's sake. You might even get Art himself."

Alex Wyse looked pensive in his homburg. Like a chastened Mad Hatter. MacSween pressed on.

"I have a railway story. Jack Pickersgill, you know, a great parliamentary wit of the Pearson government. This was when he was minister of transport and was engaged in a debate on something like freight rates. Someone shouted at him, 'The minister wouldn't know one end of a boxcar from another.' Pickersgill thought for a moment and then stood. 'Point of order, Mr. Speaker. What *is* the difference between one end of a boxcar and the other?' ''

''That reminds me of Ellen Fairclough,'' Wyse countered. ''She was our first woman minister at the federal level, you remember. An opposition member was taunting her. 'Doesn't the minister wish she were a man?' he said. And she shot back, 'Don't you wish you were one?' ''

They told each other stories until we arrived at the small house where Wyse and his wife lived, near the governor-general's residence. We sat in the living room and the sculptor poured us each a little glass of scotch.

''I like the blinds you've put on these windows,'' MacSween said. ''Roman blinds, aren't they? Guess you gotta have something to stop the rocks.'' Wyse had just shown us a cannon he kept pointed at his neighbours in the back yard.

''Say, maybe I can get some help here,'' MacSween began again. ''I was looking through the dictionary this morning. We need a new name for the Art Centre's restaurant. It's gotta be bilingual, so Latin would be good. I came across the word cunctator. But I think it sounds rather scatological. You dirty cunctator! See what I mean?''

''What is a cunctator?'' asked Wyse.

''Apparently it's someone who procrastinates.''

They agreed the meaning, if not the word, would be fitting for an Ottawa restaurant.

''It puts me in mind of a BBC talk show I saw recently on pornography,'' Wyse said. ''There were three panelists, and a commentator.'' He launched into an impromptu performance of all four parts. The commentator introduced Mr. King of the King newspaper chain, which ''publishes at least one magazine of what I believe I can safely say is rather widely regarded as pornographic.'' Mr. King, in an educated British accent, eloquently put forward the market-demand argument for smut. ''I am not in favour of anything that might be construed as pornographic, but I do not pass judgement on the tastes of my readers.'' Then Mr. Barker, ''whose specialty we must hasten to emphasize is really architectural photography, but who is known to have published photographs of the female form in some of the most popular of the King magazines,'' submitted a Greek-statue defence of nude photography. ''I mean it is true,'' Wyse/Barker concluded in perfect cockney inflections, ''it is true that these are pictures of the human form, but that's only incidental. What really interests me are the abstract shapes.'' And then the Bishop of Suffolk held forth, impaling himself on his own moral fence. ''Well, now that you ask, and I must say I don't know whether I should venture even a personal opinion on this delicate subject, because while I can speak for the Church, this is perhaps not quite the time or the place for any opinion at all. I do *have* a personal opinion of course.'' Wyse took off his navy-blue pinstripe suit jacket and put it on inside out and backwards. He made a credible senile cleric as he alternately grinned and grimaced in his makeshift soutane. ''I will say that I have some concerns. For one thing, we cannot know for certain, but I do firmly believe that our young people may be growing up with a very false view of the female body. Young people today may be growing up with the idea that the naked female has a fold down the middle. And a small tin staple in the abdomen. I think this may explain some of the very odd behaviour we see our youth indulging in. Very odd indeed.''

MacSween's large belly was jiggling with laughter. ''Alex, you understand the nature of humour. I've always thought that it's like making love.'' He demonstrated, rolling his ample torso forward and then back in the Wyses' armchair. ''You keep rolling the audience up to the edge and then pull them back, right to the edge and then back again, until finally you can take them anywhere you want.'' MacSween turned to me. ''Alex's brand of humour is a little different. You hit the ball over the net to him, and instead of hitting it back he bats it over the fence and you watch it go over and up and around and under, zoom, zam, shoosh, bang, and then between five and fifteen minutes later it comes flying back and hits you in the ear, dead on.''

The next day I wandered through downtown Ottawa thinking how the city had changed since I used to visit my grandmother in the 1950s. She would tell me how different it was from her own youth at the turn of the century when the few sidewalks were made of wood and it was still a rough and unformed place. By the 1950s Ottawa had cement sidewalks, but was regarded as dismal by anyone who enjoyed good restaurants or the arts. Murray's, one of the few eating establishments downtown where three edible courses were served, and probably the most popular, ran the kind of earnest kitchen that gave you mashed potatoes shaped by an ice-cream cone scoop. The city seemed stifled by a Methodist-Presbyterian conspiracy which even my grandmother, a devout and abstemious Christian Scientist, found a little too unyielding. MacSween, though not a typical public servant, played an influential role in the new cultural bureaucracy; it had been people like him who had helped free Ottawa from the stranglehold of dullness.

Before catching the midnight train to Toronto, I attended the gathering MacSween had mentioned. At a fashionably renovated house in the New Edinburgh district, it was a dinner party in honour of Mordecai Richler, the author, who was giving a public reading the next day. Richler, looking typically rumpled, shuffled through the crowd in his shirt sleeves while the guests stood by admiringly in suits and blazers. After dinner an Ottawa man wearing a club tie and blazer confessed stiffly to a spirited French-Canadian woman who had come from Montreal with Richler and his wife, ''You know, when I was growing up in Ottawa, I thought French-Canadians were all street cleaners and milkmen.''

"Tu n'as pas connu beaucoup de monde, n'est ce pas?" she answered dryly.

In the background I could hear MacSween, "What do you think?" he asked. "Are we headed for Armageddon? I'm sad that all this may end soon. I'm enjoying it. What I'd really like is to come back after I die. Even if it had to be as a stone or a snake or a pterodactyl. I'd just like to come back and see how the play turns out."

The train was small, one coach and one sleeper. Lying in a windowless upper berth, I could feel only the three glasses of cognac that were sloshing around in my cranium. The train moved. It was like being in a room a large crane had suddenly picked up and swung sideways. I could hear MacSween saying at the party, "It takes less now to give me the whirly-beds. If you've got the whirly-beds, you know you've had too much."

Closing Down the North

IT WAS THE END OF APRIL. I HAD STAYED TWO WEEKS IN Toronto, spending longer than I had planned with my daughter. She had not taken my absence well. "I'm going on a long, long trip on my train," she told me the second day I was back. "So you won't see me again." The weather had been balmy—eighty degrees during the day. But on the train for northern Ontario the woman opposite my berth said to the sleeping car porter, "It snowed in New Liskeard on Sunday."

In the bar men were drinking seriously, as if they were being paid to consume a quota.

"Goin' to Liskeard? Not much there," said a vast fellow in a checkered lumberjack shirt. "Excitement is a funeral." He had close to three hundred pounds on him.

"I operate big cats, any kind of heavy machinery. Don't matter if the mine's makin' money. Long as they pay me." He had two plastic cups of double rye whiskey in front of him, and four empties pushed to one side. We both had our hands on our tables. Beside his mine looked like they belonged to a child.

At six o'clock in the morning I stepped off the sleeping car onto the New Liskeard platform and back into the chill of winter. Six months ago on the same train a retired druggist and his wife had told me about this place, settled in the 1890s when the government opened the area to farmers. A fertile strip of land running about thirty miles to the north, called the Little Clay Belt, was the source of local agricultural wealth. At the north end of Lake Temiskaming, New Liskeard was lovely in the summer, the druggist had said. Today it was freezing cold as I walked down the empty main street, past the white smears of icy puddles and the lingering piles of snow.

I banged on the door of the King George Hotel, a plain white building. It was too cold to wander the streets. A woman appeared in her dressing gown and let me in. We stood in the narrow hallway that substituted for a lobby. "You have to pay fifteen dollars," she said.

There was no register, but she promised a receipt— "when I wake up." She led me to the second floor, along the old linoleum hallway to a small room with a concave bed, a wooden chair, and a dresser marked with little black potholes where guests had left their cigarettes. Outside the other doors were pairs of heavy winter boots. Some people were permanent residents here.

When the town had opened for the day, I dropped in on the editor of the *Temiskaming Speaker*. Forrest Greene told me he had answered a help-wanted ad four years earlier in southern Ontario for a reporter's job on the paper. "I got hired. So I went up to Temiskaming. But I couldn't find any sign of the newspaper. So I phoned the editor. 'Son,' he said, 'we're in New Liskeard. You're two hundred miles out.' " Forrest was dressed up to look like a newspaperman. The necktie hanging loose over his chest and the blue baseball cap pushed back on his head gave the right effect. So did the nicotine-stained index finger.

"Our population is aging," he said. "Most of the young people leave."

A local bus followed the long, thin lake down to Haileybury, and then on to Cobalt, the silver-mine settlement. New Liskeard, according to Forrest Greene, had been the home of some of the mine owners and investors. Haileybury was the managers' town; Cobalt was where the workers lived. I wandered through Cobalt, a curious, make-believe place with stepped sidewalks and dwellings built up on nobs and down in dips. It was mid-day. The late April sun had warmed the air. Off the winding main street was a patch of public grass where some historic plaques had been erected. One explained Cobalt's beginnings. "About nine hundred yards southwest of here, on August 7, 1903, two lumbermen seeking timber for railroad ties made the initial discovery of the Cobalt silver camp. Named for its discoverers, the McKinley-Darragh mine operated from 1904 to 1927. In the rush of 1905-06, Coleman Township became the scene of the most intensive prospecting hitherto known in Ontario. Though it once boasted over a hundred producing mines, the fortunes of the camp waned after 1920, owing to sharply reduced silver prices. . . ." Not a word about the con men, gamblers, whores and thieves who must have populated Cobalt in those frenetic days. The plaque was like a gravestone. It murmured cryptically and left whole lives between the lines. I knew some ore deposits were still being worked nearby, but the town seemed a sad derelict place, if not yet a ghost town, almost a corpse. The railway station, in use until a year before, had been closed and boarded up.

Back in New Liskeard I went into the public library, a handsome Carnegie building. "So many small businesses have closed," the librarian said. "The wood products mill, the iron works, the dairy. Now they take our milk away and send it back in cartons at a higher price." When the Temiskaming and Northern Ontario Railway had arrived in 1905, there had been widely held hopes of limitless growth for the region. The silver mines had been discovered when the tracks pushed up through Cobalt, and fortunes were made. But few people still nurtured grandiose dreams of prosperity now for this part of northern Ontario. The government railway (whose name was changed from the T & NO to the Ontario Northland in 1945 so their accounts would no longer be confused with those of the Texas and New Orleans Railroad) continued to maintain the operation from North Bay up to Moosonee. New Liskeard, with a population of five thousand, was the largest community on the line.

In the common bathroom at the King George Hotel, as I washed before an early supper, the old man busy at the sink beside me said he was eighty-two. "I grew up in Burks Falls, down south," he explained, referring to a small settlement north of most of Ontario's population. "I came up here in 1926. Worked in a saw mill for a good many years." He soaped his stump with the one good hand. The stump had only two half fingers. A beam of late afternoon sunlight touched his bald head and made a warm stripe across the faded red plywood cubicles behind us. "The sun feels good today," he said. "I don't even have any heat on in my room."

The librarian had arranged for me to meet a retired railway employee in the early evening. We found each other in the reading room. Len Tucker was small and wiry with a weathered brown face and sparkling eyes. He lived on the old family property outside the town. His grandfather, one of the first settlers in the area, had built a log cabin near the lake in 1895. His father had farmed farther north, he said, but that property had been destroyed in the great bush fire of 1922. (I had read about one of these sweeping fires that afternoon in the library: "It was so hot that the railroad tracks just curled up like

hairpins.'') After attending the mining school in Haileybury, Tucker went to work for the Temiskaming &
Northern as a railway gardener.

There was a time when every self-respecting railway
maintained gardens at its principal stations. They were
an early variety of corporate-sponsored public art. Tucker
tended the flower beds between Temagami and Englehart, and between Cochrane and Moosonee. "We had a
greenhouse at Englehart, and our own boxcar with special springs for a smoother ride. Quite often they'd shunt
us off to a siding in the woods. They weren't in any hurry
to get us to the next place. Didn't matter. We always took
a fishing rod along, and they paid us by the hour.'' He
told me he had a dream for New Liskeard. He wanted to
bring back the turn-of-the-century steamboats as a tourist
draw. "I can remember when those boats used to stop at
every farm dock around the lake. They'd pick up a pile
of wood the farmer had cut—the boat used it for fuel—
and they'd leave bags of supplies.''

It was easy to believe in the resurrection of the steamboats. On the face of it, New Liskeard had not thrown
away its past. If you stood at the intersection of the two
principal streets, you saw mostly low, pre-war buildings,
two or three storeys high. Only the antique New Liskeard
Hotel rose noticeably taller. In front of the Pro Hardware on Armstrong Street, a worn and scratched plaque
was embedded in the sidewalk. "Nine samples of Temiskaming grown seed were encased in this concrete block
on the occasion of New Liskeard's fiftieth anniversary—
1953.'' It was a paradox common enough in Canada. A
place could nurture its history or its future, seldom both.
For New Liskeard the future appeared to be shrinking.

I had called the druggist and been invited for a drink.
He was settled in a big living room chair. The apartment
stood over the pharmacy he had operated until retiring.
He and his wife said all their children had moved away
to find work. He was a large, leathery man, bald and
slow from age, with the cracked nails of a diabetic, and

a face so closed-up it might already have been embalmed. She was younger, and in better health.

"I built my own skidoo," he said, "years before they came on the market. We have real winter up here, not the pretend winter you have down south. I used to organize dog-sled races up the mainstreet in mid-winter." He told me about raising pigeons and mushrooms in his basement when he was younger. His wife showed me old black-and-white snapshots of the races and the skidoo. Around the room were their mementoes, an enormous conch shell, a camel saddle, a chunk of silver ore from one of the Cobalt mines, and a propeller made into an ashtray. When I remarked on this contraption, they told me about a young man they had known who had lost his arm to a whirling propeller. "It was chopped right off. Imagine." The propeller suddenly seemed ominous, as if I had walked into a stranger's living room and found a stuffed arm on display.

He liked to tell stories. "There was an Ontario provincial policeman up here. They sent him out to the bush to collect a body. He brought a box with him, but it was too small. The corpse was frozen, so he sawed it off at the knees. His superior had him transferred to the detachment at Pembroke. There he shot at a drunk who was evading arrest. The drunk staggered into a reservoir and drowned. After that they fired him. And you know what happened? He fell off the dynamo at Iroquois Falls and killed himself." The druggist, an apparently mild mannered, eighty-seven-year-old, heaved with laughter. His bird-like little wife chuckled. I remembered the mine worker on the train: "Excitement is a funeral."

I lay in bed at the King George trying to envisage what New Liskeard would look like in a hundred years. Would the railway still be running, and would there still be jobs? Or would civilization be obliterated in the meantime? People here would not survive nuclear winter any better than those in the south. Perhaps this place would be all grey ash, indistinguishable from the tailing heaps around

Cobalt. Or perhaps it would revert to green bush. The druggist had illustrated how such things could happen. "When I first came here, there was an abandoned Hudson's Bay Company post at the narrows on Lake Temiskaming. You could go in and see everything just as they had left it. Even the old ledgers were still there. Then gradually things disappeared from the site. People pillaged the buildings themselves, probably to use the lumber. If you passed it now, you wouldn't know anything at all had been there."

At dawn my travel alarm clock roused me for the six o'clock train going north. I had allowed fifteen minutes for the walk up the main street to the station. As I banged the door of the hotel behind me, I heard my train go toot, toot. The alarm clock was slowing down in its old age. My intention had been to connect with the train from Cochrane up to Moosonee; if I missed that one, I would have to wait three days for another. With my bags I trotted up the sidewalk, hoping for a taxi or a friendly lift. There were no cars, but as I approached the station I saw over my shoulder a pick-up truck heading in the right direction. He ignored my outstretched thumb and sped past. A couple of minutes later I heard a final toot, and from five hundred yards I watched my train pull away. The man in the truck, with the passenger he had just collected, passed going the other way as I turned down the little station road. He looked at me sympathetically and gave a sheepish shrug. I cursed and grumbled. Yet there is exhilaration in missing a train. It derails you from your one-track plans, and calls for you to improvise. I went into the waiting room and asked the clerk how far the next station was.

"Englehart," he said, looking amused. "Takes the train about half an hour. You could catch it in a car, if you left this minute." I called a cab.

When I explained my predicament to the driver, who was charging me thirty-five dollars—two nights at the King George, plus change—he said, "No problem. We'll boot it." And he roared up through the little clay belt on a fairly good road with no traffic and no witnesses except a few cows, so still and uncomprehending that they looked like plaster casts of themselves.

"Been having a little trouble with my valves," he said. The engine was clanking. There was a dot on the map between New Liskeard and Englehart, a place called Earlton, and I did not much want to include it in my trip across Canada.

"Keep those valves pumping, pal," I said, "or whatever it is they do."

"You're not from around here, are you?" he asked.

"I grew up in Montreal," I replied. I had discovered the day before that to mention Toronto in New Liskeard was to invite a storm of abuse, as if I were personally responsible for all the pimps on Yonge Street and the industrial waste in Lake Ontario.

"I went to Montreal once," he said. "The draft beer in the taverns, you know what it tasted like? Christmas trees." Keep those valves pumping, my man. I did not want to sample the beer in Earlton where I imagined the few residents wore suspenders or polka-dot dresses, baseball caps or kerchiefs, all descended from great-grandpa Earl who chopped his way through the forest with a broad axe on days when he was not begetting. But we clanked in and out of that dot on the map in no time. Everyone was asleep. We arrived at the white clapboard station in Englehart ahead of the train.

Next, a pleasant-looking track-stop by a waterfall. Swastika. The Ontario Geographic Names Board had recorded that this settlement was called "after the good luck charm on a lady's necklace." Ontario loves good news and shuns bad. Describing the swastika as a harmless bauble, although it did have harmless pre-Nazi associations, seemed to me like pretending the hurricane was only a sunshower when your neighbour's roof had blown away. But the town's people had resisted all suggestions that the name be changed, and there the matter rested.

We reached Cochrane mid-morning, four hundred miles up from Toronto. Above the town stood a water tower with a polar bear painted on it, the only one of its species to be seen here since the last ice age. If you lived in Toronto Cochrane was cold and northern, but for a polar bear this was still the melted south. The railway ran a tourist train from here in the summer and called it the Polar Bear Express, but that too was wishful thinking. Even from the end of steel at Moosonee, not far from where the Moose River emptied into James Bay, it was necessary to charter a plane and fly farther north to see the white bears. Most people had to be content with the hyperbolic picture on the water tower, part of a make-believe package for tourists.

On the mixed freight-and-passenger train destined for Moosonee, the coaches were as I remembered, shabby and utilitarian, with hard seats. Inside, the six-hour ride was uneventful. Outside it was a dream-like journey back into winter, the snow piled imperceptibly higher as the train dragged slowly north, a long gentle toboggan slope down to the sea, beginning in spring and ending in winter. When we arrived, Moosonee's main street was crowded with Cree Indians evacuated from villages farther north on James Bay. Both Fort Albany and Kashechewan had been flooded by the swollen Albany River. The natives had been flown out in government helicopters. I heard one man saying his house had been moved thirty feet by the water before he had joined the airlift. In the shops and in the hotel the flood was the focus of all discussion.

My last visit, in the fall, had been relatively quiet. The Moose River had been free of ice, so the freighter-canoe taxis had been running across to Moose Factory Island, the Indian reserve. But now break-up had made the river impassable; too late for trucks, too early for boats. An expensive helicopter ride was the only way over the water. I remembered the island. Behind the government-issue housing, many families had erected teepees where they stored hunting gear or smoked the geese their men shot. The reserve, with its dirt roads, run-down dwellings, and silent, brown people, reminded me not of any place in Canada, but of Peru.

Across the river, on the Moosonee side, lived mostly white people. The town was an administrative centre for the vast area of sub-arctic running up to Winisk. It looked the same as it had in November, the day the snow had begun to fall. The unpaved streets were a slurry of mud. ("In the summer, it's dust," a shopkeeper told me. "What it boils down to is you can't walk or you can't breathe.") Moosonee was a rough, hard place: the low, box-like, northern utility architecture; the reckless truck drivers (no driver's licence was required) hurtling along the dirt roads that ended in the bush outside of town; and the chip-chop murmur of the Cree language that drifted out of the huddles on the main street, often punctuated by a suspicious glance.

This was where dreams conjured from a distant map had come to a dead end. In 1897 Charles T. Harvey proposed the Great Northern Ontario and Northwest Canada Transit Route, just one of many northern glints in a southern promoter's eye. Harvey's route, a combination of rail and boat lines, was to have traversed the north from Sault Ste. Marie, through Moose Factory and Chesterfield Inlet, up the Mackenzie River and on to the Bering Strait, a grandiose fantasy, but no more unlikely in its first flash than the transcontinental railway had been. Ninety years later most people took the emptiness of the north for granted, like an unfinished room in the attic—nice to have the extra space, but you wouldn't want to spend the winter up there. In 1932 the railway had reached Moosonee and stopped. There was talk of a salt-water port for Ontario, linked by the rail line to the south. A population increase of a hundred thousand was predicted. But the port never materialized, and Moosonee remained a small curiosity on the fringe of the national rail grid.

Where the white man's dreams of conquest ended, native ambitions could begin. Moosonee and the government installations at Moose Factory had been stepping-off places for James Bay Indians who wanted to leave the reserves. I walked off the street into a government office and spoke with a man who had grown up in a Moose Factory family. He was employed as a social services counsellor for the provincial government. "We're not all drunken Indians," he said. In the sensitive, intelligent face I read some anger and disappointment. He expressed regret that school teachers thirty years ago had turned him away from his native tongue. "Educators now have realized that it's not a good idea to cut people off from their language." On a table in his office sat a Cree syllabic typewriter. Despite early discouragement, he had mastered the written form. He said he helped some of the older natives in the area correspond with government agencies. He was, as far as it is possible, bicultural, and so had no objection to the powerful white presence in Moosonee. "My first job was in the kitchen of the Moose Factory hospital. It was there I began to hope and dream of ways to get off the island."

My mind kept turning back to Peru as I walked the muddy roadways of Moosonee. The Cree Indians were physically more like the Quechua and Aymara Indians I had seen in the Andes than like European Canadians. As the Peruvian natives did, most of the Cree lived close to the land, without many material possessions. A few, like the educated man I had met, broke into the white world, but they were exceptions. Those who stayed on the reserves were poor, though less dispossessed than their South American counterparts. Medical care and housing on the Moose Factory reserve were superior to anything available in remote Andean towns. The human squalor and degradation in Peru and Bolivia were not comparable to what I had seen on the island. Yet Moose Factory was not comparable to New Liskeard either, except that many people in the more northern community could speak some English. To step off the train in Moosonee was in some ways to step off the Canadian map into a less technological, less literate, less self-confident domain, though what confidence and skills there were on the island reserve my southern eyes might need a guide to see.

I woke early to catch the return run back down to Cochrane. The evacuees were shifting and murmuring in huddles along the main street. They had been billeted in the school. Enough food and blankets had been found, and the children seemed to be enjoying themselves, but the adults looked displaced and bored. An old man in a blue vinyl parka and green baseball cap explained sadly in slow English. "They took me down here by a plane. I live up the coast. Maybe my house went down the river. Maybe I could save it."

I looked into the ONR storage shed beside the station. One wall was stacked high with cardboard boxes. The stencilled black letters on each one read POTATO CHIPS. "Austin Airways will fly those up to Winisk one of these days," the young freight worker told me. "Food comes up here once a week, beer every two weeks." He said there were about thirteen hundred cases of beer in a load. That worked out to one case of beer for each man, woman, and child in Moosonee.

It was a slow haul back down to Cochrane. We were on northern time, less a matter of minutes than of moons and seasons. The train averaged about forty miles an hour, back across the fifty-first parallel, past Coral where the tattered scarecrow I had seen in the fall was still standing in snow, through stretches of tiny trees—the kind of woodland in which Hansel and Gretel lost their way—and on to Otter Rapids, exactly halfway up the line, where you could see a hydro dam out the window. A man with crinkled skin and silver hair spoke to his seat companion about all the workers who had been transferred from hydro sites now that the dams and the power grid in the area had been automated.

"My brother used to work at Fraserdale," he said, "but jobs aren't there any more. They're closing down the north." It was an exaggeration. The hydro dams, like the railway, were providing the same service with fewer employees. In a more subtle way, though, the old man may have been right. The visionary zeal for northern development that could be found in prospectuses and planning documents until the 1960s had faded. Settlements like Moosonee, once regarded as centres of economic promise, had been assigned a more modest role as outlying government service centres.

The two half-empty coaches rolling slowly through stunted bushland seemed unconnected to any departure point or destination. Most of the passengers were Cree Indians. Several times we made unscheduled and unannounced stops where one or two Indians, clutching cardboard boxes bound with twine, jumped down onto the rail bed and disappeared into a nameless bank of trees. An elderly Cree called Bert sat on the bench behind me.

"I remember coal-oil lamps on this train," he said, "and coal stoves at either end of the car." We passed an empty clearing and he pointed. "Used to be a sawmill there. We had horse teams to haul the logs."

I had not paid much attention to the white man and his young daughter ahead of me in the coach until I heard her high voice as we entered Cochrane. He had told the conductor he was bringing her out for a holiday.

"Look, Daddy! What are those pretty birds?"

"Pigeons."

"Pigeons!" she exclaimed. "Just like in my storybook."

We Don't Have Locusts
in Toronto

NO TRAIN RAN FROM COCHRANE TO TIMMINS, SO I caught a bus. "Come to Timmins, the city with a heart of gold," pleaded a sign along the way, but after wandering for two hours I began to question the metaphor. Gold was a heartless thing and Timmins had the rough, hard look of a city whose main industry was digging for rocks. I bought a ticket for the train south in the morning, and found a room across from the station in the Empire Hotel—twenty-three dollars with a private bath and colour television. In the lobby the Italian desk clerk was swatting mosquitoes. The hot noonday sun had brought them out. Yet the streets in the early evening were cold.

Enormous fortunes were made in the mines around Timmins early in the century. I went out to look for some evidence of that frenetic time. I remembered the long, stately mansion one member of a Timmins family had owned in Westmount, not far from where I lived, so big that the developer who acquired it took out a chunk from the middle, sealed the open ends, and sold the truncated pieces as two large houses. A friend of mine at school was heir to a fortune built on royalties from the Hollinger mine near Timmins. His father dedicated much time and money to the shooting of birds and other bigger game. His uncle was noted for eating glass at parties. A few families had lived lavishly on wealth extracted from rocks mined here, but few benefits appeared to have accrued to Timmins itself. My friend's family had taken their pile

131

first to Montreal and then to Bermuda. Sir Harry Oakes, another gold mine millionaire from this area, had removed to the Bahamas. It was a Canadian pattern, not rigid, but familiar: find the ore, drop a mine shaft, sell out, move south, a good index of the entrepreneurial sense of place—or lack of it—that had prevailed in our wilderness from the earliest days of the fur trade. You took value from the hinterland, furs or trees or rocks, but you were not obliged to give anything back, not any more than a woodland hiker incurred a debt by drinking water from a stream.

The only residue from the boom years that I saw on my walk around the little city were a few blocks known as the Hollinger Housing. Among the street names in this neighbourhood were Laurier, Borden, and Vimy. Some of the miners for whom the houses were built would probably have fought and lost friends at Vimy Ridge in the First World War. (The population of Timmins jumped from 935 in 1914 to 13,000 by 1929). To call these buildings houses was generous. Row after row of identical wooden shacks clad in red and green tarpaper, they were tiny, though some had been expanded with small additions. The picture of the magisterial stone residence in Westmount hovered in my mind's eye as I wandered the miner's neighbourhood. A fable-like simplicity informed the contrasting images: a prince-and-pauper tale with not many happy endings beyond the big house on the hill. You could imagine some kinds of richness in the lives that were once contained by these cramped shacks, but also much penury and hardship.

On my way back to the hotel I went into a store with a new sign—Renaissance Health Food Oasis. The owner told me he had travelled for four years in the Middle and Far East. A small, wiry man with wisps of facial hair, he had the unanchored look of someone who doubts the power of material reality. "It's a hard, hard town," he said. "Mining people, they're into heavy drinking and smoking. We appeal to maybe 2 or 3 percent." I paid for some muffins. He lifted a jar of scummy water onto the counter. "I practise macrobiotics. I'm telling you, the muck I've got out of my body! But after thirty years, what do you expect? Look at this. I distilled only thirteen gallons of my mother's water. Do you see all that dirt?" He held up the jar and shook it. A dark cloud of sediment rose. "That's what they're all drinking here. And they say it's clean in the north!" Underlying the health-food optimism was a morbid despair.

In the early morning the air was wintry, as if we were in another time zone far from spring in Toronto. I paced the platform to keep warm. The low slung, brown brick station with standard ONR blue trim had pleasant lines. Cut into the cornerstone were the characters "Hon. William Hearst Premier Province of Ontario 1916." I had the choice of going down to North Bay and waiting half a day for the train to Sudbury, where I would again have to wait half a day for the transcontinental, or of going all the way back to Toronto, staying the night there and then boarding the cross-country train the next evening. I bought a ticket for Toronto. The train out of Timmins, called the Northlander, was the most comfortable in Canada and I was looking forward to the day-long ride.

My guide book told me the Northlander cars had once served as first-class accommodation between Paris and Zurich. The European-style compartments had six seats. A few minutes after we left the station a waitress came down from the dining car and asked if we would like a drink. A throwback to the railway age, the Northlander was unlike other Canadian passenger trains, except that like the others, it lost money and required a government subsidy. There were four of us in the compartment, one middle-aged woman with red hair, one older woman turned grey, and a younger woman opposite me. The red and grey ladies appeared to be travelling separately, but they were talking. Red was from the north. She had taken a bus over from Cochrane to catch the train. Grey had been visiting her daughter in Timmins and was going home to Toronto. It was early in the morning. We left the station at seven-thirty, and by eight o'clock the red lady was deeply involved in an investigation of Toronto wildlife.

"I hear they have these insects called cockroaches inside the buildings. Even in winter." She wanted to know how big they were, what colour, and at what speed they ran. "They don't get in the beds, do they? My goodness, I hope I don't have one in mine." She made them sound exotic. I could imagine a huge water tower with a cockroach painted on it by the Toronto rail yard to match the pictorial polar bear in Cochrane.

"I can't understand why God created them, unless some day we might need them for food."

"No, you can't eat them," the grey lady replied. "But I read about somebody doing art work with them."

After a pause the lady from Cochrane wondered aloud, "What's a locust like? I read about them in the Bible."

"A locust is just a grasshopper gone crazy. We don't have them in Toronto."

Maybe it was not going to be such a pleasant ride after all. This kind of Biblically inspired discussion reminded me of the frustration I felt as a toddler when I was tied by a rope to the garage door so I could get some air but could not run away. Bible talk was always tightly circumscribed. Leave the circle and you might fall off the edge of the world—into the dark abyss where cockroaches have no purpose. It occurred to me that my bug-ridden apartment in Toronto must be located somewhere in that abyss. Turning this thought over for its possibilities, I managed to fall asleep, and when I awoke, the two ladies were gone.

It was ten o'clock. The bush was higher and thicker. Between the trees and on the stubbled fields were occasional patches of snow. We passed New Liskeard and the rows of green, yellow, and red hulls stacked outside its canoe factory. Then Haileybury's red brick station, plywood on the windows, and Cobalt's station, also closed.

A few minutes later, a bull moose stared impassively at the train from a marshy meadow. He looked at us the way my child looked at a picture of the cow jumping over the moon—we were diverting, but not quite real.

The dark-haired woman across from me began to talk. She said she had been born south of Naples. "Not on the toe. Around the ankle. We left when I was two and emigrated to England, then came here to a small fruit farm around Niagara-on-the-Lake. My father worked on construction and did farm chores in the evening." Her name was Lucy. She had married into Wasp Ontario, and her husband worked for the provincial government. They had just completed a posting in Timmins. "I liked it up there. Toronto people are closed. They'll stab you in the back with a smile. Up north they're warm and friendly. You feel safer." I said being closed seemed to me characteristic of most Ontarians.

She agreed. She had uncles and aunts in New York state, she said, who were more outgoing and expressive than the family members who had settled in Ontario. "My husband's family, that's another thing. They're part United Empire Loyalist, and part Scottish-Irish-German, very different from us. They'll talk to you up to a point. But they have their family secrets." She smiled.

South of North Bay, past a placed called Powassan, Lucy exclaimed, "Oh, the water's running south now." At Burks Falls the frame station appeared to have been dragged away from the tracks onto private property. It was now the centre of a dense junk yard with an extravaganza of garbage beyond the imagination of any cartoonist. Then Huntsville, and cottage country, the beginning of southern Ontario. The fields looked greener, there were lily pads on the trackside ponds instead of ice, and what had been green tips two hours before were now baby leaves. The journey had been a time-exposure film from winter into spring; it reminded me of the train ride in Peru down to the jungle, all the dry mountain browns changing into thick wet greens in half a day. There was something unsettling in such an abrupt turnabout. It seemed to violate some primordial inner law.

Two blue herons lifted off a Muskoka lake south of Gravenhurst. As we skirted the western side of Lake Simcoe we saw trilliums in bloom, then fruit trees beginning to flower in suburban back yards.

"Cherry," said Lucy, "and crab."

Down the Don, Toronto's little river, floated a lone canoeist.

The Transcontinental

THE TRANSCONTINENTAL DEPARTED FROM UNION STAtion at midnight. By seven I was awake, watching the rain out my lower-berth window. We passed through the barren rockscape around Sudbury. People seemed to accept this desolation as easily as they accepted baldness. Some men lost their hair; some landscapes lost their trees. From the train Inco's big stack was visible. Then the stack dropped out of sight and air pollution became abstract again. A train creates its own train of thought, the endless footage of unpredictable images flickering past the glass. At nine-thirty the village of Benny appeared briefly, a prisoner of the surrounding waterlogged scrubland. "So small there is no official population," my guide book noted. From the window you could see five shanties with propane cylinders propped by the front doors. Then Benny was gone, a precarious dot of life made by the rails which would be erased the day the train died. There was an air of stoic defeat about the place. The railway brought dreams. Some clusters of shacks and tents prospered with the arrival of rail. They grew to be successful cities like Regina and Calgary. But there were many more places like Benny.

Stralak, Pogamasing, Metagama, and then mid-morning to Biscotasing. "Population of eighty," said the trainman in the tail-end car. "All retired." An open steeple with a shapely bell pointed up from the village church. We went on into the bush, clickety-clack, clacketty-clack. This was some of the most unforgiving country penetrated by the CPR, and the isolated villages along the line seemed as unlikely as remote settlements in the South American jungle. Lift a banana tree frond, and there you were in a clearing made for the little schoolhouse on stilts. Carved out of nothing, dependent on the train for their supplies, the small railway towns seemed half illusion and half the unremitting reality of a country that spread itself paper-thin. Until about fifty years ago, this was what most settlements in Canada looked like, small towns connected to the outside by a single rail line and a dirt road. If you were old in the 1930s, you might remember your grandparents talking about the days before the train came through, before fresh milk and daily mail were widely available. Towns like Biscotasing must have been prosperous and enlarging compared to the pioneer settlements their older residents could remember.

The trainman, who lived in Chapleau, told me he had made thirty-eight thousand dollars the year before. He did not like to give any of his money back to the railway. He used his pass every year to go down to Toronto with his wife and children. "But I never pay these prices for a drink," he said, holding up a menu card. "I bring a dozen beers on with me in an overnight bag." A man in a blue jacket, the passenger service assistant, (whose primary function was to speak the official language—usually French—not spoken by the service manager) announced the first call for lunch. "Don't go," counselled the trainman. "The food's terrible." He said fresh hamburgers were available near the station in Chapleau. The man in the blue jacket gave a mock-scowl and then smiled sheepishly. No one made a move for the dining car. Against the reputation of Via Rail meals, a good hamburger sounded attractive. At the Chapleau stop several passengers hurried to the fast-food stand and returned clutching their little piles of fried beef tucked inside buns.

"Isn't this great?" gloated an American who had brought back lunch for his two small children. "The burgers in the dining car are made from old shoes."

I remembered Eric Wilde, whom I had met on this train a year earlier. "There's a fundamental rule in life," he told me. "You can go anywhere in a tux." He always packed one on his train trips, and always wore it for the evening meal in the dining car. The steward had sat me opposite him, I in my plaid shirt and jeans, Wilde in black tie. Watching him drink mediocre wine from a plastic wine glass and consume the watery vegetables and instant mashed potatoes served by the Via kitchen had been like watching a talented concert pianist reduced to making plink-plonk music in a piano bar. A computer programmer in his early thirties, Wilde loved trains and could not get his fill of them. He had flown hundreds of miles to experience far-away railway rides. "Trains are a disease," he told me, "like computers. I like talking to people. Here I have a captive audience." After dinner we had gone back to his room for a liqueur. He had the drawing room in the tail-end car, with space for several people to sit. "The biggest window on the train," he gestured from his armchair, placed where he could admire his vase of flowers on a shelf by the couch. They had been delivered to the train by a florist. He was going to spend the night in Thunder Bay, put his flowers in a locker, and pick them up for the return trip in the morning. Solitary and theatrical, the traveller in him had belonged to the railway age. "I only have two ambitions in life," he told me. "To live in California and to have a private railway car."

I once rode through the bush in the locomotive from

White River to Schrieber. When the engine reached high speed, it felt like an enormous weight slamming through an unalterable trajectory, a rocket on rails. There were a hundred and eighty degrees of visibility from the cockpit. The train seemed to be eating the bush with great relish and spitting it out behind. It was the kind of hostile country that inspired Canada's second prime minister, Alexander Mackenzie, to call the proposed Pacific railway "an act of insane recklessness." The builders were not much more optimistic. William Van Horne, the CPR's general manager, despaired that his crews faced "two hundred miles of engineering impossibilities" around Lake Superior. Repeatedly they would pour crushed rock into the muskeg and lay rail, and then the rail would sink, and they would have to begin again. Some steam engines sank too, adding more fill. Where there was no need for fill, rock cuts had to be carved, tunnels dug, and bridges built. A hundred years later it was easy to take this passage for granted. Yet in its day the railway around Lake Superior was as daring as the launching of spacecraft in the space age.

I had decided not to try for another engine ride this time. Instead I loitered in the park car (the tail-end recreation car, each one named by the CPR after a different national park) on the prowl for someone as eccentric as Eric Wilde. No one appeared wearing a dinner jacket. I listened to the grumpy trainman who had replaced our good-humored hamburger enthusiast at Chapleau. "When you married your wife in those days, you married a washing machine. There was no pressure to buy all these appliances you gotta have now." Oblivious to the stiffening backs in the lounge, he went on. "The two-cent letter. We used to pick up mail at all the stations along here and you'd get it in Toronto the next day. Then they gave it back to the donkeys in the post office. The train used to deliver lake trout from up here fresh in New York. We threw that whole life away. And I'll tell you what for. Drugs and women's lib."

A genteel, middle-aged matron who had been listening quietly placed her cup of tea in one of the holes in her drink stand and spoke to the trainman, several seats away. "My father was injured in a sawmill accident before he was fifty. There was no compensation and no pension. Don't tell me your old-time stuff. I don't want to hear it." Like a dignitary on a dais, she rose, picked up her handbag, and calmly departed. The trainman smirked, as if he had been proven right: *another woman spoiled by too many appliances.*

Up in the dome all you could see were trees and rocks and water. The landscape was repetitive and confining. But under the transparent canopy, sipping a beer, I felt this was an excellent way to travel; no need to look for a hotel or a restaurant, nor to think about the distance or the time. Across the aisle an Englishman, who had spread a map and asked me where we were, expressed more than contentment.

"This is a fabulous train," he extolled. "I've seen these American trains on film. Somehow I never thought they were really in use." He talked about the Billy Wilder movie *Some Like It Hot*. "Do you remember that scene where, I think it's Jack Lemmon, is in drag, desperately trying to bring it off, and is repeating to himself 'I'm a girl I'm a girl I'm a girl I'm a girl' in railway rhythm, with cutaway shots to the wheels and pistons? These cars are identical to the ones they used in it. I couldn't believe my luck when I got on board." He spoke with childish glee about the bunks that folded away on Canadian trains, and about the dome cars. Had I seen the female black bear and her cubs alongside the tracks? I thought again of my railway rides in Peru. You had to work harder to see things in your own country. The figure and the ground were always starkly defined in foreign places. At home there was a familiarity to shake off.

I went down the narrow stairway from the dome section to the lounge, where people were reading the magazines in plastic folders. Then down into the bar under

the dome level, sometimes the place to find good conversation. But it was empty. On the front of the bar itself,
two carved linoleum ducks were depicted in flight. I remembered taking this train, The Canadian, with my
mother and father in 1958 from Vancouver to Montreal.
It was then only a few years old, and the CPR proudly
touted it as the last word in luxury train travel. For our
passenger trains The Canadian was the last word and the
eulogy too, though we did not know that at the time. The
hand-tooled bar and other interior surfaces beguiled me
as a child. Fantasy and reality merged on that train, an
endless succession of mobile rooms with improbable floor
plans, like the dreams a child has, in some ways larger
than life, in other ways wonderfully child-sized. The
sleeping compartments, for example, seemed made to
measure for a ten-year-old, small, private, with pockets
for hiding things and a panel of switches for the lights
and the fan.

This end of the train was for people who had enough
money, the comfortably middle-class, or those who had
saved for a holiday. Even the least expensive sleeping
accommodation was not cheap, unless you took your
chances and tried for something half-price after 10 P.M.
The difference between the rear part of the train (where
people slept lying down) and the forward part (where
they slept in their seats) was the difference between an
old luxury hotel gone to ruin and a youth hostel. I walked
up eight cars, bobbing and weaving as the train lurched,
and took a seat in the forward bar. No Presbyterian ladies
drinking tea at this watering hole. I went into the steward's kitchen and asked for a beer.

"Siddown," he snapped. "I got to carry it to you."

The beer arrived at the same price it had been eight
cars away, but without the faded luxury. A man about
thirty, who said his name was Max, sat opposite me. He
was coming back from Halifax with two hundred pounds
of luggage.

"Halifax is shallow," he said. "A very bad music

scene. Very conservative drinking laws. I wanted to open a pub there, but the liquor commission wouldn't let me." He had been a disc-jockey, a farm labourer, a bar-tender, a cab driver, and now he waited in formal restaurants. "I make two thousand a month or better," he said. That was another difference between the forward and the tail-end bars. People here talked easily about money. In the back of the train more was hidden. Passengers could retire with their secrets behind the closed doors of bed-rooms and roomettes.

Max was dressed in tight blue jeans, cowboy boots, and a shirt with a wide-open collar. He wore a gold chain around his neck. "I could make good money with the right kind of bar," he said. "But I'm always ahead of the place I'm in." He sounded like a stock promoter. "Life-style is the key to making it in the bar business." I won-dered what he meant. We ordered a second round, and then a third. In the tail-end car I had been one of the younger passengers, but here it was the reverse. Walking the train I had seen row after row of them, just out of university, looking for adventure, no itineraries, the fu-ture wide-open. And others, a few years older, playing the same game, but for the older ones, like Max, the future had begun to close a little, fantasies were turning into disappointments, and they liked the train because they could borrow for a few days the enthusiasm of the students.

It was after five o'clock. Most of the seats in the li-censed lounge had been filled. We passed Mobert, one of those curious, railway-coined names (originally Mon-tizambert), and then we broke out of the enclosing bush onto the lakeshore, though you could not see it well from the bar and even less so through the rained-out light. A pretty woman, dressed like a college student but closer to my age, entered the car and looked around. There were no free tables. She sat beside me, small, slim, bright-eyed, and said her name was Linda. Her hands were flecked with little cuts.

"They say the track ahead is sinking," she told us. This happened some years in the spring between Thunder Bay and Winnipeg.

Max had heard the same. "They might reroute," he said. "We'd go up north onto the CN line. That would make us a day late." The transcontinental could still be buffetted by weather. Two years earlier an engine's steam-heating system had been frozen in mid-winter by prairie winds. The train's arrival had been delayed by a day.

Linda had just completed a welding course on a government grant. Unable to find work in Montreal, she had bought a ticket to Smithers in the British Columbian interior where her uncle owned a cannery. "He had a farm in Quebec when I was growing up. Whiskey bottles and big apples is all I remember." Another woman took the fourth seat at our table. She was good-looking too, with green eyes, curly blonde hair, and a mouth like Jane Fonda's. A designer in the theatre at Thunder Bay, Susan was on a tour with her portfolio, looking for work with one of the prairie companies. Like most theatre people in Canada she had to watch her money, and so was sitting in the coach. Susan was a measure of how the country had changed since I had taken the train west in 1970. The chances then of coming across a theatre professional in this or any other bar outside a few in Montreal and Toronto were slim. Theatre in those days was something you went to New York to discuss. Susan spoke intensely of being drawn to the stage, of the energy she found there. To the side I could hear Linda, with an incipient slur, telling Max about her uncle.

"He's been trying to get a piece off me for years."

"It's the way actors connect with the people in the house, the way they offer themselves totally, that fascinates me."

"I never let him though. He picks women up and throws them away."

"They're magnetic, the good actors."

"Where in hell is Smithers anyways?"

We continued, beer on the table, the women doing most of the talking. The train passed Marathon and Schreiber, and went on into the dark. I felt inspired by Susan's green eyes, and by her perceptiveness, but she gave no sign of similar inclinations. *Too many beers*, I thought. *Put yourself to bed*. Linda, who had pulled her legs up onto the bench beside me, was hugging her knees. Cheerfully intimate, like the women in beer ads, she had lodged her toes under my left thigh. The toes began to wiggle as she continued talking to Max, and Susan to me. The squirming feet seemed detached, little female feelers looking for affection. *Romance with a welder. And the possible dire after-effects*. I decided against it. In this case silence could only mean consent. I made a move to go, and Linda asked where I was sleeping.

"I have a berth," I said.

"Is that one of those little rooms?"

"Just a bunk bed with curtains," I replied, trying to make it sound uncomfortable.

"Curtains," she murmured. "Couldn't get a piece off in there very easy."

True, if you wanted absolute privacy, although coupling in a berth was not all that awkward either. I staggered back to mine wondering whether I ought to have grabbed Linda's toes, if only in the pursuit of literature.

Grave Markers for a Way of Life

THE SLEEPING CAR PORTER REACHED INTO MY BERTH AND tapped me awake, saying it was eight o'clock. We had rolled slowly over the sinking track, he said, and were running two hours late. In the dining car I sat with Richard, a white man, and Ricky, who was black. She worked as a show business agent, a big-boned, handsome woman who turned heads when she rose to go.

"She was in the armed forces," Richard said. "Married a French-Canadian. In two weeks she's getting married again, to Mr. Taylor in Toronto." This might be true, I reflected, and it might not. It would be easy to fabricate a false life on the train. Beyond the last stop we had no shared future with one another, no one to verify our claims.

We passed the gigantic statue of a fish outside Kenora. Richard was asking me about myself. Lingering over tea after breakfast, he seemed unnaturally interested. Like a writer, I thought, or a homosexual on the make, he's working hard to cultivate me. But Richard was neither literary nor gay, as far as I could tell. Originally from Britain, he sold computer software and had a Kenyan wife, of whom he spoke admiringly. We talked about our children, and then he asked, "What do you think the true nature of reality is?"

I looked out the window. The rain had stopped, but the light was still grey. We were travelling above the view, on a ridge overlooking a series of ink-blot lakes punctuated by woodland. "Whatever you manage to hold onto," I said absently.

"But there's something beyond all this, don't you think? An after-life?"

I realized I knew the pattern well. "You're a Jehovah's Witness," I concluded. And he said yes.

"This world you see around you, this is Satan's world." He would have made a compelling pitchman for Via Rail, with a variation on their current television ad telling people to "Come feel the magic."

"Jehovah's there for everyone," he continued. "No one should be denied." I said I'd had an excess of religion growing up as a Christian Scientist, and that I wasn't convertible.

"Christian Science. Is that Ron Hubbard's thing?"

"Christian Science has affinities to ancient gnosticism," I replied. Which ended the discussion. Walking back to the sleeping cars I felt Richard was my opposite in some way, the antithesis of all travellers who went for the sensuous experience of new sights and sounds and smells. Satan's world, as he described it, was self-reinforcing. You narrowed your perceptions to focus on it, and left out the sources of joy. This could be the ultimate Pyrrhic victory, cheating death by reducing life to its equal. I did feel as though I had just peeked inside Richard's coffin, and found him there repeating a Domesday prayer.

"The right train of thought can take you to a better station in life," read a hand-painted message scrawled in the raunchy rail yard outside the Winnipeg station. "Fuck you," read another. We had arrived almost three hours late. People in Toronto often spoke ill of Winnipeg, but on my previous visits I had liked the city. I was born in it (though I left as an infant), and I had antecedents here going back to the late pioneer days. Just before the CPR laid rail through the province, my paternal grandfather rode across the southern Manitoba prairie on horseback looking for business opportunities. His father, a judge in Toronto, must have had enough money to give his son a small stake. This was how many established Toronto families extended themselves into the west. With a little financial backing from Ontario, an astute and energetic entrepreneur could make a tidy fortune in Winnipeg during the boom years between 1885 and 1914. My grandfather and his cousin started an importing business, and they prospered. He resided in the city until his death in 1928. As a child I had heard stories from my grandmother about life in the mansion they had built on Wellington Crescent. The grand ball they held for the Prince of Wales was a favourite memory of hers. She told stories about my father in his nursery, about the chauffeur and the kitchen help, about taking her two children abroad after my grandfather died. Later I met people who remained bitter about the disparities between life on Wellington Crescent and the less privileged experience of Winnipeg's north end. Of this the family stories told nothing. By chance as an adult I discovered in a library that eccentric and aloof Uncle Alec, whom my grandmother would occasionally mention in her anecdotes, was the judge who presided over the jury trial of Fred Dixon, a leader of the 1919 Winnipeg General Strike and a name well known to students of Canadian labour history. Dixon was charged with seditious libel and acquitted. Reports on the trial proceedings in the Winnipeg Free Press included a cartoon of Uncle Alec asleep at the bench.

It was late in the afternoon by the time I had bought my next train ticket and found a hotel. I prowled the old warehouse district, said to have the richest concentration of nineteenth-century industrial architecture in Canada. At six o'clock the district, now a mix of offices, stores, and unrented lofts, was deserted except for a few hookers. Past the handsome warehouses I came to Chinatown, an agglomeration of low, run-down buildings. Poorly dressed Indians, some of them drunk, hung around the entrance to a hostel. They looked at me carefully, sizing up my meaning: a possible mark, a possible agent of the law. For me they separated east from west. Winnipeg was where the native people became visible in urban Canada. Indians lived in Montreal, Ottawa, and Toronto, but their numbers were relatively small. In Winnipeg you could ignore them, as most people did, but you could not forget they existed. Their faces stared at you ambivalently from every sidewalk in the downtown.

I went into the King's Palace restaurant which occupied the downstairs of a small two-story brick building. In the cramped space—only nine tables—groups of Chinese were eating. Until an Indian entered I was the only outsider. Dressed in traditional native style, his thick black hair braided into pig-tails, a bone talisman around his neck, his black jacket colourfully embroidered, and his broad-brimmed hat adorned with feathers, he strode into the room holding a small boy by the hand. They sat at the table next to mine; the child and I said hello. The man looked at me impassively, as if I were a stuffed animal, not a flicker in his eyes, and then he turned away.

The next morning, booked for Churchill on Hudson Bay—a long journey back into winter—I left my bags at the station and walked in the good weather. A butterfly circled and alighted on my arm, opening and closing its wings. The sun was giving the air and the sidewalks a sharp spring heat. On the butterfly's black surface were tangerine stripes and little drops of white. A pubescent fuzz of green thickened the seedlings along Broadway Avenue. I continued up it to the provincial legislature and went inside to hear the daily question period.

The elevator operator, who carried one limp arm, closed the gate with the other and pushed the button for the third floor with his nose. In the legislative chamber questions were asked about the possibility of closing down Churchill. There had been a shrinkage in the volume of wheat shipped out through the port. The minister responsible blamed his federal counterpart, an old Canadian game. Heated exchanges followed on other issues. The questioners were artificially indignant and the ministers insincerely self-righteous. There is no end to hollow hyperbole in a provincial parliament; interminable debate about gravel pit regulations and electric power rates are imbued with all the false pride society can muster. The richly made Manitoba legislature suggested highminded eloquence, but the architecture had been deceived. Looking down from the third-floor gallery onto the grand staircase fashioned from Carrara marble, you could see the two life-size bronze buffalo which greeted visitors at the bottom of the steps. They were both male, their enormous brass testicles visible from the railing above. The sculptures injected a fresh animal sanity into the place, but also announced an ethos of masculine authority and male power. Most of the buffalo in western

Canada had been slaughtered years before the staircase had been constructed. These two brass bulls, trapped in the legislature, were symbols of pioneer freedom and a wish for the continuation of early prairie values, but they could also be viewed as grave markers for a way of life.

There was still time before the train. I went into Dalnavert, the restored home of Hugh John Macdonald, only son of Canada's first prime minister, Sir John A. Built in 1895 in the eclectic Victorian style, it stood on a side street between the legislature and the station. I looked at the dinner gong, the ice-box, the fire-fan, the speaking tubes, the servants' bells, the golden oak panelling in the dining room, and the art nouveau chandelier. A local historical society maintained the house in impeccable period condition. Their guide took me through, speaking in hushed tones about the trappings of Victorian gentility that had been preserved here. She spoke as an anthropologist would speak of the lost tribe, marvelling at the implements and housekeeping habits of the Macdonalds. I could hear my grandmother ringing her own gong for dinner in her equally dark house in Ottawa. Already part of me was in a museum. Walking through the rooms was like being taken back in a dream to a place long ago put behind, with a suggestion that you had not really left. I told the guide I had a train to catch. Could I not stay until tomorrow, she wanted to know? The great-grandson of Sir John A. came in on Wednesdays. "His reputation has suffered," she added anxiously. "He wasn't really the heavy drinker that some people think."

"We Like the Countries with Big Spaces"

CHURCHILL WAS A THOUSAND MILES BY TRAIN FROM Winnipeg. "One of the most diverse, wild, and desolate stretches of track in Canada," said my guide book. The cars were less than half full. At the first sitting for dinner I was alone, one pair of eyes in a railway car crossing a limitless expanse of flat terrain. The impression of space was overwhelming. Or could one speak of an impression of space? The sensation was more like impending self-annihilation, as if the train were being sucked into a vacuum—the Canadian north—and about to disintegrate. Occasionally some sign of life would tumble into the vacuum, a solitary farmer running a machine over his vast acreage, or a few ducks, or a lone grain elevator. Where there was grass, it was palpably green. We passed some spring calves scampering from the train. But most of the land was given over to grain farming, huge tracts of ploughed black earth, silent and empty. To the west hung a purple haze.

"You'll have a quiet ride," said the steward in the bar, which occupied the other half of the dining car. "Not many on tonight. I've had trips where they had to lock the day coach on this train. Just lock'em in there and let'em fight it out." Four Indians, all of them over six feet, came into the bar a few minutes later. The steward, a soft, rotund man, sold them beers quickly and retreated to his canteen, bolting the door behind him. Every ten minutes he opened it enough to stick his head through and see if anyone needed a drink. This peekaboo service gave the bar a mock-jailhouse atmosphere, which seemed to get under the skin of the natives.

"Hey mister," shouted one. "Why you lockin' yerself up?"

"Hey," said another, waving at the steward, whose black face was poked half-way through the doorway. "Hey. C'mere."

"You want a beer?"

"He needs something," called out the first Indian.

The steward came down to the table. "Don't shout at me," he said.

"I got ten dollars," boasted the one who had waved. "Bring me dinner."

The black man shook his head. "Peanuts and chips. That's it."

"Other people had dinner," protested the Indian. He was holding up his money.

"Dinner is over," lied the steward. I could see through the galley that the waiter was still serving the second sitting.

The Indian dropped his head and looked up sideways. "Then gimme four beers."

The engine was pulling four cars, one for baggage, a coach, the bar-diner, and a sleeper. I went back to my berth. Across the aisle sat a German couple, about sixty, on a cross-country tour.

"We have been to Australia," said the man.

"And Argentina," said his wife.

"We like the countries with the big spaces. Big strong countries." They looked at each other and he chuckled. "You are strong here, yes? You have many commodities."

"Our economy is not as strong as it used to be," I replied.

"At home for us is very crowded. You have the land." He thought about it for a moment. "Maybe you need more people." He said his sentences looking straight ahead, then punctuated them with a furtive glance in my direction.

I asked them why they were going to Churchill.

"We think that is really Canada," he said. "Up north."

"We like to travel far," she added.

When I woke at six-thirty in the morning, the Germans were up and their beds had been folded away. They appeared to be dressed in hiking costumes. He sat with one arm across his chest, and she with her hands planted firmly in her lap, neither looking at the other. Their apparent determination made me feel slothful. It also gave me the odd sensation that I was about to be arrested. I clambered down the little ladder provided for upstairs sleepers, and was thrown off the last step by the lurching car. Off balance, I met his steely, neutral stare.

"You must find the shoes," he remarked. I looked at his feet. They were encased in well made walking boots with thick laces. His wife wore a similar pair. I reached up for my inferior footware and padded down to the washroom, as if following orders. There was an advantage to rising early. The linen towels piled beside the tiny sink were still clean and dry, and the floor was not yet sloppy from spills. I washed and then pocketed one of the wrapped pieces of soap for later in the day when soap would be hard to find—people like me kept stealing it.

At seven o'clock we reached The Pas and the Germans disappeared. The train stood in the station for an hour and a half as scheduled. I sat with a marine engineer for breakfast; we were the only passengers in the car. The crew were lounging on the stools, two of them arguing about whether they would meet their colleague Bennett on the way up.

"No, no, no," sang the waiter in a high, homosexual voice. "You'll see. Bennett will be there."

"I'm telling ya," boomed the black steward. "L. D. Mackay runs with Bennett. L. D. *follows* me up every time. Him and Bennett. I'll bet ya twenty."

"I shoulda bet that thousand last time," shrieked the waiter. "I shoulda did it."

"Well you didn't. You didn't have the nerve." They went on needling each other with their patter through the breakfast hour, like cell mates killing time. The marine engineer had been working on the tugboats out of Nanaimo in British Columbia. When he had been laid off there he had taken a contract in Churchill and moved with his family. I asked how he liked the northern town; a litany of complaints ensued. Food cost almost three times what it did in the south. The permafrost made housing expensive—all the underground pipes required heating wires. The schools were bad. The stores stocked inferior merchandise. The weather was abominable. And there was nothing to do at night but drink or watch video cassettes.

Walking the train as we pulled out of The Pas, I looked into the second coach we had taken on there. It carried a single passenger, one old Indian woman huddled in a corner. In the first coach sat an Indian couple with a child, one Indian by himself, and a white woman and child. The train appeared to be almost as empty as the wilderness it was traversing. Back in the sleeping car the Germans were carefully eating slices of apple. They had walked around The Pas. I was surprised to see that he had lost an arm. I had formed a four-limbed picture of him earlier and it seemed for a moment that he must have suffered a nasty accident on his morning stroll.

We entered a watery part of the world north of The Pas, even more liquid now during the spring melt. The tracks ran along Cormorant Lake and beside countless shallow pans of water without names. Past the town of Cormorant, an old wooden railway car, hauled off the tracks for a makeshift cabin and then abandoned, lay rotting in the soupy bush. We came to Wekusko. Like most Indian place names along these and other tracks, it signified water, "herb lake." A few shacks and tumbledown houses stood by the line. Outside loitered two little brown girls, and two dogs. An Indian stepped down from the train with a cloth sack over his shoulder and walked toward the dwellings. Then we drew away into the scruffy, spindly trees.

At Wabowden, another one of those curious railway-made names (W. A. Bowden was an engineer with the department of railways and canals), the southbound train was waiting for us. Both crews gathered on the platform to gossip. I stepped down, thinking I would buy a paper. "I'll sell you mine," said the clerk at the counter. "The stores are closed for lunch." But it was yesterday's paper, which I had bought in Winnipeg. He shrugged. "This is the freshest paper you'll see from here to Churchill." I wandered onto the main street of Wabowden, population two hundred and eighty-four, about half-way up the line from Winnipeg. The buildings were unadorned and utilitarian. It was an ugly place. People worked for the railway or ran small businesses. I imagined they hunted and drank, and now watched satellite television. They came here because they did not want to be bothered. There might be other reasons, like inheriting your grandmother's grocery store, but even then you would have a choice. Wabowden did not have the look of a permanent settlement, though it had survived almost seventy years since the railway had gone through.

We started again, back into the dwarf bush. Thicket Portage, in the early afternoon, was a typical Indian village: a log cabin, some one-room shacks and unpainted houses, dirt roads, a simple wooden building with a sign that said GENERAL STORE, an outdoor rink, and two satellite dishes. In front of the store five Indian men stood idle, staring at the train. By the door of one of the shacks, a ragamuffin girl, plump and doll-like, stared too. I remembered Al Purdy's poem about Indian boys watching trains.

> *Boys with their mouths open*
> *some missing part supplied by trains*

*Thought will not come to them nor speech
they have no words for department stores
or pictographs for elevators going fifty
miles an hour into the sky*

Three times a week the white man's train rolled through,
mobile and rootless. I would have been hard pressed to
explain to these Indians why the train was here today.
Megalomania? Force of habit? Certainly we had too few
passengers to justify sending five railway cars into the
northern bush. Did the Indians perceive the train as a
pretentious folly? They rode it too, and it brought them
supplies. But it stood at the edge of their world, and it
belonged to someone else. The train led to the white
man's alcoholic cities and the wrong side of the tracks.
And in their collective memory the Indians surely knew
that just as the railways meant opportunity and wealth to
white people, the first trains had signalled poverty and
defeat to the Indian.

We took the spur line into Thompson, Manitoba's
nickel capital. It had been built from raw bush in the
1950s by the International Nickel Company, an instant
town and now a city of fourteen thousand. With an hour
and a half of station time here, I walked down the highway into the settlement. The clerk in Wabowden had been
right—no fresh papers. I bought a copy of the weekly
Thompson *Citizen*, six days old. A front page story de-
tailed recent cases tried in the itinerant provincial court.
Orville Clemons had been convicted of assault. He had
punched his ex-girlfriend in a dispute. Linda Jawbone
(not an associate of Mr. Clemons) was excused from pay-
ing restitution for a forgery. A man was ordered to stay
out of Thompson for three months because he had stolen
a bottle of orange extract from a grocery store. And then:
"Frederick Brightnose was fined $1000 and put on pro-
bation for two years with an order to abstain absolutely
from the consumption of alcohol. . . . Brightnose, 41,

was picked up on May 1 drinking from an open bottle of liquor in front of the Thompson Post Office.''

''The most common reaction of newcomers to our city is one of amazement!'' bubbled a pamphlet in the shopping mall. ''They can't get over being suddenly dropped into a slice of suburbia after driving through or flying over hundreds of miles of wilderness.'' Amazement would be the neutral reaction. If you considered 1950s suburban architecture a high point of western civilization, then Thompson embodied the perfectability of the northern bush, and it would delight you. To my eyes the whole place was a desecration, the legacy of post-war quick-and-dirty design, a triumph of expediency over taste. The commercial strip, the faceless mall, the look-alike houses, all were functional, nothing more. I was reminded of pictures of the new Siberian towns, the similar surfaces. And beneath the surface people were working, coupling, fighting, making and unmaking families, living as they did in places I found aesthetically richer. Some would claim the shape of the built environment had no consequence. The owner of a shop on the main street said as much.

''Fourteen thousand people can't all be wrong.''

I asked if he would stay on after he retired.

''I've got my piece of land in Florida.'' He had started work on a house there. I remembered a Greek restaurateur in Toronto saying to me, ''Canada is just a waiting place. Even people who are here two, three generations, they are waiting to get out to somewhere warm.'' His judgement was too sweeping, but believable in Thompson.

The train crawled out on the spur line and switched back to the main track. A road had been washed out not far from the junction. You could catch glimpses of pavement underneath the floating ducks. Some ponds were clear, but as we headed north the water had more frozen patches.

''Candle ice,'' said the man opposite me in the diner.

"You pick it up and it's just like candles. Gets that way in the spring around break-up time." He was a heavy man with a roll of flesh hanging over his belt and two surplus chins squeezed up by his closed collar. He had lived in Thompson for seventeen years, working as a meat salesman.

"It's a good town. We have everything we need."

"Will you stay when you stop working?"

"When you're older it's different. Some people can't take the winters."

He said he knew all the villages from Thompson to Churchill and beyond. "That's my territory. Mostly Indians. All the way up to Rankin Inlet." He looked out the window. The trees were growing even smaller and thinner as we pushed north. "This is where nature smiles for miles and miles."

The villages were small. Some appeared to have only four or five shacks. The few Indians we saw were dressed for cold weather and the bush retained a dead, wintry look. But the light was May light; you could see out the window until after nine o'clock. At dusk we came to Ilford. Beside the stopped train a beautiful Indian girl with thick, braided pig-tails, a delicate face and confident bearing poked a boy's chest, grabbed his crotch lightly, and then jumped back to laugh. About twenty natives watched the freight being taken on and off, their breath making streams of frost. A rush of cold air filled the bardiner as the cook put out garbage and spoke to the Indians through his little loading door. Then we rolled back into the darkening bush.

The Blue-Engine Bullet Train to Yellowknife

MY GUIDEBOOK NOTED THAT THE TRIP TOOK TWENTY-TWO hours, but we had ridden the train for thirty-seven when we reached Churchill early the next morning. The schedule had been stretched. "We run it like a freight train now," the steward said. At seven o'clock one restaurant was open. The meat man and I sat at tables decorated with plastic flowers. The low-roofed room was windowless and dark, a white man's igloo. Outside yawned limitless space, but you could make habitable only small pockets of it. The train berth seemed generous compared to a winter spent in rooms like this.

The cars would sit in the Churchill rail yard all day, and start the return trip at six in the evening. In two days another train would come. I tramped around the frozen dirt roads, feeling the chill. I had brought no heavy clothes, thinking the cold was behind me. But it was still winter in Churchill. Crusted piles of plowed snow clung to the roadsides, and the sky showed a dull grey.

POLAR BEARS PUBLIC MEETING MAY 22 announced a notice posted in public places around the town.

POLAR BEAR ALERT PROGRAM
POLAR BEAR RESEARCH
POLAR BEAR IN GENERAL

This was not the season for bears, I had been told by the Germans. "Too late for the bears," he had said. "And

158

too early for the whales." I had not hoped for whales—
this was the first I'd heard of them—but a polar bear, yes.
The German couple were marching in unison around the
town. As well as matching boots, they wore similar
tuques, and carried identical wine-coloured satchels.
Each was pulling a little metal cart onto which matching
black leather suitcases had been strapped. I found a movie
on polar bears playing at the Parks Canada office. When
I entered the theatre the Germans were already seated
and waiting.

"Some people," intoned a gravelly voice-over at the
beginning of the film, "refuse to acknowledge that polar
bears are dangerous, wild carnivores."

Behind me the German man laughed loudly.

"We will stay for the next train," he told me after the
lights went on. "Do you know, is it possible to find real
Eskimos here?" I envisaged him marching over the tundra with his wife, baggage buggies in tow, in search of
an Inuit encampment.

"You'll have to take a plane," I said. "We are not
very far north. And you may be twenty-five years too
late." In the lobby I pointed on a map of Canada to
where I thought the Inuit lived. They began to squabble
in German.

"She doesn't like small airplanes," he apologized.

The wife looked indignant. "We take only the railway."

At the mouth of the Churchill River was one of the
oldest European settlement sites in English Canada. The
Hudson's Bay Company established a post nearby in 1685,
a year after an installation had been built down the coast
at York Factory. Fort Prince of Wales, across the river
mouth from Churchill, was built over forty years beginning in 1731. The historic remains could not be visited in
May. Neither float planes nor vessels were safe with the
ice breaking up. A Parks Canada employee imparted this
information while pointing to pictures and models of the

inaccessible sites. The German couple sat attentively, like well-behaved school children. When the lecture ended they said it was after twelve o'clock and they could now check into their hotel. I watched them pull their carts down the frozen street to the Tundra Inn as I made my own way to The Bay store, the last of the company's structures in use here. The oldest incorporated joint-stock merchandising company in the English-speaking world was represented by a utilitarian shed without windows. It was a miniature department store selling clothing and appliances and food. The Florida oranges and grapefruits were turning brown in the refrigerated bins. There were pineapples and coconuts for sale, four kinds of apples, and boxes of decaying strawberries. After the bleak, brown streets of Churchill, walking by the piled fruit was like visiting unhappy tropical animals at a zoo.

Outside I could find no sign of vegetation. The yards around the houses were covered with dirt or gravel. So was the school playground. Along the main street small businesses operated out of aluminum and wooden sheds. In a climate of absolutes there was everything you absolutely needed and very little else. Fifteen minutes of walking along the main road took me to the last windowless aluminum barn. It was an easy stroll; the cold wind blew from behind and my hood was up. I walked a while more onto the featureless sub-arctic barrens, then turned around. Churchill looked far away. Beyond it hulked the huge concrete grain elevators that were the port's reason for being. I had lost track of the distance and the time. The wind blasted across the flats into my face and through my clothes. It was an effort to move into it and back towards the centre of town. A numbness and an unpleasant tingling. Naive, I thought, to have wandered away not knowing the temperature and wearing the wrong clothes. The iceman cometh. It was true that death hung in the wind here, curling around the tight dark houses and sheds, waiting for you to make a mistake. Later in the day a pamphlet informed me that average May temperatures were below zero Celsius, July and August the only months without snowfall.

I went into the Eskimo Museum and warmed myself. It was housed in a plain, rectangular building beside the Holy Canadian Martyr's Church. Around the perimeter of the one exhibition room stood glass cabinets filled with stone and ivory carvings by the Inuit. On the open floor brooded an out-of-season polar bear, stuffed. The curator, an old priest, sat alone and idle at his desk in an alcove. His eyes were pale and watery, unfocussed. Apparently his thoughts were far away.

We exchanged a few words. Then he said in French, "I'm eighty-five. Today is my birthday." Brother Jacques had first arrived in Churchill in 1927, two years before the railway. "Life is easy here now. In those days we travelled by dog-team, or we walked. The natives showed us how to live." He spoke reverentially of the Inuit. They knew things about the north, he said, that no one else would ever know. "My first year up here I was making a trip with a native guide. We were hauling our boat across an ice drift. Everything looked okay to me. Suddenly my guide stopped still, as if he was listening for something. Then he pulled me away. The section of ice we'd been standing on broke off and capsized." Brother Jacques said he felt lucky to have survived the north without injury. "A friend of mine fell into a deep crack in the ice once. The only thing he could do was take off his mitts and claw his way out. He lost his fingers."

The collection in the cabinets had been started long before mass-market selling had given Inuit art a commercial value. The quality of the work was high. Until the 1950s missionary priests must have been able to acquire artifacts without competition. Many of the pieces were endowed with a delicate whimsy absent from later Inuit carvings. Brother Jacques' clerical career covered the period when Canada's far-northern natives had been assimilated into southern culture by education and resettlement. These carvings embodied some of the naiveté lost in that process. Several pieces recorded the coming of airplanes (aloft on thin ivory poles) to the north. Others showed the strong influence of the missionaries.

"That's Pope Pius XII," said the priest when I asked about a tiny ivory figure wearing spectacles made from green glass. He looked at my notebook. "I don't like anthropologists. They want to destroy Christianity."

Behind the museum I hummed "Frère Jacques" and stood on a snow-crusted rise to see Hudson Bay, an undefined expanse of lumpy white, not the neat blue horseshoe I knew from maps. Once, in the Peruvian jungle, I thought I understood the urge to explore uncharted terrain, the danger and rewards of the green unknown. Why any traveller would want to go against the vapid white infinitude north of Churchill was more difficult to comprehend. Maybe it was only the simple need to make a mark, like a child's irresistible impulse to doodle on a clean white page, lines across the unmarked snow, furrows in the mapless sea. The charting in Canada had been done, which seemed a good reason to turn away from the frozen whiteness and revert to the warmer unclaimed ground of the clean white paper in my pocket.

After eleven hours in Churchill, the train started south. I went to bed early, reading the novel *A Candle to Light the Sun* by the Winnipeg writer Patricia Blondal. "Jacob heard the way-freight cry frostily of cruel loss and sudden loneliness." The train as a metaphor for sadness, bringing people into our lives, and taking them away. Coffins used to be shipped by rail. And full trains were devoted to funerals. On the other hand, honeymooners travelled by rail, and so did party-goers. Yet the train whistle is a mournful sound. We hear it grow faint and die, and it reminds us of our physical limits.

In the morning I woke at a remote halt called Pikwitonei. This was the same journey as two days before, in reverse, and at the same slow pace, forty miles per hour. It summoned from memory a high-speed train on the central corridor in France, and the slow train from Sucre to Potosi in Bolivia, where there was more to see. For a curious traveller the problem with the Hudson Bay Railway was not that it went north, but that it did not go far enough. Below Churchill the land had an indeterminate character, part sub-arctic and part northern bush, vacillating somewhere between spring and winter. We passed ice-free pools from which rose flurries of Canada geese. Then we swung back into winter and cruised along a stretch of snow-covered tundra. Five light beige caribou were startled by the engine and loped away across the flats. The trans-Canada railway had been considered by most observers a hopeless folly when first conceived, but the railway that would have given new meaning to the term lunatic fringe would have been the line to Yellowknife. Regrettably, it was never built. For one thing, Great Slave Lake lay in the way. For another, there were never enough people in Yellowknife to make such a line profitable. But dubious profitability had not prevented dozens of Canadian railways from being built. Many lines had fallen into bankruptcy and been taken over by the government. In my mind I laid track up across the sixtieth parallel for the blue-engine bullet train, achieving in fantasy what Via Rail's number ninety-two failed to provide. I decided it might be simpler to move Yellowknife than to circumvent Great Slave Lake, although a railway still existed that crossed one of the world's larger inland bodies of water. (The train from Peru into Bolivia traversed Lake Titicacca by ferry boat.) For the Canadian winter a snow train might be installed, like the one outside Montreal in the last century; it was a seasonal railway laid when the ice grew sufficiently thick. But more likely the tracks would end on the south side of Great Slave, perhaps generating a new town, Lower Yellowknife. In any case, my bullet train was not an engineer's proposal. It was an easy way up the map of a country that suffered from cartographic encephalitis. The blue-engine bullet train was an imaginary trepanation of the bloated north, a small hole drilled to relieve the pressure of all that white volume high up on Canadian charts. The ride south of Churchill gave a taste of what a tundra ride would be like—vast stretches of snowy flats, with occasional caribou and birds. In the summer the rich tundra plants would flower. And to travel on the bullet train people would come from far-away places. Life in the cars would compensate for the sparsely inhabited landscape. Sadly, this was not so on the Churchill train. It supported only a little more life than the tundra did, though the crew assured me their passenger numbers increased in the summer. They were content with the light work load, and in some ways would have preferred to have had no passengers at all. After lunch I noticed the cook and stewards cutting into a fresh apple pie. The passengers had been given jello.

"You didn't mention you had apple pie."

"You didn't ask."

A plumber who had been working with his son in Churchill was talking to a man who had been visiting friends there. They were in the bar waiting for The Pas, which we would reach around four-thirty.

"The place I hate," said the plumber, "is Mattashawa. I don't go there any more unless I can tie the pilot to a tree." They were trading stories about survival in the northern bush. "Last time I went in, the pilot dropped me off and said he'd be back in a few hours. I only had half a day's work to do. As soon as he left, it fogged over, and didn't lift for a week. I found a cabin with a case of tuna fish, and that was my food for six days."

The other man said he had once been unable to fly out of a place called God's Narrows. "We were stuck there four days. I've never seen so much booze come out of the walls in such a short time. Someone produced a full case of whiskey." He shook his head, feigning dismay.

"God's Narrows," echoed the plumber. "We had real trouble there once. They thought we had liquor and they started shooting at the building we were in. Christ, I hid behind the boiler and held on till it was over." Two tables away a group of Indians were drinking beer. The plumber spoke of *them* in a nineteenth-century way, as if they were beyond redemption.

We rolled over the Saskatchewan River into The Pas. Most of the graffiti on the bridge had been painted over, but you could still make out a few shrill slogans, including an insult hurled at the railway: CN SUCKS. I walked a couple of blocks to the main street. Miss The Pas Restaurant caught my eye, but through the dirty plate glass I saw it was a dreary short-order joint. The New Moon Inn had been changed to the New Moon Indian by a prankster with a can of paint. Several shops were closed; so was the Canton Restaurant. The town looked as if it had been hit by plague or drought: dusty, leached, makeshift. On one corner the Bank of Montreal occupied a standard-issue concrete box. Other businesses operated out of buildings with false fronts. The older structures appeared unkempt and broken-down; the newer ones looked hastily built. I had often wondered about this place. The Pas. An early centre of the fur trade, a historic site. It possessed a name that invited speculation. But seeing the poverty, the lack of imagination, the ugliness, I wanted to leave. Perhaps the dull, cracked face of The Pas was unconsciously reassuring to the Indians. A civilization that produced shiftless, semi-occupied settlements such as this might not be invincible after all.

As the train left the town, dinner was called. I looked at the menu and ordered sole.

"The sole tonight," said the steward, "is halibut."

While I waited I heard the cook say in the kitchen, "There's something wrong with the fish." He consulted in whispers with the steward, who nevertheless looked unruffled when he brought the order out. It was obvious what was wrong with the fish. The sauce had curdled and tasted off. I scraped it away.

A few minutes later the steward came back smiling. "How's the fish?"

"Great," intoned the people at one table.

"Very good," replied the woman in front of me. Her companion nodded meekly.

"The fish was okay," I said. "But the sauce was no good."

"What do you want me to do about it?" he demanded testily.

"I'll have a piece of pie."

"Sorry. No more pie. Want some jello?"

I zig-zagged down the narrow hallway to the other end of the car for a drink. A CN worker who had been cruising the corridors over the course of the day came in and took a seat.

"Used to have passenger trains with twenty-seven cars on this line," he said. "I've got my conductor's papers, but I'm working the baggage now. That's enough for me." He was a good-looking older man, with bright, dark eyes, and silver hair. "My name's Walter Goshulak. Like Cadillac. I was the conductor for the royal train in 1970." He opened his wallet and took out the I.D. card he had been issued for the Queen's visit. "In the old days we used to carry everything up here. You name it, milk, butter, eggs, salesmen. If I had a car full of Tide, I knew I had a soap salesman on board. The roads just came into places like this a few years ago." We were passing a town called Endeavour. "Until then the train was it."

Like many railwaymen I had spoken to, he grew sentimental about the past, and showed some bitterness about the new order that had replaced the old railway-connected world.

"Women don't know if they're women any more. Men don't know if they're men. You got these goddamn feminisms and liberators and what all. The system's gone haywire."

Blue Ribbon Tea

HARRY HAD COME TO CANADA FROM POLAND AT THE AGE of eight. The family was sent to a Jewish farming village in Manitoba. His father had been a merchant in the old country, but was allowed into Canada on the condition that he take up agriculture. In the village, they lived in a small wooden house with a log shed beside it. When he was sixteen Harry moved to Winnipeg to work for his cousin Albert in the fur business. He was paid fifteen dollars a week for sixty or seventy hours of work. This arrangement continued for two years, and then Harry asked for a raise or a reduction in working time. His cousin said no; that was when Harry had begun his own family fur business. After his parents had sold their farm and moved into the city, he had operated out of their North Winnipeg basement.

I was introduced to Harry through a friend of mine, a local city planner. Harry now owned properties in the exchange district (also known as the warehouse district), so named because it was where the grain and fur exchanges had started. My friend had been encouraging Harry to renovate these buildings. The city was trying to save its architectural past. Much remained that would have been torn down in other Canadian cities. The economic growth of the 1960s and 1970s that had changed the look of urban Ontario had been slower in Winnipeg, allowing the survival of more antique structures. We walked into Harry's fur and clothing emporium, a large corner warehouse with a purple sign. Wearing a perfectly fitted sports jacket, pressed shirt and pants, and patent leather loafers, he glided across the purple carpet of his

167

showroom to greet us. I had on my travelling clothes, jeans, an unpressed shirt, a wrinkled corduroy jacket, and a necktie stained with flecks of Via Rail sauce. I could see clothes meant something to Harry, and that I had failed his sartorial test. The three of us walked to a restaurant called Bottles in the 1909 palazzo-style edifice once occupied by the Great West Life Assurance Company. My friend pointed to the Kootenay-marble finishing work as he showed us in. Looking at the menu, Harry said he did not want anything rich. He had developed a stomach ulcer at the age of eighteen. "Poor eating," he explained. There had not been enough money for decent food.

"I don't know what's happened to Winnipeg," Harry said. "Thirty years ago Portage Avenue was full of life. Now in the evening the whole downtown is dead. Thank God for the girls in the exchange district." He believed the prostitutes who hung around his store at night discouraged burglars and vandals. "Those girls offer a service. It should be legalized and regulated." He was a tough man, but he had a sensitive side. With silver hair and one drooping eyelid, he looked a little tired. The complexity, a softness and gentleness mixed into the steely resolve, showed in his face. Over lunch he reminisced about the fur business.

He had bought his first raw pelts in 1952. There had been a thousand people employed in the fur trade when he began. Now he thought there might be a hundred. The fur manufacturers in Montreal and Toronto, many of them Greek immigrants, had taken the business. "We used to work like dogs. One of my parents' neighbours reported us—you weren't supposed to work out of a house—so we had to rent space downtown. People said we'd be broke in no time. But slowly we expanded." Harry was among the inter-war immigrants who had given Winnipeg's north end its special character. North Winnipeg had been a seat of political ferment and of Jewish immigrant culture. Its history had acquired a romantic patina because so many talented people had escaped its poverty into business or the professions or the arts, both here and in other cities. But Harry was one of the last. Many of the old Jewish families had moved across the river into more expensive neighbourhoods. There was a new underclass made up of Filipinos, Vietnamese, and Canadian Indians, dispossessed, but without any visible sign of the pride and conviction that had once emboldened the north end.

After lunch I walked again through the warehouse district. Between 1880 and 1920 most of western Canada's wealth in one way or another had flowed through these blocks. My friend had given me a pamphlet with a map and pictures of the architecturally notable buildings in the area. On Princess Street I found the warehouse my grandfather had built, beginning in 1887. It was his business headquarters for thirty years. I read in the pamphlet that "the G. F. and J. Galt Company were importers and dealers in teas, cigars, wines, brandies, and general groceries, and established the Blue Ribbon line of teas and coffees. The building is a 'pre-Richardsonian' warehouse in the early English baronial style"—but an addition had altered its character. I knew almost nothing about my grandfather's everyday life. He died forty years before I was born. Among other books, he owned a luxury edition of Dickens; inside the front cover of each volume his nameplate was pasted. At a duck marsh outside Winnipeg he hosted shooting parties. The mansion, the shooting lodge, two wives, seven children, and this warehouse—which brought me no closer. I walked along Princess Street, past a row of well preserved turn-of-the-century commercial buildings, and looked at the 1902 Thomas Scott Memorial Orange Hall, commemorating the man whom the Metis leader Louis Riel had ordered executed—or murdered, depending on whose history you read.

As I crossed the city hall plaza, a storm of pink petals blew back and forth on the concrete. Some pink flakes were caught in puddles left by the night rain. Spring had stepped back a little. The air was cool. Along Main Street I passed a collection of handsome antique office buildings erected by financial institutions when Winnipeg was the economic centre of the prairies. In front of one stood a government plaque, gold script on red. "The skyscraper was a by-product of technological advances and increased urbanization of the late 19th century. Steel frame construction, the elevator, and rising land values made multi-storeyed buildings structurally and economically feasible. Between 1900 and 1916 twelve skyscrapers were built in Winnipeg, imposing on the city the verticality and density of a modern urban core." The old financial centre ended abruptly as you walked north on Main, and the dark side of the modern urban core appeared. There were seedy bars, with signs that said BEVERAGE ROOM, and coffee shops, and run-down hotels. The windows of the stores were caked with grime. Along the sidewalks Indians meandered, many of them inebriated in the early afternoon. "The drunkenness of Winnipeg is notorious," a line I had noted from George Grant's book on Canada, *Ocean to Ocean.* He had passed through here in 1872. Since then the plight of the Indians had probably worsened. They had lived now for three generations in the shadow of skyscrapers. As the white man's architecture had grown taller and fatter, they had remained on the sidewalk, empty-handed, with nothing to do.

Winnipeg's CPR passenger station was no longer in use. In a sad act of symbolic reconquest, the stretch of Main Street around the closed railway building had been taken over by down-and-out-natives. Going north along Main and then east to look at the station, I was conscious of being watched. The red brick and white stone structure, built in 1904, stood idle. If Winnipeg was the Gateway to the West, as the early slogan claimed, this building had been the door. Hundreds of thousands of Europeans had passed through it on their way to prairie settlements. I entered through the unlocked front entrance. Dark and silent, the enormous lobby had the mood of a lost tomb, or a place quickly evacuated for mysterious reasons. Four thick pink pillars supported the gently arched ceiling. A sign on one wall said TICKET OFFICE. Others said BAGGAGE and PARCEL LOCKERS, though the lockers themselves were gone. I listened to the echoing click-clack of a woman's high heels as she walked across the mosaic tile floor and disappeared up a stairway. The old P.A. system speakers were still dispersed throughout the hall, perched on top of the high panelling that dressed the perimeter. The speakers were black wooden boxes, as I remembered from the 1950s, with a circle of soft cloth in the middle protected by three natural-coloured wooden slats. A light shone from the baggage room. The man I found there was using it to sort the CPR mail. The station, he said, had been closed for seven years. THIS WAY TO THE TRAINS beckoned another sign. I tried the doors up to the platform. They were locked.

Before leaving Winnipeg I asked my friend to drive me over the bridge to St. Boniface. I wanted to see Riel's grave. The tombstone gave nothing away.

Riel
16 Novembre
1885

Wreaths of plastic flowers, red and white, were leaning against the polished red stone. Around it in an almost closed circle stood a knee-high fieldstone wall. The sign nearby identified the "Tomb of Louis Riel President of the Provisional Government of 1869–1870." I was reminded of the solitary grave of Kazantzakis on the island of Crete, not because of the settings, which were only faintly similar, but because both men were iconoclastic visionaries, impassioned and forsaken. Kazantzakis had been ostracized by his country's clerical establishment and forbidden a burial in consecrated ground. Riel rested here in the cathedral's cemetery, but he had arrived by way of the noose. From his grave you could see across the Red River to the green copper dome of the CN station, now used by Via Rail. It was the train, as much as anything, that had buried Riel. He had foreseen the changes it would allow. The train would encourage full-scale agriculture and industry, ending the free life of the Metis as freighters, boatmen, guides, and hunters. Riel sought to protect his people from the powerful white interests that were pressing in from the east. Metis land rights, he insisted, should be acknowledged and guaranteed. On the train soldiers travelled to put down what became known as the Riel rebellion. The train was given the right of way, across the land, across history. If Riel's small marker was the loser's monument, the railway station on the other side of the river was the victor's.

The Middle of the World

IN THE TAIL-END LOUNGE AS WE LEFT WINNIPEG I SAT with Americans in their sixties and seventies. Some of them wore buttons: AMERICA BY RAIL. They were travelling in a group. Their escort displayed a name-tag: BILL GREENLEAF. Beside me, the retired marine who had been discussing the Russian threat, World War II, and Ronald Reagan, said, "Our part of the world's gone soft." He was adamant but not specific: somewhere American bombs should be dropped. An elderly matron, big-boned and fleshy, with a large magisterial face, moved slowly up the narrow stairway into the dome observation seats. Encased in a closely fitting red dress and laden with big pearls, she carried a polished black cane. The retired marine and some of his compatriots, I noticed, were wearing bedroom slippers.

The first time I had left Winnipeg by train had been in 1948, at the age of six months. I have always claimed this event as my first visual memory. There was only one scene, but it remains as clear as anything I have ever remembered. I was in a shallow basket. To my right glowed natural light, a window, which would have been facing south (we were moving east to Montreal, where I would grow up). To my left, on the north side, was a doorway, and in it a tall uniformed figure with a peaked cap on his head. A girl appeared, my five-year-old sister, and she and the railway official, perhaps the conductor, exchanged words. The uniformed official and the girl leaned over my basket and gave me a pleasant greeting. Then they backed away and closed the door, and I trapped no more memories for several years. My associations with the scene are excitement and fear. The uniformed man was not entirely reassuring. I sensed power and a degree of benevolence, but also threatening indifference: the emotive and unruly infant up against the cold eye of Mr. Rulebound. Sometimes on a train this old memory would break into consciousness, as it did when I saw the pairs of feet wearing bedroom slippers in the tail-end lounge.

Up in the observation dome I recognized the pink, chubby face of Ken Smith, a trainman I had met on the same run the year before. He had shown me then a yellow dispatch alerting the crew to gumbo conditions, which he had explained meant soil drift. "Very fine prairie dust that sticks to the tracks and can make the wheels slip. The engineer has to take it slow." Today the line was gumbo-free. I asked why we were not hearing the familiar clickety-clack. Smith said we were travelling on new quarter-mile rail. The click-clack had been caused by the frequent rail joins. Soon all the old rail, and the regular percussion, would be gone.

"I'm retiring in November," he said. He was a cheerful man, but you could hear the note of sadness. "My father worked for the CPR as a switchman. My grandfather, who was from Germany, worked as a blacksmith in the railway shops at Winnipeg.'' It was the end of a progression.

We passed Brandon, with its symmetrical yellow brick station and McKENZIE SEEDS painted on a tall warehouse; the old stone station at Virden; and the tiny red frame station at Moosomin, all settlements created by the railway just over a hundred years before. At Moosomin, population 2300, you could see the main street from where the train stopped. The grain elevator, the hotel, the government liquor store, the Lyric Theatre. And you could see that the buildings diminished in size as the street unfolded to meet the prairie. A place called Wapella (Indian for ''white snow''), a place called Whitewood, and then we stopped at Broadview. The crew entered the derelict station. Across the road stood the rigorously plain World Cafe. ''Good Chinese food,'' said Smith. I asked about the condition of the station. ''There's only one guy there now, an all-round Joe. Pretty soon he won't be there either.'' After fifteen minutes we rolled on across the flat earth.

Beside Indian Head on my schedule was printed the number 49. ''Stops to detrain passengers,'' explained the key. I told the conductor I wanted to leave the train there. He radioed ahead, but the engineer did not receive the message and we overshot our mark by almost a mile. ''We don't stop much at Indian Head,'' the conductor told me as we backtracked laboriously to within an easy walk of the station. I stepped down onto the rail bed, the only one to get on or off at this settlement, and watched the other passengers stare down from the windows as the train hauled itself away. The station was locked and boarded-up; the town was nowhere in sight. When the train disappeared I felt an eerie quietude. In the distance a power mower growled faintly, and close to my ears sawed the buzz-buzz evening crescendoes of darting insects. I had asked the train crew for directions to the trans-Canada highway, where there would likely be a motel. To the south, they had said. A dirt path penetrated the dense bushes that screened the south view. I followed it out to the road. At the intersection stood the predictable filling station, fast food restaurant, and motel. The man at the motel reception desk offered me a room for thirty-one dollars. I asked for something cheaper.

"I'll give you the one with the leaky tap for twenty," he said. The plink-plink-plink of dripping water was barely audible if I closed the bathroom door made of unpainted plywood. In the ashtray sat a book of specially printed matches which told me my hosts were Ivar and Mary Orenchuk. On the wall hung a message: "By grace are ye saved through Faith; that not of yourselves: it is the gift of God." I returned to the front desk and telephoned the wheat farmer whose name had been given me by a friend in Toronto. Yes, said his wife, they had received my letter. She would pick me up the next afternoon. Through the window, out in the parking lot, I could see a car hooked to a trailer, and on the trailer a handmade sign: HILDEGARD'S WALK FOR THE BLIND.

I had never set foot in a prairie town. For a few hours once I had been on the main street of Brandon, west of Winnipeg, but Brandon was a city of thirty-five thousand with an airport and a university. The population of Indian Head, my guidebook noted, was eighteen hundred. I started up the road in search of something to eat. The rim of the deep orange sun floated an inch off the edge of the earth. An old man looked up from clipping grass as I walked by his small frame house.

"Nice day," he said, "but we'll have the bloomin' wind again. There was a dust storm last week. I couldn't see across the road." He wore a hat that advertised the Indian Head Credit Union. In his upper jaw glistened a few needle-thin spikes, the remnants of a set of teeth. When he spoke, dark red streaks showed on his tongue. "Yep, we've got some wind in this place. But I like it. Only the trucks are a bother. And the bloomin' trains, hangin' onto their whistles for grim death. Regina passed a by-law. No more whistles. There's talk here, some of them, of a petition." He was eighty-five. In 1917 he had come to Indian Head from Ontario, and had settled on the section and a half of prairie that two of his sons were still farming. "This here," he gestured to his front yard, "this was all a farm when I came."

On Grand Avenue the hotel, a brick building painted white, was about to close its beverage room. At eight-forty-five light still lingered in the sky, but the main street was deserted.

The Rainbow Cafe, the Chinese restaurant, was locked. I peered in through the blinds and thought I saw a 1930s diner, dark red stools along a wooden counter, and two rows of booths. No cars passed, nothing but mosquitoes. Even the Nite Hawk Theatre was closed. I walked back to the highway and found the restaurant lot there full of dusty cars and pick-up trucks. Inside men were sitting with men, and women with women. I overheard conversations about farm machinery and seeding.

In the morning I returned to Grand Avenue. Away from the buildings you could feel strong gusts of cooked air hurling bits of dust. At one end of the wide street stood four grain elevators. I went in the other direction under a dry, hot sun. Abruptly the town ended, recalling W. O. Mitchell's *Who Has Seen the Wind.* "He looked up to find that the street had stopped. Ahead lay the sudden emptiness of the prairie. . . . And all about him was the wind now, a pervasive sighing though great emptiness, unhampered by the buildings of the town." Beyond lay the government tree nursery where seedlings for wind breaks were grown. Men in blue work suits were pulling baby evergreens out of the ground for shipment to farms. I turned to walk back, and the four elevators appeared, white with red roofs. At the base of Grand Avenue's long perpendicular, they made a graceful interplay of angles and planes. The elevators defined any notion of height here. Everything else looked flat, the prairie and the town. Only the hotel and a couple of commercial buildings rose to three levels. Some stores had been built with apartments above them, but most of Grand Avenue was one-storey high and flat-roofed. The antique gas station, the art decoesque used-car lot office (boarded-up), the absence of new buildings, and my memory of the Rainbow Cafe the night before gave a 1930s mood to the street. Perhaps I had seen too many photographs of the dirty thirties on the prairies, and the region was too closely linked to that time in my mind. When I entered the Rainbow Cafe, it was not a 1930s diner at all. The dim light the evening before and my dense associations had constructed something false. With its pink vinyl upholstery, fake wood panelling, and aluminum-grey table legs, the Rainbow Cafe contained no suggestion of nostalgia. Its pastel murals of Chinese peasants and fishermen removed it even further from my fantasy.

"Chinese family be here for long time," said the owner. He had worked for twenty-two years in Indian Head; there had been others before him. "Juss about every taow i Sascashawhan have one Chinese family." He lived upstairs with his wife and children.

In the window of the newspaper office next door hung an advertisement. "Oak Whiskey Barrels direct from Central Canadian Distillers Weyburn (Barrels were drained April 15th)." I bought the Indian Head-Wolseley News and took it back to the Rainbow Cafe. "Thunder echoes in Wolseley," announced the front page headline. "Dating back to last Wednesday and Thursday," the article explained, "there were no clouds or sunshine prevalent throughout both days, however thunder echoed within the confines of many buildings." I turned to the section on Indian Head. The first item listed under "What's Happening in Town" caught the paper's editorial tone. "A number of Elementary students made some fascinating little buildings out of popsicle and revel sticks and gave them to the business establishments in downtown Indian Head." Another piece recorded the opinions of eleven students who had been asked why Indian Head was "a nice place to live." All of them mentioned the town swimming pool. On the dry prairie water was prized. "Indian Head is the best town in the world," wrote one girl. "It is in the middle of the world because everything is around it."

The Wheat Farm

THE WOMAN, WHO RAN A WHEAT FARM WITH HER HUS-band, drove through the Qu'Appelle Valley and along The Fishing Lakes to Fort Qu'Appelle, where she stopped for groceries. Green hills rose around the lakes, and the water was clear blue. Turning west we found prairie again, not the sheer flatlands you saw from the train window, but gentle rolls and dips. Ducks paddled in the green sloughs. The farms were vast plowed rectangles. Infrequently we passed a house and barn, or a row of seed bins. In the dusty town of Abernethy, dirt roads and wooden buildings, we stopped for the mail, then travelled four miles south to the Lyster farms. The woman, her husband, and their two daughters lived in a small frame house that had been built as a Methodist parsonage in a town called Kenlis. It had been moved to the Lyster property in 1926.

"You didn't waste wood in those days," she explained. "Every board had to be hauled across the prairie from the rail line." Her name was Pat. She had married Bryan Lyster, whose family had worked these farms for over a century. Before that the land had been unplowed prairie.

"I think Bryan's out seeding lentils," she said. I walked down the long straight driveway to the public road. The land was dry, and the road, graded but un-paved, threw up spirals of dust when a car passed. The smooth fields looked to me like one big farm, acres of plowed land, but no people. I came to a coulee, a gash in the prairie deep and wide where bushes and trees grew. The air was dancing with mosquitoes. If you looked into the middle distance, you could see a thick screen of them, like rain.

The two girls and their mother and I ate stewed lentils from last year's crop. She talked about her work as a part-time remedial teacher for a blind student. Then we were silent. A bird sang out in the yard. I asked about the winter.

"I was storm-stayed twice this year," she said. "Then you get so you don't want to go anywhere in the snow. And that's not a good feeling."

I said I found it quiet.

"Do you think so? I don't notice any more." She had met her husband at university in the east. They had lived in cities, but he had wanted to return to the family farm. She had moved often as a child. Her father had worked in the armed forces.

"Farm life has given me a kind of stability I never had."

In the guest room she showed me a history book on the Abernethy area. I read that Bryan's great-grandfather, Edwin Lyster, had been born near Melbourne, in Quebec's Eastern Townships. Edwin had come west in 1879 through Chicago and St. Paul. The Canadian Pacific had not then reached Indian Head. In 1888 Bryan's grandfather Chester was born at Kenlis, near Abernethy. He had taken over the family farm in 1929; Bryan's father had done the same about twenty years later. Marion, Bryan's mother, had taught in the local primary school. The book said that Marion had first arrived in Abernethy on a rainy evening in the fall of 1942. Enquiring at Quong's Cafe, she had been directed to the people who boarded the teachers. Quong's Cafe. *Juss about every taow i Sascash-awhan have one Chinese family.*

The next morning Pat drove me out to the field where her husband was at work. I had asked to watch some planting, and he had smiled. "I think of rice paddies when I think of planting. It's seeding here. We put seeds into the ground.''

He waved me over to the tractor. At nine o'clock he had already seeded for several hours. Using the good weather, he was working from before dawn to after dark. We continued to drag the seeder and disks around the field in bigger and bigger circles. He was not given to idle chat. I asked what he thought about up in the cab all day. He had to watch the disks, he said, and monitor the seed. ''I'm hopping in and out a lot, to refill seed or fertilizer. When it's going well I have my classical music.'' A tape deck had been installed in the cab.

We stopped at his blue and red three-ton truck, parked in the field near the road. From the truck we blew grain into the five boxes of the seeder, using a wide, pliable plastic pipe. It was like holding a fat fire hose. Several loaves of bread were spilled on the ground when we had finished. ''I'm doing Glenlea this morning,'' he said. ''A utility wheat.'' Slapping mosquitoes, we climbed back up to the cab. In half an hour the field was done. We emptied the seed that remained in the boxes into burlap sacks and swung them onto the small pick-up truck. The last of the grain he sucked out of the seeder with a portable car vacuum cleaner.

He said we were going to move to another field. ''And do canary seed.'' But first he needed to buy more fertilizer.

Rumbling in the half-ton on the road to Abernethy, we passed his house and dipped sharply into the green coulee. ''This is where our wildlife lives. Deer, foxes, rabbits, raccoons.'' In a few minutes we were back up on the dry flats. Some fields showed the unplowed buff stubble of the previous fall. Others had been turned over. A truck and a seeding machine stood in a distant field. Otherwise the country looked empty, except in the direction of Abernethy where a small collection of low buildings were spread around the two elevators. SASKATCHEWAN POOL was painted in big letters on one, UGG on the other. They made a strong vertical statement, both defying and reinforcing the flatness of the earth. And more than anything here they proclaimed the presence of humanity, though not in the same way as the spires of rural Quebec. The elevators did not dominate their landscape. Like lighthouses they survived and performed a task, but any sense of control they conveyed was illusory. Prairie farmland, like the ocean, could be badly disturbed by erratic weather. The elevators stood against the wind and rain and snow, separating man from nature while making an accommodation between the two. With its little birdhouse superstructure for a head, the elevator assumed an organic humanesque shape, an announcement that the far-reaching emptiness was populated. I found as much visual pleasure in their simple lines and graceful proportions as in any hand-carved Quebec barn or gingerbread Ontario farmhouse.

We turned into the fertilizer yard where he kept an account. Parked under the conveyor belt, he pulled his shovel out of the cab and strapped a dust mask over his face. The ash-coloured chemical flowed onto the floor of the truck, making a grey cone. He shovelled hard at the pile, spreading it across the fertilizer compartment. On the other side of the divider was a larger area for seed. The fertilizer left a cloud of fine, parching dust. Above, through the broad sky floated tufts of cirrus cloud.

On the way back we stopped at the old Lyster homestead. He shared a row of cone-capped metal seed bins there with his father, who still occupied the nineteenth-century farmhouse. Bryan emptied the remaining Glenlea grain and we wheeled the forty-foot gas-powered auger to a canary-seed bin. "This machine is super dangerous. It's a foot remover," he cautioned. We shoved one end of the auger into the seed and started the motor. He stood at the back of the bin shovelling grain toward the churning metal bit. Into the back of the truck spiralled a rain of golden kernels.

Over lunch he told me his fields all had surnames. "But

a field doesn't take your name until you die. Or until you sell it.'' He worked five quarter sections (eight hundred acres) acquired over the ten years he had been farming. Later he would have his father's three. Work and family appeared to be the totality of his world. An experienced journalist, he wrote articles in the winter for a farm magazine, *Country Guide*. I looked through a recent issue in which his article ''Watch Out For Cutworms'' had appeared.

In the afternoon I had agreed to speak at a school. Pat and I drove to the town of Balcarres where she commuted several times a week to teach her blind student. I was introduced to Myrtle Love who taught ten- and eleven-year-olds. Myrtle said a few words to her class, and then I spoke. She had unfurled a wall map over the blackboard. I remembered the Canada I had known at the age of ten, this same paper abstraction: at the top a lot of ink-blot islands and one that looked like an upside-down dog's skeleton, but a smooth line along the bottom border. And below the border just three letters—U.S.A.—on white space that did not belong to us and about which we did not have to learn, though draining it of colour and expunging the dots of its cities seemed even then like risky bravado.

Myrtle Love's pupils asked why I was crossing the country. I said I had wanted to make the map real for myself, and that I had found a publisher who would advance me some money. They wanted to know how I remembered what I saw. ''What do you think of Canada?'' one child asked. ''Which is your favourite part?'' queried another. I said Canada was different from South America, where I had last travelled. But after the talk, wandering down the dusty main street, I found echoes of Peru. The buildings of Balcarres were low, many with false fronts. In the dark restaurant where I sat for a cup of tea, Indians lounged in the booths, dressed shabbily, idle and poor, reminiscent of a South American scene. And back out in the street mosquitoes swarmed.

"Excuse me, sir, you do a survey on my building?" enquired the Balcarres Chinaman nervously. (Peru as well, I remembered, had a large Chinese population from its railway-building years.) I closed my notebook and shook my head. "My place almost the town centre. Lottery tickets. Video. Liquor. Everything you want." He rushed back into the store, but business looked slow, even with the government liquor franchise.

In the late afternoon Pat dropped me at the Motherwell homestead, about halfway on the dirt road between Abernethy and the Lyster farms. W. R. Motherwell had been provincial minister of agriculture from 1905 to 1918, and federal minister during the twenties. His property had been declared a national historic site. I walked through a hedge into the quiet nineteenth-century scene. A couple in period costume were hoeing the large vegetable garden. At the end of the path I came to a building with didactic displays on prairie settlement and the scientific farming methods Motherwell encouraged. Like many of the pioneers in this part of Saskatchewan, he had come from Ontario. As much as they could they had brought Ontario with them. "The Ontarians," said the writing in one display, "believed that hard work, Christian living and individual enterprise were the only sure roads to success and prosperity. Men were to be masculine and self-reliant; women, the supportive 'fairer sex.' " On another panel were enlarged photographs of an old train. The text read: "A unique method Motherwell used to inform the province's farmers was the Better Farming Train. It travelled the province in the summers of 1914 to 1918, eighteen cars long, filled with exhibits on all aspects of western farming. Thousands of men, women and children visited the train, attending lectures and demonstrations."

Outside I was greeted by another young woman in period costume. The long smock and high boots looked uncomfortable in the heat. She had blonde hair pinned at the back, and a Nordic face with large blue eyes. We

walked alone onto the back lawn. It was early in the
season—there were no other visitors. She began talking
about Motherwell in a voice that sounded rehearsed but
genuine. I found myself mildly interested in the dead
farmer, but distracted by my guide's blue eyes. She spoke
of the design of this place; the shelter belts that Motherwell had planted around the farmstead; the Ontario barn
behind us with its double-pitched gambrel roof; the lawn
tennis court; the dugout where snow collected in winter,
providing water for the house and garden. Motherwell
had come from the town of Perth where stone was favoured as a building material. He had brought this taste
in architecture with him, and had erected a cut fieldstone
dwelling that could have been lifted off any residential
street in his home town. I knew Perth. There was a
dream-like sensation in seeing a piece of it here on the
dry prairie: a turn-of-the-century Italianate stone house—
immaculately restored, the green lawns, the tree lines,
the genteel ornamental garden. There was nothing like it
for hundreds of miles. A breeze ruffled the smock of the
blue-eyed woman. She did not mind the mosquitoes and
seemed content to be living in someone else's clothes.
She was a traveller. After the summer season the house
would close, and she would return to Greece.

Inside we went through the kitchen, the study, up the
back stairs to the servants' quarters, and into the room
where Motherwell slept. The house suffered from a dark
Victorian interior, but standing by the bed you could see
out the window far across the prairie; light, the broad
sky, space. She led me down the front stairway into the
living room, where we looked at the Indian beadwork
Motherwell's wife had collected.

"Indians have come to look at the site," she said. "But
they don't always like to see their things here. Some say
Indian artifacts don't belong in this house."

I set out on the dirt road to the Lyster property. Before
the coulee a man in work clothes stopped his car and
offered a lift. It was a few minutes to six. He was on his

way to the fields. "I'll be out there till midnight," he said.

After supper Pat and I visited an older woman on a neighbouring farm. "Yes, I knew him," she said of Motherwell. "And her too. She was just right for a politician's wife. She knew how to do it. But I'll tell you something. Quite a few in this area were against what they did with the house. It's the eastern government, you see, coming in and spending all that money. Waste and interference, that's how many here saw it."

Changing Stations

REGINA. ON THE HOT SIDEWALKS THE WIND CARRIED BITS of sharp dirt. I walked the streets, which were arranged in a grid. The year before I had met an editor with the Regina *Leader-Post*. He had said the Indians were organizing themselves, becoming politicized. But I saw them on every downtown street, wandering slowly, apparently without a destination. I went back to the La Salle Hotel and made some calls. After the wheat farm Regina was depressing.

When I telephoned Rex Deverell, the local playwright, he asked me over to his house. I found him padding through his rooms in bare feet, a plump, affable man with a soft voice and gentle, hooded eyes. He had a story that he thought illuminated Saskatchewan's social structure. "Not long after I came here from Ontario we arranged to have a Christmas goose delivered by the Hutterites. These geese are hard to buy, but we managed to get on the list. Anyway, the Hutterite arrived at my front door one day with our goose, and asked, 'Can I come in and use your phone?' He dialed, and said, 'Hello Al?' And

proceeded to give the premier, Allan Blakeney, a piece
of his mind. That kind of intimacy would be impossible
in the social hierarchy of Ontario.''

I went out to a suburb to talk to a journalist. On the
bus there the driver said, ''We got a big native problem.
Thirty-five or forty thousand of them in Regina. They're
into what they call heritage now. See that guy? A feather
in his hair and dirt all over him. That's what they call
heritage.''

Later, on Rose Street, I saw the Indian hookers, some
of them young girls. And the drunks. I had imagined a
morally neater place. This was the province where Canadian medicare had been conceived and first put into
practice. The co-operative movement was strong here.
Social democrats had governed Saskatchewan for most of
my lifetime. But the neatness I had imagined was an abstraction gleaned from reading, and a reflection of how
little could be learned about contempory natives from
conventional Canadian histories.

In the morning I walked along Victoria Avenue, crossing Halifax, St. John, Ottawa, Toronto, Montreal, and
Quebec Streets, then down Winnipeg Street to the tracks,
and into the empty station. The eastbound train had come
and gone. The westbound one would not arrive until ten
o'clock at night. A few Indians shuffled in and out of the
men's toilets. They huddled, slowly scattered, then
drifted together again. Some small packages changed
hands. I sat in one of the rows of broken wooden benches.
It had been a grand station. Six green pillars with ornate
plaster crowns still supported the ceiling in the cavernous
lobby, counterpointed by twelve suspended lamps. The
marble ticket counter, with its built-in wooden bureaus
and brass handles, had been abandoned. I decided not to
stay in Regina until late in the evening. The next stop
west was Moose Jaw. I would take a bus and wait for the
train there.

In the bus station restaurant an Indian sat down at my
table. He said his name was Victor. He mumbled an or-

der several times to the waitress. "Beepslabder." Finally she understood and brought a beef sandwich.

"Hell of a wind out there," he said. "A dusty wind."

I nodded. My mouth still tasted gritty from walking the streets.

He leaned forward, grinning. "Have a good trip!"

I went into the men's room. "Goddam wind," said the man standing next to me. He wore wire-frame dark glasses, and had an unclipped goatee. "Cans are filthy here. Probably got crabs." He paused. "There's one crawling right up your leg, son." His laugh turned into hysterical coughing.

The bus left Regina in the middle of the afternoon. We crossed country that looked as if it had been fashioned with a carpenter's level, smooth and tranquil. The spring sloughs made swimming pools for ducks. Out of the flatness poked up the occasional row of seed bins, rectangular huts if they were the old wooden ones, or round with conical hats if they were metal. We went off the highway into a town called Pense. There were two elevators, some stores, some houses, a compact Anglican church on a corner with street signs saying Press and Ontario, and then the town was gone, and we were back on the immense table-top prairie. We passed a potash mine. It was a series of connected boxes and cones that looked foreign and sterile, a gigantic assembly of beakers and retorts set down in the middle of someone's wheat farm.

I put my bags in the deserted train station and found a Chinese restaurant up the street where copies of the Moose Jaw *Times-Herald* were sold. Front page reports included a mine blast in Japan and slow progress in the U.S.–Canada hog war. The Philadelphia Zoo announced the birth of a Malayan tapir that looked like a watermelon with ears. And I saw a brief item under the headline "Washrooms to be ready soon."

The exterior of the new washrooms in Crescent Park should be completed by June 15, Stuart Lazear, Heri-

tage Canada Main Street project coordinator, said Friday.

  The new washrooms is the former loo located in the first block Fairford Street West.

I remembered a Stuart Lazear from Ottawa. We had met briefly through our work ten years earlier. I retained a vague memory of some festering disagreement. Or had it been with another person from that time? The more I searched my mind, the more I seemed to forget. From a phone booth I called the Lazear listed in Moose Jaw's directory. Yes, he remembered me. He would be down to pick me up in fifteen minutes.

We rode around the city together. If there had been a falling out, he seemed to have forgotten. As the newspaper had indicated, he was administering a demonstration project designed to revitalize Moose Jaw's downtown. He knew the surfaces of the city well, and its history, and talked about it as we drove.

"No bones about it," he said. "Moose Jaw was founded on speculation and greed."

"No bones about it," I repeated. He showed me the old commercial buildings on Main, High, and River Streets. There had been tunnels he said, built under River Street between the hotels as escape routes from the gambling raids. Moose Jaw had been Saskatchewan's city of sin in the early part of the century. Brothel-keepers, bootleggers, and gamblers had run the town, though no compelling evidence of this past remained. You could see there had been money. The old buildings were well made. Now it was a quiet place on a Saturday night. I remarked on the number of churches as we drove up and down the streets.

"There are only eight families left in the Jewish community," he said, after pointing out the synagogue. "All older people. I went to high holidays last year. They need a quorum of ten."

We drove over to South Hill on the other side of the tracks. The houses were small, some of them not much more than amplified shacks. You could see the tall concrete grain elevators in the background. South Hill was where the railway workers had lived when Moose Jaw was a major rail centre. The city had been the terminus of a line up from St. Paul, Minnesota as well as a CPR divisional point. The end of steam in the 1950s had hit the local economy hard. An air force base was now the principal employer.

Lazear stopped the car at the base of the Fourth Avenue bridge on an unused laneway. He looked out his window into the silence, a tall man in a sky-blue sports shirt. The light was growing dim. I did not know why we had parked on this deserted road and I felt uneasy.

"This is my favourite undiscovered heritage site," he murmured. His eyes took on a soft-focus glaze, and I let go of my door. "Look at the painted column capitals." It was nearly dark but you could still see the bizarre Egyptian-revival ornamentation on the side of the bridge. "They call it the Thunderbird Viaduct."

He left me at the station. I sat and waited, once again the only passenger in a vast, abandoned lobby. It was a handsome old building, erected in the 1920s, the third station on the site. I went into the men's room, reached through an anteroom off the lobby. The cubicles still had wooden doors and slabs of stone for dividers. I silently nominated the urinals for historic sitehood. Fashioned of thick porcelain, with rich networks of black hairline cracks, they seemed about to fall to pieces. In the lobby: rows of wooden benches with armrests. High on the wall the old station clock encased in brass. Eight heavy lanterns suspended by brass chains from the ceiling. And polished red terra cotta tiles on the floor. You could still pay your fare at the antique wicket with its vertical brass bars. And you still went under TO THE TRAINS when you passed through the wood and glass doors to the platform.

TELEGRAPHS FIRST DOORS LEFT said another sign, but the telegraph operator had gone home years before.

I heard the train hooting as it approached the station. A man came out from behind the ticket wicket. ''West-bound train,'' he shouted into the empty hall, not looking at me. ''For Swift Current, Medicine Hat, Calgary, and Vaaaancouver.'' I boarded and took a seat on the coach. About half the passengers were in their late teens or early twenties, many with back packs. They looked bedraggled. If they had come from Montreal or Toronto, this would be the end of their second day on the train.

At 3:30 A.M. the conductor shook me awake. I jumped down onto the rail bed and felt the cold wash of night air. This was a place called Maple Creek.

Cow Town

TWO RCMP OFFICERS WERE SHINING FLASHLIGHTS ON A small house down the road from the station. They went behind the house and reappeared on the other side, flashlights still glowing. After the train pulled away the night was still. I walked across a dirt lot and over the road to the Commercial Hotel. Sprawled on the floor of the vestibule lay a drunk. The inside door was locked, so I banged on the plate glass. I had called ahead for a room. The Indian on the floor stirred. I did not want to rouse him but I did want to go to bed. I banged again. He rolled over. It was too cold to wait outside, so I kept hammering. The Indian opened his eyes.

''What're you want?'' he grumbled. Then he dropped his lids abruptly, as if someone had hit him over the head.

Down the stairs came a woman in her dressing gown. ''Saturday night,'' she said, ''you sometimes see them sleeping outside.'' I went to my room and discovered a twenty-four-hour movie channel. *The Dresser* was playing, a film about an aging Shakespearean actor and the illusions he found it necessary to sustain. The images were bouncing down from one of the pay-TV satellites. Outside in the cold, stepping over the intoxicated Indian, I had experienced a strong sense of place. But the little screen in the darkened room took a traveller far away from the town. I fell asleep with the sense that I was nowhere at all.

In the late morning, on the street, Maple Creek asserted itself again. I had stopped here partly to look at Fort Walsh, a national historic site, but I had wrongly assumed it would be accessible by bus. A pamphlet in the hotel told me the fort was thirty-eight miles away. I walked down Maple Street and turned right, the direction of the fort. The day was sunny and warm. A car or truck passed every few minutes. Most of the people were dressed in good clothes, going home from church, perhaps visiting someone for lunch. I had my thumb out, hoping for a lift. Half an hour later, when I was well out into the country, a small grey-haired woman driving a blue Chevrolet slowed to walking speed beside me and rolled down her window. We said hello.

''I'm sorry,'' she smiled. ''I'm not supposed to pick you up. You know that.'' She rolled up her window and drove away.

Another half hour passed, with sour looks from the drivers who sped by me. I had washed and shaved and put on a clean shirt, but perhaps a man without a car was by definition a vagrant here. Stopped by the side of the road, I was considering my options when a touring wagon with a man and woman in uniform approached. They looked hard at my thumb and pulled over. When I got in I saw they were Salvation Army people on their way home from Sunday service. I asked if they had a farm. No, you didn't have a farm here. You had a ranch, and they were ranchers. If I didn't mind stopping at their place for lunch, they would drive me to Fort Walsh in the afternoon, they said. They liked to take Sunday afternoon off from ranch work.

We rode down the long dirt road to their buildings. "Look," said one of the children. Four antelope grazing on a hillock had heard us and were bounding away. Ron and Clara, the parents, had just finished their new house. From inside you could see the old dwelling where Ron had been raised—empty since his mother and father had retired into Maple Creek—and the log house his grandfather had built.

They all changed into their ranch clothes before lunch. "I've lived on this land all my life," Ron said after the youngest child had recited grace. "My grandfather came out from La Chute, Quebec in 1883, about the time the railway reached Maple Creek. They went to Winnipeg by train, and then I believe they went down to Denver to buy horses. He was the first white man to settle on this ranch." The buildings sat in the middle of gently rolling terrain. The ranch stretched everywhere you could see, except up into Cypress Hills provincial park. Ron owned six sections, almost four thousand acres. They raised beef cattle and kept horses. A taciturn man, he knew ranching and he knew his land. There was no need to learn about many other things.

They had visited Fort Walsh several times before and remembered the way. A little bus took us from the parking lot down a steep hill to Farwell's trading post. In and around this national park the land was all up and down, the Cypress Hills. We entered the trading post, a reconstruction. Abe Farwell and Moses Solomon, two American whiskey traders, set up seasonal encampments along Battle Creek to buy hides from the Indians in the early 1870s. Americans freely roamed the Canadian prairie then, as if it might soon be theirs. But near these posts it was American-style wild-west uproar that triggered the imposition of Canadian law and order. A plaque outside the stockade commemorated the Cypress Hills massacre.

"Here on June 1 1873 a party of American and Canadian wolf hunters, searching for stolen horses, attacked a large Assiniboine camp. They killed twenty or more Indians, put the rest to flight, and returned to Montana. This incident hastened the recruitment and despatch to the Territories of the North West Mounted Police." As at the Motherwell House, Parks Canada had put people in period dress to complete the scene; at the trading post they also had speaking parts.

"I notice some of the women are wearin' britches," said the Farwell character. "Maybe you'd like some material to make yerselves skirts." The little girls in jeans giggled. Farwell, designed to look like a nasty piece of business, wore a shapeless floppy hat, high boots, and suspenders. A wood stove smoked in the yard, "for making bullets." Animal skins were hanging under a shelter. But all this was a re-enactment of distorted white man's history. If you thought about it, you had to wonder why the Canadian government had chosen to recreate an American trading post rather than a Canadian Indian encampment. The answer was that while the Indian encampments in the Cypress Hills were history, the historic feud between white settlers and Indians was still cooking. Parks Canada had discreetly elected to give a voice to neither side in this continuing dispute. Instead, perhaps unwittingly, they had made theatre of an equally old Canadian neurosis, fear and suspicion of the Americans.

We took the little bus back to Fort Walsh and entered the palisade. The first fort had been built here in 1875, but was dismantled and abandoned in 1883. The wooden buildings on the site dated from the 1940s when the RCMP had reacquired the land and built their remount ranch on it. A pamphlet said the horses for the Musical Ride had been bred and raised here until 1968, when the force ceded the property to Parks Canada. What you saw if you stood by the flagpole in the middle of the fort were some wooden buildings, painted white, about forty years old, enclosed by a wooden palisade that was modelled after the one built here in 1880. There were no actors in period dress. Mounties forty years ago looked much as they do now. Period dress would only have added to the contemporary atmosphere of the fort, which was no fort at all, but a leftover home for horses with a wooden fence around it.

"I had an uncle," Ron said, as we walked back up the hill to the information building, "who was shot and killed by an Indian horse thief."

We drove the long way back to Maple Creek. They wanted to show me the Cypress Hills, miles of undulating plateau; most of what we saw was closely cropped ranch land. Ron named the trees when we ascended a forested summit: lodgepole pine, white spruce, aspen. He said very little as we drove, a few spare comments on this sparsely populated terrain.

They dropped me at the Commercial Hotel late in the afternoon. "I hope you'll remember us," he said. His wife added, "We wouldn't usually pick someone up." The children waved. I went inside and bought the Maple Creek News.

Three Day Rodeo Planned

Maple Creek's Cowtown Rodeo has been developed into a three day format with weekend action scheduled to begin with the Bucking Horse sale Friday . . .

The Pony Chariot and Chuckwagon races start at 6:00 P.M. Saturday and the Kinsmen have indicated they will operate a beer garden on the grounds Saturday. "Haywire" has been engaged to provide the music for the big rodeo dance Saturday night at the skating rink. During the afternoon, a Heritage luncheon tea has been planned for the Armouries followed by a Family Dance to begin at 9 P.M. with music by the Old Tyme Fiddlers.

Walking the empty street at dusk I saw a poster advertising the rodeo in a store window.

PANCAKE BREAKFAST
CHUCKWAGON RACES
BAREBACK STEER WRESTLING
LADIES BARREL RACE

Through the soft air the scent of spring lilacs came in waves. An RCMP car crawled up Cypress Street. At the tracks Maple Creek's two grain elevators stood in silhouette. (Across the road the Bel Air Gardens restaurant sign: a tiny Chinaman with a plate of food.) The cars of a freight train pulled through the station without stopping. From the caboose a man hung out, his crooked arm extended over the platform. A woman on the ground held out a hoop with a message clipped to it. In one continuous motion it went over the man's arm, he picked off the piece of paper, and threw back the hoop five yards on.

I went into the hotel and sat in one of the carved oak armchairs. Their lumpy seats were covered with old black leather, creased and cracking. On the wall hung the heads of a moose, an antelope, a deer, and a buffalo. Around the room: stuffed owls and hawks. An old wooden hat stand. Small white bathroom tiles on the floor. And a dark wooden banister up the stairway. On the landing a sign told you YOUR SHOES MUST BE CLEANED BEFORE GOING UPSTAIRS THANK YOU.

The train would arrive in the middle of the night. As I waited in the lobby, a man appeared from the back room. "Those chairs are over two hundred years old," he said. "I've been offered over thirty-five hundred dollars apiece for them. These originality paintings, I've been offered a lot of money for them too." On the wall hung scenes of Indians, buffalo, old Fort Walsh, and a frontier version of the Commercial Hotel. "That's the first hotel, built in the 1860s. This here one is over a hundred years old. They hauled the wood from a ship in Vancouver." A newcomer to town, he had recently bought the building. "One of the best towns I've been in. No cliques. Had people sleeping on this floor in a surprise storm last winter. Dancing and singing in the lobby all night.''

He spoke about the Indians. ''They don't have alcohol bred into their system like us white people. We've had it in us three or four thousand years. They've only had it two hundred. I know how to handle the bad ones. You have to throw 'em out of the bar and rough 'em good, so they remember. I did that about the third day I took this place over. I don't have no trouble now.''

The train was late. At four-thirty I boarded the coach for Calgary. Through the black night I could make out a long barn by the tracks, in between the Pioneer and Saskatchewan Pool elevators. A sign said COW TOWN LIVE-STOCK EXCHANGE. On the other side of the train, near the hotel, was a road excavation marked by little oil pots shaped like bowling balls, flickering in the dark.

Alberta to the Coast

AT CALGARY I CHANGED TRAINS AND RODE THE DAY-liner to Edmonton. ''The views on this north-south run,'' said my guidebook, ''are stereotypically Alberta.'' Isolated farmsteads, spring calves wobbling on the short grass, flat wheatlands. Past Leduc, near the end of the line, the sky divided into black and blue. We charged on into the shadow, leaving the blue behind. Torrents of rain whipped the coach, and thunder banged above us. As we entered Edmonton the downpour softened to a drizzle. From the old South Edmonton station in a raunchy neighbourhood I took a wet walk to the run-down Strathcona Hotel. Inside this pale yellow wooden building a one-eyed woman stood at the desk. ''No telephones and no

TVs,'' she snapped. I went upstairs and fell asleep on the sagging bed, tired after Maple Creek.

The train for Jasper left the next morning from the newer downtown station. This train originated in Winnipeg and came up through Saskatoon on the northern transcontinental tracks owned by Canadian National. A CN official called out that the train would be half an hour late, then an hour, then an hour and a half. I walked outside under a grey sky, wondering if there was time to visit the Edmonton Mall, the world's largest shopping centre. On the sidewalk an Indian asked me for twenty-five cents. My dislike of shopping malls, verging on phobia, did not diminish with the thought of exposure to the largest one on earth; I made a circle of the downtown, which appeared to be faceless and dull. Outside the station a glass crypt sheltered the polished wheel of an old locomotive. ''The steel wheel rolling on the steel rail carried Western Canada to greatness,'' read the inscription.

Late and slow, the train pulled through Evansburg, then Edson. The conductor confided that he had once hit a herd of pigs on the Calgary-Edmonton run. ''So I always have an answer when I'm asked can pigs fly.'' Within a year an accident would kill twenty-three people near Hinton, which we were then approaching. But on this day the train moved uneventfully and unhastily ahead. The clear prairie and bald foothills of the south were gone; instead we saw a few farms and miles of bush. The magazine I had bought in the station offered an article by an eminent scientist decrying the Star Wars defence system. Another piece charted the short history of satellite TV. The sky was changing, and with it our fate. Crawling along the earth's surface on this old train and contemplating the hardware orbiting above was something like an Asian peasant in an ox cart looking at his first motor car.

In the afternoon I went forward to the bar. We were running two hours late and were now stopped on a siding in the woods. Some people had been drinking since opening time. "I think I've had enough to tell you the kind of entertainment we need here," said a tall blonde woman wearing a sweater and aqua slacks. She had a healthy, self-respecting look, not the droopy face of an alcoholic, but she was talking too loudly. "There was this dancer in Vancouver who put tennis balls inside herself and then could shoot them out across the room. I figured the act would be perfect if they could find a guy to bat them back. Know what I mean?" Stuck in the woods—"in the hole" as railwaymen called a siding— hearing a blow-by-blow description of genital tennis, I badly wanted to detrain. There were only trees outside. As so often happens on a Canadian railway, we were miles from any place marked on a map. The woman continued her monologue. I remembered the remark of a friend who had come to Canada from abroad. "Some Canadians tell you nothing until they've had too much to drink. Then they tell you more than you ever wanted to know."

We arrived late in the day, two and a half hours off schedule. Enclosed by mountains, Jasper was a bowl of light, scrubbed clean. After the sour bar car, the air smelled crisp and sweet. Walking the town you saw people with relaxed, almost vacant faces. Nordic women wearing halter tops and long blonde pony tails carried bags of groceries, or strolled together, or sat on the grass. Europeans, mostly single men in their twenties, with hiking boots and back packs, walked slowly through the central park. And everywhere the Japanese men, not so relaxed, straw cowboy hats too big or too small on their heads, bearing heavy cameras with long lenses that stuck out obscenely like phalluses from their ample white-shirted bellies.

In the morning I caught a bus out of town to the Jasper Tramway advertised on a poster. Trains had become a habit. On the bus I thought of the mountain railways in Peru, steep and frightening. But up Whistlers Mountain the line was a tramway in name only. The car ascended on an overhead cable, no different from a gondola ride up any high skiing mountain. Dangling from a wire three thousand feet in the air, we could look at the pretty lakes below, though there were distractions. I wondered when the grip had last been overhauled. The man beside me had begun the trip with his head bowed, gradually lowered himself to a crouch, and finally sunk to his knees below the window. "Oh sheesh, oh sheesh," he gasped. The woman with him bent down to rub his neck.

"You're going to make it, Hal," she said.

"I don't know," he moaned. The two red setters an American had led onto the car began to whimper and growl. They were straining to get closer to the man on the floor; their owner, pulling their leashes taut, looked concerned.

"Alright, it's over Hal," the woman murmured. "He's getting better," I heard her tell a passenger on the boarding platform. "We never used to be able to do things like this."

From the terminal you could walk above the tree line. The little map we had been given said it was five hundred feet up to reach the snow. I found that the dirt path became a mud slick there and so turned back to cross the lower summit, thinly covered in alpine grasses and small flowering plants. Through the clear air the sun hit the mountaintop hard. Across the valley the bald peaks, grey and creased, looked like old elephant skin. On the valley floor tiny Jasper hugged a rectangular turn in the tracks. I had wanted to write about people, but as I had come west, there had been fewer and fewer, and more and more space. The mountains were pleasant to look at, but there was not much to say about them unless you were a naturalist or a climber.

Lise and Danielle, the two French-Canadian sisters I had spoken with the night before, appeared down at the base of the tramway. They asked if I would come camping with them, but I said I had decided to leave. We had met at a table in the hotel nightclub with three young couples, all of them Albertan, though none had been born in the province. I had said to one, a municipal bureaucrat from Grand Prairie, that Albertans seemed to stand lightly on the land, as if they might soon be shifting venue, "like aliens on a new planet." It was speculation on my part. But he agreed.

"You don't often find an Albertan who's been here for two or three generations."

Lise said, "We think that's true for all of you. For all of English Canada. Isn't it like that?"

The bureaucrat took umbrage. "No. It's not true. People put down roots in Alberta. There's pride here."

His girlfriend said she had a Newfoundlander joke. "Did you hear about the Newfie who became a moron after a series of operations? First he lost half his brain, then half of that, then half of that. He came out the fifth time with one thirty-second of a brain. And burst out singing *Alouette*."

The French Canadians looked uncomfortable. I said in French, "These people have had similar operations."

"We only came to see the mountains," smiled Lise.

The next day I went back down to southern Alberta on the train, and two days later my daughter, Vanessa, arrived. I was to look after her while her mother attended a meeting in Calgary. We visited the Glenbow Museum, and the zoo, and walked the streets.

"Is this Calgary?" she asked. And then, "What's Calgary?" I said I didn't really know. It was a place. Each place was a little different.

"Is this different?" she persisted. But Calgary was distinct not because of what you saw. On the surface it was an ordinary Americanized city, without much history, straightforward, open for business. The deep conservatism, the drive for wealth, the rivalry with eastern business interests, these were not immediately apparent.

"People do different things here," I said. "They drill for oil."

"Why?"

I explained what oil was and how it came from the ground.

"Let's dig a hole," she said. "And get some."

Her mother invited us to a party at a house on the Elbow River. The cottonwoods were sending their seeds across the gardens, a storm of tree fluff that looked like fallout from a pillow fight among the gods. It fell on the grass, on the swift river, in hair and on clothing.

"Is this tomorrow?" Vanessa asked, running back and forth on the lawn. Tomorrow, she had been told, we would take a train.

I spoke with Whitney Ellsworth, the publisher of the *New York Review of Books*. He knew Ottawa, but had been dismayed, he allowed, when this meeting had been called for Calgary, a city on the far edges of his consciousness. "I'm pleasantly surprised," he said. It was in fact pleasant standing on this lawn with a glass of punch, watching the Elbow shimmy past, slightly screened by the fluff storm which acted as a coarse gauze filter. I asked if his paper supported the people who worked on it. "The financing was a bit thin twenty years ago. But we do well now. To tell the truth, I inherited money, which allowed me to take this kind of job." He had a degree from Harvard and spoke in well-rounded sentences, a gentle man endowed with the self-assurance and self-esteem that imperial cultures produce.

The next day I took Vanessa to the railway station. We waited an hour on the benches for the train to Lake Louise.

"Is it later yet?" she kept asking.

An announcement was made that the arrival of the train would be delayed for five hours. Not even the demands of literature could induce me to keep a three-year-old in this dismal lobby for half a day. We walked up the street, rented a vehicle, and drove with her mother to Lake Louise.

"Did you come from Toronto in your car?" asked the clerk at a hotel near the lake.

"No," Vanessa said. "We borrowed it from a gas station."

The lake, perfectly still, with steep mountains plunging down to frame it, made an oriental watercolour. And here again were the Japanese tourists, heavy with cameras, swarming over the boardwalk and through the old railway hotel overlooking the water. My daughter called them the "trapeze people."

In the morning we travelled up the highway between Lake Louise and Jasper to look at the mountains and the wildlife. There were bighorn sheep, mountain goats, deer, and bears. In the back seat my little girl fell asleep; her eyes were closed when a baby elk wandered out of the woods onto the side of the road with its mother.

"You missed an elk," I said when she woke up.

She blinked and replied, "I bet you didn't see the elephants." She had it all inside her, from storybooks, a world full of animals; they lived in little houses, sometimes wore clothing, scolded their children, and sent them to school. The naked, speechless animals in the national park she seemed to eye with disappointment.

We drove up a mountain and threw snowballs at the summit. "Is it winter now?" she asked. And later when I left them at the airport, she said, "We'll be up, Pappa. And you'll be down. Because you don't know how to fly."

I boarded the westbound transcontinental in Calgary. Today it arrived on time. We rolled over the bald foothills, past the Cochrane ranch—the first big cattle ranch in Alberta—with its brass cowboy on a rise, and through the Stoney Indian reserve, where *Little Big Man* was filmed. The tracks followed the Bow River valley into Banff and on to Lake Louise. As we rose, the river took on the milky-jade hue of glacial water. Mule deer and coyotes scampered to find cover when they heard the engine.

At Lake Louise I went forward and joined the engineers. Jack Murphy, the senior man, was known for his singing. He crooned over the radio, ''I've bin workin' on the railroad.'' After thirty-four years of service he was about to retire.

''First year I worked was the worst scare I ever got. Someone left a switch open. We tore into a fifteen-mile-an-hour curve at quite a clip. I jumped out with the train-man and rolled over and over, ass over tea kettle. Cleared a fence and kept on going. I thought the train would be rolling after me. In the days of steam, that was.''

From Lake Louise over the railway's highest point at Stephen B.C., and through the spiral tunnels to Field was only twenty miles. It took us an hour and a quarter of laboured chugging. We climbed steadily past Grotto Mountain, Pigeon Mountain, Mount Rundle, and the Three Sisters, the beginning of a stretch that the railway had made the most popular landscape in Canada. Around Stephen we were as high as the clouds and slid into them like a tongue into cotton candy. I remembered Van Horne's quip that if he couldn't export the scenery, he'd import the tourists. The CPR's first manager was also the country's loudest barker, a tireless promoter who pulled customers by the carriage load into this huge alpine theatre. Nineteenth-century trains provided our first motion pictures, silent movies framed by windows. Perhaps it was no coincidence that the popularity of film rose in tandem with the decline of pleasure travel on railways. (The CPR enjoyed its most profitable passenger decade in the 1920s.)

Jack Murphy took us down through the spiral tunnels slowly, snaking first through Mount Stephen and then through Mount Ogden and then on down the Big Hill to Field, a one-in-forty grade. The throttle had eight positions. As we descended he held it in the first groove.

''See that yellow stuff?'' He pointed down the steep bank to our right. ''A dozen cars went off the rails here a couple of months ago. They were hauling sulphur. You can see the mud slide up on the left.'' A vast avalanche of mud and gravel, shaped like an alluvial fan, rose steeply from the tracks up the mountain. Technology had not tamed nature here. Despite a century of steady improvement, there remained an edge of danger.

The mid-afternoon sun shone brightly on the platform at Field. I walked the length of the train and boarded my sleeping car near the tail-end. In a bag I had the old CPR pamphlets a book dealer in Regina had sold me. "The traveller of today follows the trail-blazing of a glorious past into a boundless future," said one printed in 1965. No brochure writer for the railways would say the same two decades later. It was odd to think of Canada as a country where the past conferred more than the future promised. Yet on the railway this was true. The land of boundless opportunity had become a place with a golden age that had already been lived. The older men on the railway had entered the working world when most Canadians thought of passenger trains as an essential part of everyday life. Trains were associated with land development, a Canadian preoccupation for much of the country's history; they kept until mid-century their reputation as vehicles of hope. The straight-forward optimism generated by the making of new towns, the seeding of new land, the harvesting of forests, and the opening of mines was intimately connected to, and literally conveyed by, the railways. When people, of necessity, began to look beyond these simple first promises, the future had lost its gleam. The railway, its primary purposes of settling and binding the country accomplished, grew old and backward on the job.

Another pamphlet, published in 1937, gave what the title predicted, *Canadian Pacific Facts and Figures*. "There are approximately 750,000 pieces of linen required for cars operated by the Sleeping Car Department, the laundry bill amounting to around $20,000 per month. In order to maintain this linen in the best condition a Linen Repair Shop is maintained in Montreal, where a staff of expert seamstresses is kept constantly at work." The book was full of such prosaic facts, a token of the public's fascination with trains fifty years ago. A comment on food quality from the 1937 publication was no longer heeded. "The traffic officers all over the continent know that a satisfactory dining car service at comparatively low prices must be given if people are to be encouraged to travel by railway." Fifty years later good food in the diner had gone the way of all railway optimism. At the back of the little red book a section subtitled Publicity began: "Sir William Van Horne may be considered the pioneer of transportation advertising in Canada, with his celebrated posters carrying slogans such as *'How High We Live,' said the Duke to the Prince on the Canadian Pacific Railway."*

Back up in the dome I watched the passing mountains. On the seat beside me someone had left a recent *New Yorker*. In it I came across a strange story about a semi-fictional country called "the new Canada," by Bruce McCall. Glib, post-modern humour, the piece treated this "new Canada" as a metaphorical antipode to the third world: a bland and unperilous place devoted to material comforts, where nothing was more than it appeared.

The Ross Farquaharsons . . . dwell, like most families in this new Canada, indoors. Yet for all the official government statistics "proving" a huge leap in living standards since confederation, in 1867, the Farquaharsons live little differently from the way Canadians have lived for most of this century.

Ross Farquaharson, his wife, Helen, and teen-age daughter, Kelly, all share a single living room without running water. To use the only swimming pool requires a trip outdoors. Dogs roam freely indoors, begging scraps from the meals, taken communally at a table hewn from a piece of wood.

But there is no wood to burn in the fireplace. "Ran out in May," Ross Farquaharson says with a shrug. May is now three months past.

Was Canada really so earnest and dull? Sometimes it appeared to be. But that was in part because we had no insistent national myth and no rigorous dogma to trumpet. Canadian quietude and stability could be laughable, as the *New Yorker* writer evidently believed. It could also be the seed bed of excellence. At its worst our culture had suffered from a failure of imagination and energy, conservatism to a fault, political apathy, and moral smugness. At its best Canada had allowed political experimentation, eccentricity and high achievement in the academy and the arts, and moral tolerance. If the dominant beliefs remained too closed and unambitious for my taste, it was also true that compared to most other places you could go about your business and speak your mind in relative peace. And in the peaceable kingdom, as long as you did not shout, you could express whatever unusual vision you might cherish. On a good day, you might even find an audience.

The mountain sun made the dome section an oven. By late afternoon all the seats had emptied. I moved to the dining car and sat by the window until there was no more light. We stopped at Golden, went through Calamity Tunnel, passed under snowsheds, and crossed narrow bridges high above alpine creeks. Little patches of snow clung to the mountainsides, but the trees were breaking into leaf. Green rushed into view at every turn. The brown prairie spring seemed part of another time.

At dinner the steward grouped me with a Florida boat dealer and a Kamloops woman with military bearing. She told us about her job with Canada Customs. The world was apparently divided into two camps—violators and other people.

"You can tell just by looking in their faces," she said.

"What we got in Florida is a problem with illegal aliens," worried the boat dealer. "They should hire more immigration officers."

The woman from Kamloops agreed. She wanted to keep undesirables out of Canada. The regulations were too lenient. "We're getting too many of the wrong kind," she asserted. "In twenty years people won't be able to recognize this country."

Pole Vaulting God's Clothes Line

"IF YOU'VE BEEN ON BOARD SINCE MONTREAL," said one of my guidebooks, "you've travelled 3045 miles and will probably be ready to walk around. Don't miss Chinatown." It was early morning. People spilled out of the coaches looking groggy but relieved. The year before on the same platform a member of the crew had shouted to the others, "Hey, wanna go for a Cobalt treatment?" Nobody did. The bar in the derelict Cobalt Hotel had had more appeal when they were younger. Today the parade along the platform was quiet. The crew disappeared in taxis for their one-day layover in a hotel, and the passengers milled around in the lobby until they were picked up by family or friends. Some back-packers set out on foot. A few of us drifted into the cafeteria for a station breakfast. Vancouver. The end of the line. There was the feeling of let-down that came with fatigue. Pierre Trudeau's remark in his essay on wilderness camping came to mind: "Travel a thousand miles by train and you are a brute." He went on to recommend canoeing; what I wanted was a bed. After breakfast I found one at the run-down Patricia Hotel near Chinatown on East Hastings Street, a raunchy neighbourhood where the rooms were cheap.

It had been fifteen years since I had spent more than a day or two in Vancouver. Then I had rented a room in an old house off English Bay. One of us had to go down to the basement every few hours and shovel sawdust into the furnace, which looked like a big tin can with a door cut into it for fuel. In the room next to mine were two Saskatchewan farm girls who had run away from home and found jobs as waitresses. Down the hall lived a visionary madman on amphetamines. He claimed to be able to talk to his mother and girlfriend in Ontario by using his doorknob as a microphone-transmitter. The ground floor rooms were rented by out-of-work loggers. They sold drugs to supplement their unemployment insurance benefits.

I called an old friend who advised leaving the Patricia. "Someone was stabbed near there a week ago," he said. The district had an unsavoury reputation. We arranged to meet the next day—I said the hotel looked safe enough. And went for a walk along the streets down by the water. The air was warm and damp. A marine smell came up from the harbour.

A ragged man lurched out of a doorway and confronted me. "You look like you could use something." His eyes shone urgently.

"I don't think so," I replied.

"You're lying," he said. "Everybody does." He stood a little above me, but was slightly built. The warehouses on the street were quiet. We were alone on the sidewalk. I stepped around him to get away, and he grabbed my shoulder.

"I've got something for you." The leer was homosexual.

Curious, I waited.

He wore a pair of stained green work pants, heavy brown boots, and a dirty white T-shirt. On his left arm was a tattoo of Mickey Mouse. I watched him pick up a paper bag from among a pile of belongings he had stashed in the deserted doorway. He came back and held it up.

"There's a dead thing in here. You and I could cook it together."

I said no and walked away.

"Hey mister," he called down the street. I turned and saw him shaking the bag, which had smelled of dead fish. "You're lying." And then a roll of mad laughter.

On Powell Street a shaggy-bearded man moaned and beckoned at the door of a mission house. Inside five derelicts seated in pews were doing their best to sing a hymn, "Abide With Me." They sounded like an old record, scratched and warped. Whoever finished the hymn earned a meal. I gave the deaf-mute at the door a dollar bill and went on. People drifted to the west coast, some of them to find jobs, others just drifting. If they were down and out, the climate was easier to bear here than elsewhere in Canada. Vancouver had a tradition of boom and bust, of winners and losers. This was where people had come, often on the railway, with a dream, and where they had ended when their luck ran out.

Downtown stood the old CPR station I remembered from fifteen years before. High on the walls the elegant clocks still kept time, but there were no more trains. The building was being used now as the depot for the seabus across Burrard Inlet. It housed boutiques with names like The Sandwich Tree and Franks For The Memory. The Ionic columns, the highlighted squares in the ceiling, the new peach-coloured paint, all gave the lobby the look of a memorial.

In the afternoon I passed through Chinatown, the only neighbourhood in Canada that really deserved the appellation. For several blocks you saw a preponderance of oriental faces and signs, and heard only Chinese words. This was almost their sovereign place, not merely an agglomeration of Chinese restaurants catering to the rest of the city, but a self-contained quarter. Unsure of my way and wanting to talk to someone, I asked directions from a bent-over old man with a wispy white beard. He stopped and studied me with guarded interest, as if I had just washed up on a raft from the China sea. I asked again and he replied in what I took to be Cantonese. "No Ingrish,'' he concluded with effort. For a moment I felt enclosed by foreignness.

The Patricia was not far away. Outside the entrance a man shuffled along the sidewalk in a pair of faded cotton pajamas and white running shoes. Two heavy women wearing black leather mini-skirts and loose blouses were looking for business. ''Want some company,'' they both called out. Inside the hotel a small, grey-haired man with a cane was waiting for the elevator.

''Slow coming,'' he said. ''Like Christmas.'' But when the door opened he stood still and watched me walk in.

Upstairs I drew a map that looked like the beginning of a musical note. I would visit here with friends, then proceed across the strait to Vancouver Island, travel up the island railway, loop back down to Vancouver from Nanaimo, and take a northbound train through the interior on the line up to Prince George. From there I could make a treble clef note and explore eastward on the northern transcontinental line. Or make a bent golf club and head west. After three months on the road I was casting ahead to the end of the trip, the first sign of travel fatigue.

Sounds of traffic and drunken voices in the street woke me. I flicked on the TV to check the time. Across Canada the familiar late-night images from this piece of talking furniture went where the railway went. Here it was again, the lined face of Johnny Carson, telling TV in-jokes from southern California for the insomniacs of an entire continent, a man who grew noticeably older but would never rise from wisecracks to wisdom, a star also in the ancient sense of a marker in the night sky, a light to see your dreams by. Some light. The show was a talking comic strip with a revolving cast of characters. As with comic strips that survived their creator's death, some day another artist might have to draw Johnny, but the show would go on. My sense of place, so strong across Canada before dark, was mocked after midnight by these far-reaching pictures from Los Angeles.

1993 Johnny drops his false teeth during his monologue.

1997 Johnny forgets his last name.

2001 Johnny dies laughing on The Tonight Show.

2002 Johnny reappears after rejuvenating surgery, slightly taller, and with a deeper voice. "It was a lotta fun. After the day of judgement I woke up in celebrity heaven. A guy greeted me and said they were going to give me my own show. 'Does everyone here have to work?' I asked him. 'No,' he said, 'but you're going to need money to pay the lawyer who got you in.' When I asked how the lawyers got in, he said, 'We had a choice between lawyers and NBC producers.' "

In the morning I bused to the art gallery on Granville Street where my old friend Patrick sold paintings. Recovering from a serious illness, he looked pale and weak. Outside, a fine wet spray floated down. We looked at watercolours by Tony Onley, soft, grey mountainscapes. "These paintings helped explain B.C. to me when I first came out here," he said. I could see in the light washes of colour a cool, fluid, ethereal quality that matched my memories of rainy days on the beach outside Vancouver. My friend had settled here after exploring Asia in his mid-twenties. As teen-agers we had been close in Montreal, but what I remembered now was the time we had travelled together on a Swiss train. After an evening in bars I impulsively joined him on the coach to Paris— where he had a job—rather than continue my studies in Switzerland. I fell asleep on board, with neither passport nor money. My friend bought me a ticket, and the passport problem was solved in an unusual way. A stout French immigration official very much regretted poking me awake and demanding to see my identity documents. I have a dim but indestructible memory of his polished black shoes over which, at precisely the right moment, I became spectacularly ill.

Down the street from the gallery was the Vancouver Press Club, not much more than a seedy pool hall, where

I read an appeal for the local food bank. In one month
the year before more than ten thousand bags of food had
been distributed to the city's hungry. Farther along the
street I turned down toward False Creek. The graffiti in
the underpass reflected the politically polarized atmosphere as well as the individual wackiness that had long
been characteristic of B.C.

> INDUSTRIAL PROFITS ARE WORTH YOUR LIFE
> FREE THE SQUAMISH FIVE
> STATE THE REASON FOR THE CANCER PLAGUE
> ZEN MAN SAYS POLE-VAULT GOD'S CLOTHES LINE

In the creek, off Granville Island, floated a dozen
houseboats, vines growing up their walls, shrubs and
flowers growing in boxes and barrels, sailboats moored
by some of the back doors, and a brick cooking fireplace
built on one of the decks. It looked pleasantly sybaritic,
a long way from life on the streets around the Patricia.
Every city in Canada had these contrasts; in Vancouver
they were more pronounced.

The Island

I HAD SPENT THE EVENING WITH PATRICK AND HIS WIFE,
talking in their garden. They cultivated rhododendrons,
colourful azaleas, and cedars that grew three feet a year.
The soft climate, he said, was one of the things that held
him to Vancouver. Now, late the next day, the ferry had
snaked across the strait and docked on Vancouver Island.
My bus was rolling into Victoria where I had arranged
to meet another friend, a woman I had known growing
up in Montreal.

My first memory of Norah Deane was from thirty years ago, a small child on the beach throwing stones at me and running away. I had not seen her since the early 1970s. When she came into the Victoria bus station she looked the same, the fine hazel eyes and dark hair, but self-assured now. Shiv, her husband, was an architect from India. They had no children; she worked in a school. Over supper Shiv talked about himself. Born in Kashmir, he had lived in a mountain village until the age of eight. "Grandmother used to sing legends in my ear," he said. Then the family moved down to Delhi, another language, another culture. From an early age he had experienced life as an outsider. His arranged marriage had chafed, and when he had emigrated to Canada in search of economic betterment he had gone without his wife. In Toronto, after he had begun an affair with an Australian woman, his wife had joined him. He described the troubled period during which he had lived in a triangle. Then he had gone west, again to look for work, leaving the women behind, and had fallen in love with my friend and with the mountains.

"I never really felt comfortable after Kashmir," he said, "until I found this B.C. landscape."

The next day we drove through sleepy Victoria and took a ferry across the channel to Fulford Harbour on Saltspring Island. The earth there spilled over with dense greens. We stopped at Ganges, busy with a Saturday market.

"Just another junky town," said Shiv. The island setting—clement, fertile, rolling—and the suggestive name of this place made the slap-dash, eyesore architecture look worse than similar places on the mainland.

"It's quite awful," I said.

Norah Deane seemed annoyed. "What did you expect? This is the west. We don't have pretty old nineteenth-century streets like you find in Ontario."

From Ganges we went along a quiet road with a few isolated houses to a place named Vesuvius. We passed yellow broom and splashes of the delicate blue camas flower. There were no signs of industry, no trains on Saltspring. The island was only twenty-five kilometres long, and most of it not more than five wide. People came here to retire or to retreat. Sheep farming was a favoured occupation, and I knew of some writers and artists who had made their homes here.

At Vesuvius, hungry for lunch, we spotted a genteel old inn with tables looking across the water. Shiv was pleased with the menu. By the look of the place we had expected meat and potatoes, but were offered Indian dishes only. He ordered curry. The quaint old colonial hostel serving curry on Booth Bay, a town called Ganges, the Indian architect, my long lost friend—for me it had been a morning of magic realism. These island havens on the edge of a cold country tempted you to believe that anything was possible. Here it might be easier to appreciate the mischievous, transcendental tales of the writer Jack Hodgins, who had grown up on Vancouver Island. Somewhere between fatigue and hallucination I sat dazed on the verandah—and remembered verandah was an Indian word accepted into English during the British Raj. As my friend's husband spoke of his homeland again, William Blake's lines danced in the background,

> *Tyger! Tyger! burning bright*
> *In the forest of the night.*

and something in me wished for an orange tiger to pad across the lawn under the flaking red arbutus trees.

Shiv was saying that his cousin, who smuggled hashish, had bought a car. "Owning car there—it's hard to imagine for you. It would be like owning spaceship here." The cousin had built a bridge so he could drive the car into his village. I wondered how often Shiv had to build such bridges in his heart and mind to join the two parts of himself, Indian villager and new Canadian. The curry aside, was there anything on Saltspring that reminded him of home? "In India," he shook his head, "we have so much dust." The heavy sky thinned and the clouds parted, letting an instant of sun flash down on us. In the bay a blue heron walked slowly, his shadow perfectly defined on the varnished water. The arbutus trees looked senile, leaning and twisted and old. An early botanist had called them oriental strawberry trees, nomenclature which suited our mood on Booth Bay.

"Do you find yourself in India in your dreams?" I asked Shiv as we rode back on the ferry. We were standing on deck, looking at the small islands in the channel.

"After two years, I begin dreaming and dreaming. And then I know it's time to go back," he said. We talked about the difficulties of seventy-five and a hundred years ago, when most immigrants could not return home and were obliged to seal off that desire. The sealing-off helped to explain why Canada had suffered from an amputated sense of history. For many immigrants who had been forced to break with the past, history became painful and unrewarding to contemplate. Or it became folklore, rich in memory, but alive only in dreams.

At their stucco cottage on the outskirts of Victoria, Shiv put on high rubber boots and went into the garden to pull weeds. It was late afternoon and the cloud cover had lifted. You could hear the gentle sound of water in the back yard, which dropped abruptly down to a small cove. On the grass, shifting shadows cast by the tall Douglas firs played with depth perception, making stepped levels out of the flat ground. The breeze rustled the foliage, and minute by minute the lighting changed, a natural *son et lumière* show. Past the hawthorns in front of the house, I went out onto the road and down to the head of the cove. There was a plaque, laid by the "Thermopylae Club of Victoria" in 1959. "When Vancouver Island was an infant colony nearly a century ago, it was here that the gallant sailing ships from the old world stopped to replenish their supply of fresh water." A pair of Canada geese flew over. In the cove stood another blue heron. This was a suburb, with houses up and down the street; the thick scent of lilacs planted in the yards perfumed the air.

At dinner Norah Deane said she did not read many books any more. Nor did they go out to see films. She had been the first of my circle in Montreal to read James Joyce, but now she said something curious. "Most people live through borrowed images, other people's thoughts, other people's perceptions. I'd rather work toward my own." Her husband talked about "living correctly" and "seeing clearly." They believed in a natural order that would be revealed if you worked at clarifying your vision. I found these views alarming, and shook off my wine-induced drowsiness to protest. There was no natural order, I argued, beyond the evolutionary systems of life produced by eons of trial and error. If order and meaning graced our lives, it was because we had arranged it thus, or because we had inherited them from our culture.

"Culture is superficial," Norah Deane said.

"Culture is fundamental," I argued. "It's what we are." But they believed in something larger and perhaps inexpressible. It was not instinct. They were speaking of a kind of pan-human empathy that transcended place and personal history.

Across the candle-lit dining room I heard dark-eyed Shiv say, "Universal level is most important." And they spoke of an experiment with rats in one part of the world that had inexplicably influenced the behaviour of rats thousands of miles away.

They had told me of first meeting at a Krishnamurti discussion group. Awake early in the guest room, I reached for one of his books by the bed. I knew almost nothing of this thinker's philosophy. The oriental wisemen who had caught the attention of people I knew in the 1960s and 1970s had never appealed to me. In *Questions and Answers* by J. Krishnamurti I found this passage:

Do not quote me—or anybody—for it is not yours and
you become a second-hand human being, which we all
are. That is the first thing to realize, because that dis-
torts our thinking. We are the result of millions of years
of the pressure of other people's thinking and propaganda. If one is not free of all that, one can never find
the origin of things.

The second-hand human being, following a path through
the dense growth of inherited words and carving a few
of his own along the way, seemed to me an admirable
creature. Roses from dung. I remembered Yeats, who
knew the value of the picked-over detritus inside us.

> Now that my ladder's gone
> I must lie down where all the ladders start
> In the foul rag-and-bone shop of the heart.

It was Sunday. We drove along quiet streets to the station
in Esquimalt, where we said good-bye. The sky was grey
when I boarded the one-car train. This was the old Esquimalt and Nanaimo Railway, which the CPR had acquired in 1905. Every morning it ran half-way up
Vancouver Island to the town of Courtenay, stopped there
for under an hour, and made the return trip in the afternoon. We passed a bright blue and yellow drydock crane
towering over Esquimalt harbour, and across the harbour, the naval shipyard. Out in the country the sun broke
through the clouds, illuminating our climb up the Mala-
hat mountain.

I went forward and stood in the cab with the engineer.
Yellow broom glistened by the tracks. Then we crossed
a high bridge over Niagara Canyon.

"The CPR would like to be finished with this line.
They condemned two of our bridges a few years back,
thinking that would be an excuse to close us down." He
spoke as if he owned the line himself and the CPR merely

held a mortgage on it. "The transport commission told them to rebuild. Cost them millions." He smiled happily.

On a curved bridge we crossed another dramatic drop, Arbutus Canyon, distinguished by the hundreds of arbutus trees lining it. "Let me show you my pictures," the engineer said. They were photographs of a train wreck. "We lifted a nice little pick-up truck and carried it down a few hundred yards. The driver had a broken pelvis and arm. Took us so long to get compensation I had to remember which leg it was I hurt so I could still limp. The CPR claimed it was a self-inflicted injury." The Island railway seemed a sleepy business, but with over two hundred level crossings, some trains suffered inevitable crunches. "If you don't have one for a while, you begin to feel you're due. When I see something in the way up there I clear out of the cab in a hurry."

Through the ties grass was sprouting. Normally the mark of an abandoned line, here it was a measure of the douce, damp climate. The rain forest around the tracks stood thick and tall. At the Ladysmith station, boarded-up and abandoned, a Brownie troop detrained, leaving the car almost empty. We stopped at Nanaimo, the island's second city, climbed up to Wellington, and coasted down to Nanoose Bay. Then there were fields of cut forest, acres and acres of stumps and slash. None of the land had been replanted. "Used to be a lot of logs on this railway," the conductor said, standing in the doorway to the cab. "Not any more."

We braked at the next flagstop, Buckley Bay. The train was running close enough to shore now for a view of the water. Beside the tracks were a group of sun-tanned men and women in their thirties, shaggy-haired, the women in loose halter tops and baggy pants, the men wearing jeans and singlets or collarless shirts with buttons. "They're from Denman Island," said the engineer, pointing across the water. "That's where the hippies and Vietnam protest people lived. Some still do. They grow good marijuana over there." One of the men hugged his woman, who stepped onto the train with her duffle bag. He winked and sang out, "Arrivederci," in a loud, raspy voice.

At Courtenay the engineer changed places for the return trip—the tail-end of the car became the front. I signed his guest book and left the train when he stopped again in Nanaimo, thinking I would stay the night. The streets were quiet as I walked down from the station toward the water. In the air was the smell of the sea. I tried the first hotel, and the second, and the third. All were locked. So too was the Globe Hotel where the marquee boasted: DANCERS THIS WEEK JESSIE BRIANNA JACKIE STACEY LIVE ENTERTAINMENT. Live perhaps, but dead on a Sunday afternoon. My bags were heavy with the books and newspapers I had collected across the west. I sat in the outdoor restaurant opposite the Globe and wondered if I could throw anything away. The waitress brought me a drink. In the bay below sailboats cruised. The blue water bounced up a galaxy of stars made from reflected sunlight.

"All the hotels downtown are closed," the waitress said redundantly. "You'll have to go out to the highway for a motel."

Was there a bus to the ferry?

No bus.

She gave me directions and I started down the road to the ferry, intending to thumb a ride. An expensive motel appeared on my left, but now a room in Vancouver seemed preferable. It was a sweltering afternoon. Someone was sure to stop. Forty cars had passed me—I had begun a count—when a frail, grey-haired lady, perambulating the road in a wheel-chair, stopped to say, "It's going to be hard. They don't pick people like you up in this part of the world." Her eyes darted at me, intelligent and fearful. And then her nurse pushed her away. I watched them dip out of sight behind a rise, feeling that my fortune had just been told.

The cars continued to pass, and I continued to walk

with my thumb out. We were all going to the ferry—there was only the dock at the end of this road. About a hundred yards short of the ticket kiosk I heard the boat's whistle blow. It began to ease away from the wharf. Leaning on the railings, the people who had passed in their cars looked down. Self-contained, uncurious, paranoid, did they think I would rob them in broad daylight on a busy road, I with my two flight bags and my drip-dry button-down shirt, my perma-press pants, my nice respectable leather shoes? Did they think I would commit indecent acts? Hijack their cars? Shoot heroin in the back seat? Or perhaps they did not see me at all. Perhaps they had eyes only for other automobiles. I bought a ticket for the next ferry, which would cross to Horseshoe Bay, near Vancouver, later that night.

Maybe the Moon

B.C. RAIL, THE PROVINCIAL RAILWAY, OPERATED A DAILY train to Lillooet, which left North Vancouver at 7:30 A.M. I woke later than planned in my bed-and-breakfast house on the north side of the city, and called a cab. We raced along the North Vancouver waterfront and arrived at the station with five minutes to spare. The bench-seats in the single coach were hard, but the view quickly supplanted any discomfort. We rolled up the shore of Howe Sound for the first hour, over streams and through rock cuts, watching the sun-speckled inlet, the boats, and the islands. Then we climbed into the high country of the Coast Range, past Mount Garibaldi and through the rugged Cheakamus Canyon, a deep, narrow cut with roaring white water at the bottom. Hugging the side of the gorge, the train ran on a narrow ledge. We crossed over the brink of Brandywine Falls, and went on past Alta Lake and Whistler Mountain. On the descent into the Pemberton Valley, a rich farming district, I went ahead to the cab. Alongside the Green River, the engineer said, "See that iron bridge? It fell into the water three years ago in a storm. No trains for five weeks. Lots of rainfall here. They grow potatoes as big as melons." In the valley we stopped at the town of Pemberton and then at the Mount Currie Indian reserve.

"They're all on welfare," he said with contempt. "See that mill? They had the place running for six weeks, then the Indians got paid and buggered off. As soon as they've got a couple of hundred bucks in their pockets, you don't see them again." He thought the Indians were lazy and negligent. "We provided a train station too, but they burnt it down. Hooch, klooch, and gramophone, that's all these guys care about." Klooch, I understood, meant Indian women.

We climbed out of the valley into the sparsely populated terrain of the Cascade Mountains, and stopped at Birken, the summit. "Here's where the paved road ends," he said. And then we descended again, this time into the arid, rocky interior. The train snaked sixteen miles along the shore of Anderson Lake, narrow, deep, dark blue, and apparently untouched. "There are only a few cabins. You either take the train or you walk in here. It's not for the family with a station wagon and three kids."

At the end of the lake lived another Indian band. Seton Portage sat on a primordial subsidence of land that had cut the ancient lake in two. We rolled around Seton Lake, another long and narrow piece of water, but milky green, a different colour from its twin on the other side of the hump. The engineer pointed into the murky deep. "There's an engine down there. You gotta watch for the rock slides. They can take you right out."

In another five miles we had reached Lillooet. The town's golden days, literally, had been during the 1850s. This was where the Cariboo Road to the interior goldfields had begun. In the Lillooet shops were pamphlets and postcards and maps that told you this had been a gold-rush town over a century ago. One book said the streets had boasted thirty-eight liquor outlets and twenty-three camels. But when I asked at the local museum which buildings had been preserved from the early days, the custodians looked blank. A house had been saved from the 1890s; the rest were relatively new. I walked the ''golden mile of history,'' the claim made for the main street. It appeared to be an ordinary mountain settlement built a generation ago. Lillooet embodied a typical Canadian response to history. The past had its place, on paper, in the stories of old timers, and set aside as token artifacts in little museums. As a material part of everyday life, though, the past was often an inconvenience to be removed. People wanted new things. They did not want to be left behind. Ironically, a penchant for current consumer fashions, for a disposable culture, had been grafted easily onto the pioneer vision that had stressed tomorrow over yesterday. But lost from the pioneer ethic was the enduring pride of place, and the notion that the old barn had sentimental value. Lillooet, to tell the truth, was an ugly little town, a mish-mash of post-war quickie construction, partly redeemed by its pleasant mountain setting. I could not help imagining what it might have been if more of its nineteenth-century architecture had survived.

On the street I saw mostly natives. Outside the hotel bar where I had eaten supper, an Indian caught my eye. We fell into step together, and told each other our first names. That was how it had been with the Indians I had met, first names only. And like the others I'd spoken with—brief exchanges on the train, or in the stations—Bob traced the movements that had brought him into my company, as if he needed to situate himself in space before our encounter could be granted meaning. His first words after hello were:

"I went to Kamloops to see someone. Got a ride back to Cache Creek. Couldn't get further."

We went down Main Street and into the Golden Nugget, a small bar with one pool table. The sign on the wall said, "Everyone should believe in something so I do believe I'll have another beer." He talked about the hockey play-offs on television, and then again about his recent travels.

"My wife's in that hospital. The one in Kamloops. I've been to see her twice. Got blisters the first time. No rides. Sacked out in the ditch." He spoke slowly, spacing his words, and accenting unexpected syllables. A Salish Indian from the Bridge River band, he said he had a job at a sawmill. In Lillooet he stayed with his sister, who rented a room.

Three heavy young women and their male friends were shooting pool. They all used the word fuck liberally in their banter. My Indian companion nodded toward one of them.

"That girl's father shot himself. Blew his head right off. You know the row of little houses across from your hotel? He did it there." After a long silence Bob rested his eyes on a wooden carving over the bar.

"My cousin made that. It's either the sun or the moon. It's a sad one. Maybe the moon." Another long silence. The pool balls clacked against each other, and the players swore. "You probably think it's quiet in here. Come back tomorrow morning. Nine o'clock. You'll see a lot of people."

We parted in the rain outside. He was going to walk to his home, several miles out of town. In the morning I looked through the window of the Golden Nugget. Every table was taken, mostly Indians drinking, but a few white people too. Lillooet was the first place I had seen where Indians and whites appeared to mix easily.

The air was wet, not with rain, but with something between drizzle and mist. Clouds hung over the valley, a suspended ceiling that cut off the mountains half-way up.

The clouds looked very close to the ground, as if you could raise a long fire-ladder and tap into the large white sacks of water. On the floor of the valley, just below Lillooet, churned the Fraser River, muddy with spring run-off from the mountains.

At the station twelve cars of finished lumber waited on a siding; each bundle bore the name of the sawmill, spray-painted in red. The passenger train left Lillooet in the early afternoon, climbing up the Fraser Canyon. Far below the tracks, brown water rushed through deep russet rock cuts. Beyond Lillooet the mountains were arid, gravelly, inhospitable; smaller versions of the Andes. But here and there isolated patches of level green stood their ground in this desert, fed by vast sprinkler systems. For an hour we strained uphill, reaching for a dot on the map called Pavilion. The name was derived from the Salish Indian burial custom of placing streamers at the grave site here. To the French-Canadian fur traders the streamers were "*pavillions.*" Pavilion turned out to be one store and a wooden shelter with the letters DEPOT on it, perched on a rocky slope. The train continued its ascent for several more miles up the Fraser, and then left the river and the brilliant sun and headed into the mountains. The weather changed abruptly to cloud and drizzle, and the land turned green. This was the beginning of the Cariboo Plateau, ranching and pulp-cutting country. We passed lush meadows with grazing cattle, and long stretches of scruffy bush. And the smoking metal teepees called "beehives" where the mill operators burned their waste.

A young Englishwoman up the aisle was reading Aldous Huxley. Tall and blonde, she looked about thirty, with delicate features and pale blue eyes. She had worked as a school teacher and now lived with her boyfriend on a ranch outside Williams Lake.

"English people seem to like it up here," she said. "Some of the ranches were started by English aristocrats. I'm not one of them." She smiled. "We had a bit of money, enough for a start. This is one of the last areas in the world which is still isolated, clean and safe, and politically reliable. Why not enjoy it while it lasts?'' At the Williams Lake station she ran into the arms of a well-built bearded man waiting beside a jeep.

Up in the cab the engineer, who had boarded at Williams Lake, said this was "your shoot-a-moose-from-the-porch, red-neck country. It attracts people like that. Go-to-bed-with-a-skidoo type people. You know?'' His name was John Alexander. He wore a white hat with a PGE button on it (until 1972 the railway had carried the unlikely name of the Pacific Great Eastern) and a light blue denim work suit. A self-educated man, he said he enjoyed books.

''I saw the demographics for B.C. recently,'' he said. ''Most people in Williams Lake, they've come from somewhere else. There isn't that feeling that we go way back, that our ancestors built all this and we want to keep it as it is.'' He had read Farley Mowat. ''I don't think the whole universe is big enough to hold his ego. And I kind of admire that. I mean you hardly ever see the ego really blossom and grow.''

South of Quesnel he said, ''See that black dot ahead? See it move?'' Down the track about two hundred yards I could make out something black. As we drew closer the bear sprinted along the rails and cut into the trees. We saw another and then a third running into the dense forest. This was rough and wild bush. The ranches were behind us.

For passenger trains Prince George was the end of the line on B.C. Rail, but the city served as the major railway junction in the interior. From it the old CN line ran east and west. Via operated the Panorama train in both directions every second day. I would have to wait here twenty-four hours, and then I could go west to Smithers. A man on a ranch there had agreed to put me up. From Smithers I could take my last ride to Prince Rupert on the coast.

Outside Prince George we passed yards full of freshly cut railway ties, and raw timber piled high in rows. The forest industry had created a boom here after World War II. The small mill town had grown rapidly into a city of 75,000. On the bus from the railway station, which had been built on the outskirts, a grey-haired, solitary American said, "I *love* frontier towns. Don't you?" His soft, fleshy face looked ill-equipped for adventure. He was wearing a silky purple cravat tucked into a pink shirt, and jeans held up by a cowboy belt. The belt was fastened with a bright brass clasp. "I *love* trains. I've been in some strange places on trains. Rough towns like this."

He wanted me to have a drink with him. "I don't work," he smiled sadly. "I travel." A wealthy drifter, alone, apparently a permanent tourist, always looking in from the outside, and always, one assumed, looking for a pretty boy.

"Tell me," he said, wanting to continue, "what's the difference between CN and CP?"

"CN is the government railway," I said. "It owns this northern line."

"Why don't you tell him the truth?" interjected a young Via Rail employee, out of uniform and travelling for pleasure. "One is run by a bunch of bureaucrats, and the other by a bunch of shareholders and crooks."

The bus driver let me off at his last stop, near the National Hotel, which stood opposite the CN station. I had been told the rooms were inexpensive.

"You wanna keep your back to the wall if you go into the bar," he said as I got out. It was nine o'clock; I had been on the train from Lillooet most of the day. Before bed I sat for a beer. The decor followed a railway motif— the place was called the Iron Horse Pub. On the dance floor whites and Indians of both sexes mixed. The men, young, tough, and beefy, wore either cowboy hats or baseball caps. An electric train ran around a track suspended over the bar.

"Hey," someone yelled, waving at the bartender, who did not bother to look up. The impatient customer lobbed a glass over the counter. When it crashed the unmoved barman eyed the offender.

"Pay for it," he said.

Three Indian girls scurried past me. A man with huge biceps was holding up a chair, ready to ram the slightly smaller cowboy-hatted drunk who had annoyed him. The nearby tables were clearing fast. A loud argument ensued as the angry man's friends calmed him down.

"That's Joanna's sister," another man said later at the bar. He nodded toward a table of pretty young girls. "I asked her if she played games. She says whadya mean? I says would she do three or four guys. No, she says. How about two or three, I says. That's different, she says."

In the morning I found a barber shop beside the hotel. The woman cutting my hair said the boom in Prince George had ended but some people had done well from it. "This town is basically made up of losers who came from other places to try to make it. A lot of them did. I had three businesses. Sold them before the bottom fell out."

I described the bar scene the night before.

"It's a rough town," she said. "Biggest alcohol consumption per person in Canada."

I walked up George Street and over to Victoria, Vancouver and Winnipeg Streets, passing Indians on every sidewalk. Most of the architecture was low and hasty. Prince George looked like a third-world settlement, but with money. I found some grass in a small park beside the city hall. The sun was beating down hard.

"White man trying to get black," said an Indian. He moved closer. "How are ya? I know ya. Didn't we meet somewhere?"

"Just got into town," I replied.

"I live here," he said. "All I need is fifty cents." The smell of alcohol was strong on his breath. A group of indigent natives was lolling under a nearby tree. I did not want to become the park banker, so I refused him.

"I can give you some dried fish," he tried again.

I shook my head. He shrugged and walked over to join the others. When he arrived they began to swear loudly. A few minutes later the water sprinklers erupted. From the sidewalk I watched the group slowly realize they were being soaked. They rose unsteadily in slow motion, leaving an array of empty bottles under their tree, and staggered through the spray onto the street. Then I saw them walk down the block and into the liquor store.

JOE'S PLACE said a sign on the way back to the hotel. THREE DANCERS UKRANINE SMORGY. I wondered about the suicide rate here. It was not a city I would have chosen to live in as a writer.

Spin

THE TRAIN MOVED OUT OF PRINCE GEORGE AT NINE-thirty, and soon the light was gone. Through the dark glowed the burning beehives, orange pinholes leaking light through their thin metal skins. We passed murky lakes in the bush, silver mirrors illuminated by the moon. At 3:30 A.M. I stepped down in Smithers. The town looked prosperous, with new roads and sidewalks, and stores selling sports equipment. The first hotel I tried was locked. In the second an Indian was asleep in the vestibule. I banged on the door and woke him, but no one came. He looked at me and said I was making too much noise.

Out on the highway I found a motel with someone awake at the desk. From my room in the morning I called Gus, the rancher whose name a friend had given me. He arrived in a pick-up truck. We drove out to his property, a small ranch in the country above the town. All I knew was that he and his wife were Americans, that they had moved here in the early 1970s, and that they were wealthy enough to enjoy life in the mountains without having to turn a profit on the ranch. My friend had said that Gus was eccentric and very bright.

We put my bags in the guest cabin. He had erected several log buildings on the property. The main house was a renovated barn. "It was built fifty-eight years ago by an Estonian guy who sold ties to the railway, a tie hack. That's quite old for the west." The mountain air felt clean and warm as we sat on his deck and talked. He had grown up on a dude ranch in Colorado, and had married a woman from Kansas. At the university he had done post-graduate work in biology, and then with his wife had travelled widely before settling here. He worked for a variety of environmental causes, and spoke knowledgeably about wildlife and wilderness preservation.

"Really," he said, "there is no more wilderness on the planet. Man has touched every place now. It's become a question of degrees of civilization. A small, wiry man, he had a prominent wrinkled forehead, and eyes set slightly farther apart than most, giving him an unusual cerebral look that fit his mocking intelligence.

We walked over to the new log barn to see the cattle. "I think of these animals as a mother thinks of her retarded child," he said. "Some people have given me grief for slaughtering them. A guy once asked me if I got a sexual thrill from the killing. Obviously he hadn't owned a cow. To me killing one of these beasts is only slightly worse than pulling a carrot."

Then he said, "You know, people are wrong about the oldest profession. It's hunting. You gotta have something to bring if you want ass. It's a long way to come from that mentality to where animals have rights."

After lunch we moved the cattle across the road into a grazing field. "My friends down south would probably lynch me if they knew, but I've named some of these black cows after them."

We strolled down into the lower fields which he had cleared himself. He looked across the Bulkley Valley at the snowy mountains and then surveyed his hay lot. I said he seemed pleased with the place he had made. "Owning land just means you have the right to do your dance on it while you're there. No one can really possess it." As we walked on he added, "I think I've done just about everything I can here and it's time to hang up the telephone." His accent still had the American twang.

I asked where he would go. He answered that it would be hard to leave. B.C. had been good in many ways. He had wanted to get away from the States. "We didn't like the direction the country was taking." I asked then if he had fought in Viet Nam.

His face tightened and he shook his head. "I can't talk about it. There are areas of my life I'm just not interested in exposing."

Later, after I had gone to the cabin for a sleep, he said, "Don't you think it's easy to make money if you can just think obliquely?" We were smoking dope on the deck; I had not tasted marijuana for years. "A friend of mine in the CIA," he went on, "markets medical and health equipment. I told him they should develop a carcinogen counter. That's gotta have a very strong future."

"You could make a killing," I said, awash in the curious mixture of dull-wittedness and effortless knocking together of thoughts that this drug induced.

Gus emitted his high-pitched laugh that would have done for an insane man. It reminded me of Tom Hulce's crazy screech in the movie *Amadeus*, and it sounded even more extravagant in front of this isolated house in the woods.

After dinner, sitting in the living room, I tried asking again about his war years. He bristled. "I can't open up too much," he said, and changed the subject. He was willing to touch on selected episodes in the past, but was most comfortable talking about life here in the mountains, the environmental causes, and his ranch and buildings. The renovated barn was the most opulent house I had seen in the B.C. interior. An elegant grandfather clock stood at one end of the living room, and for his children a piano had been trucked in over the dirt roads. The walls were the old barn walls constructed of spruce logs. Overlooking the living room he had built a second-floor gallery. The spindles and runner had a warm golden hue. "It's yellow cedar," he said, "brought in from the Queen Charlotte Islands. Because it didn't rot. I just put this place together whichever way looked best. We never had any blueprints."

In his protean face you could sometimes read merriment and mischief. Other times the eyes were cold, dark, and metallic. "People take pictures of these buildings from the driveway," he said. "I used to shoot a gun off over their heads."

Most of the next day I spent in the cabin. We met again before dinner. "Have a cocktail," he said, handing me a joint. Overhead we could hear a helicopter. "Maybe on a rescue run. You pay a price to live up in this country. All the natural luxury we have, it doesn't take very many factors to change before it goes the other way." He said there were often aircraft accidents. I asked if he ever had second thoughts about flying in the mountains, but he replied coolly, "I was raised with a very realistic attitude to death. You do the things you want to do and you take the necessary risks. I'm a bit more careful, I guess, now that I have children."

After supper he put a tape on the player in the living room. I noticed when he had been smoking that some of his syllables did contortions. "Simon and Garfarble," he announced. He asked if I would like to hear his position on abortion.

"If a foetus has rights, so do sperm. And if you're going to go for one, you have to go for the other. Masturbation should be forbidden, as should copulation for pleasure."

"What are you going to do," I said, "cut off people's hands?"

"Well, that would sure solve the abortion problem."

We walked out to the barn and threw down some bales of hay to the cows in the corral below. The moon was full, lighting the yard, the log buildings, the black cows, and the white mountains. Gus's wife had taken the children upstairs to bed. In the moonlight we walked across the road into his pasture.

"There's a grizzly on the loose down here," he said. "Our neighbours have seen the tracks."

"What's the recommended course of action if we see it?" I asked.

"Do what you like. Myself I'll get back to the house real quick." He enjoyed sharpening the edges of uncertainty and fear. He talked about some of the tight situations he had experienced in South America. I told him I had fallen ill with dysentery in Peru and still could not eat milk products,

"I've got my pen-knife handy," he proposed. "The worst that could happen is we'd have to do a tracheotomy on you."

Back on the deck we rolled another cigarette. "I was in Toronto last year, in a bar called Hemingway's," he said. "Talking to a good-looking woman. She couldn't get a fix on me. Finally she asked, 'What *are* you?' And I said, 'I'm a yippie-tie-o.' Which is true. That's my background—the dude ranch, rodeos. But I thought a moment, about the house here with the dishwasher and the word processor and all the other amenities we live with, and I said, 'Wait a minute. I'm *yuppie*-tie-o.' "

He wanted to write a novel. He had sold magazine articles, but still found writing one an arduous task.

"I don't think I could do what you're doing," he said.

"You might be wrong. But I don't think I could do what you're doing either."

"Well, there it is. Another traveller who won't trade places with me, take the property, the wife, the kids."

In the kitchen he pulled out a package of sugar-powdered dough-nuts. Whiteness, I thought: the moon, the snowy mountains, the powdered dough-nuts. Everything that mattered at this moment was endowed with transcendent whiteness. Taking a bite, I felt I was chewing a piece of the moon, eating a mouthful of mountain. When I tried to explain, he said:

"Some of us know what the essence of the universe is. But no one will buy it. Are you ready? The essence of the universe is SPIN. Think about it, George. It's airtight."

World War III on Pay-TV

GUS HAD AN ARTIST FRIEND WHO LIVED AT A REMOTE railway flagstop in a concrete bunker. He described the friend as "a little crazy," which, coming from Gus, gave me pause. He suggested we all drive over to Carl's place. I could stay there a day or two and wave the train down when I wanted to go on to Prince Rupert.

On the way to the artist's house we drove through Hazelton, an old-west Indian village, and stopped at the Kispiox rodeo. Passing a truck in the ditch, Gus said, "I guess the rodeo's in full swing." We sat in the hot sun and watched men being thrown off bucking horses. "Calamity's the name of the game," explained Gus. He had won prizes in rodeos when he was younger.

We drove along the Skeena River to the Indian village of Kitwanga—or Gitwangak in the native language. At the centre of the village thirteen totem poles stood beside the road. They were weathered and worn relics of the Gitksan civilization that had dominated the Skeena Valley until the early part of the century. Once the poles had stood in a line by the river, but in the 1930s they had been moved here because of flooding. The carved spirits looked down at us from another time, another river valley where nothing was known of trains, heavy industry, the uses of uranium. As we left Kitwanga I saw that all the windows in the little red-roofed railway station had been smashed.

We followed a rough dirt road down to the isolated flagstop where Carl, the artist, lived. "Carl can grow corn here," said Gus's wife. "He gets the warm coast air coming inland through the river valley."

Gus pushed open the thick side door of the bunker, a gloomy concrete-grey building on the outside. Inside, the artist's colourful work gave some warmth to the place. From his long wooden table Carl Chaplin greeted us, a tall man with a light beard and sad, intelligent eyes. We talked and smoked together and then the artist pulled out the sketches for his "Wish You Were Here" anti-nuclear paintings, a series depicting atomic-bomb explosions in the world's major cities. He had already painted Bangkok, San Francisco, Washington, Moscow—and Disneyland—each painting crowned by fiery mushroom smoke. Art nuko, he called these pictures. He had made them all into postcards. They succeeded as a kind of agitprop art, immediately accessible images that warned against megaton weaponry. He planned to take the series on a world tour, he said, when they were finished.

"It grieves me, Carl," said Gus, "to see you destroyin' all these places."

"I add a 10-percent surcharge," said the artist, "if I sell one to anybody in a primary target area."

We turned to a sketch of the Vatican being bombed. Gus looked pained. "Carl, you're getting into dangerous terrain here. No one has ever threatened the church and survived." But the most shocking picture was one outside the city series. The artist called it "Watching World War III on Pay-TV." Reminiscent of Jack Chambers' "Sunday Morning," it showed a suburban family viewing on television the nuclear explosion that was also observable out the living room window. On the floor a little girl fingered the trigger of the toy gun she had aimed at her mouth.

"I hope you survive your stay here," Gus said to me as his family prepared to leave. "Carl is a very strange man."

When the car had disappeared, I could feel some measure of the solitude the artist lived with at Woodcock. He did not have a vehicle of his own. When he needed to travel he waved down the train to Prince Rupert and boarded the ferry there down to Vancouver. For food he had been more or less self-sufficient until this year, when the preparations for his world tour had taken priority over gardening. Now he had to walk to the Kitwanga store for groceries, seven miles away, or catch a ride in with the rancher who lived opposite the bunker. The rancher's family and Carl were the only residents of Woodcock. There were no other houses on the dirt road out to the village.

The bunker—with concrete walls, concrete floor, and concrete ceiling—had been built by the army corps of engineers in 1943. It was a communications relay station to boost power on the telegraph line from Prince Rupert to Prince George. Pearl Harbour had been attacked two years before and the army feared a Japanese invasion up the Skeena Valley. The building had been constructed to withstand aerial bombing. "I found it by chance in the fall of 1977," the artist said. "The railway wasn't even aware they still owned it." He had worked over the years to make the bunker habitable, punching out the shatterproof wired glass in the windows, repairing broken pipes that brought water in from the mountain, replacing the old boiler and radiators with a new wood furnace, and installing a generator. Canadian National Railways charged him eleven dollars a month in rent.

We walked over the tracks, past the airstrip (paved at the time the relay station had been built), and through the bush to the bank overlooking the Skeena, a rushing torrent swollen with mountain run-off. Above Carl's little pocket of land, on the other side of the river, the Seven Sisters' snow-capped peaks rose into the blue and white sky. He led the way back to the bunker and rolled another cigarette. As we smoked he showed me his nature paintings, executed in a style loosely resembling magic realism, but which he called fusion art. "It fuses photography and painting, reality and science, light and dark, ecstasy and paranoia." He worked with an airbrush, sometimes on very large canvasses. A mountain painting seven by nine feet hung at one end of the room. Aloft in one corner of the canvass floated a Jules Verne balloon and basket, the planet-like balloon casting a blue shadow on the mountain's golden rock face.

We fried some of the eggs and tomatoes I had brought. He had run out of food. One of us, he said, would have to go to Kitwanga for supplies in the morning. There was no refrigerator in the bunker, and he had eaten all the fruits and vegetables he had preserved from last year's garden. He was also running out of money. He had not sold a painting for several months. But none of this precariousness appeared to undermine his self-confidence. He spoke of his wish to take the anti-nuclear paintings around the world as if he had already been given air tickets. A clear-eyed vision of dark forces against light was propelling him. The planet would nurture and sustain us if we learned her ways and returned the favour; if we continued to abuse her we were doomed. He talked about the apocalypse: economic, environmental, or nuclear—we were flirting with all three. A widely read, articulate man given to long monologues, he covered a broad range of survival-related subjects in his after-supper dissertation. The military mind—programmed for centuries to acquire bigger and better weapons than its enemy; gaia—a philosophy of peaceful interaction with the natural world; left- and right-brain integration; the Jehovah's Witnesses who had read of his paintings and written to say there was nothing to fear if he would convert to their faith; Helen Caldicott; Jerry Falwell; the collapse of the South American economies; and the possibility of geo-synchronous communications satellites girdling the earth to monitor its survival as a single interrelated life system. Finally he said:

"How long do we have? Sometimes I think only four or five years. Other times I think the world peace movement is growing and we'll make it through these dark times." He reflected on it for a moment. "No. I don't think we will." And he chuckled.

Waking on my mat in the voluminous main room—thirty feet by sixty—I faced the large mountainscape painting with its tiny balloon-borne globe. The morning light poured in through the bunker's big windows, reflecting off the white dry-wall Carl had recently installed. I could hear him working with the airbrush in a far corner of the room. His own bed was in the basement. He had risen earlier, but not in time to catch a ride up the road with the rancher.

"If you think you're going to be real hungry today," he said, "you can walk in to the village. Otherwise we'll eat tomatoes and catch a lift tomorrow." He kept a box at the post office in Kitwanga, where he collected his magazines and correspondence. There was a radio in the bunker, with reception from the CBC Prince Rupert station. And he had acquired a radio telephone, which he treated with suspicion. Other users of the same channel could eavesdrop on his calls.

"In my worst moments I imagine they've got road-blocks out to stop people from coming here. Sometimes I think they know exactly what's going on in this place because of the radio telephone." I speculated that some degree of paranoia was inevitable if you dwelled alone in a concrete bunker at the base of a beautiful mountain and meditated every day on the approach of World War III.

We heard someone bang on the metal door at the front of the building, an entrance the artist rarely used. A young couple entered, Murko and Lorraine. They had come to collect a painting. There was no money for Carl—he had already been paid—but the visitors pulled a bottle of white wine out of their pic-nic cooler, and a pound of smoked salmon.

"I guess we were meant to have a good meal today," the artist murmured sagely. After we had eaten I rode out to the village with the couple. I collected Carl's mail, bought a bag of groceries, and began the long walk back. Half-way along the dirt road, the rancher, returning in his truck from a delivery of logs to the local mill, picked me up. He said he cut logs eight months of the year, as long as the road was good.

"Truthfully, there's not much money in it. Price of logs hasn't changed in ten years. But it keeps me out of trouble."

I asked if the isolation bothered him, and if he ever wanted to board the train when he saw it pass.

"Took a train trip a few years ago. Got on down there by Carl's place and went to Edmonton. I drank beer and celebrated for the cars on the highway slippin' and slidin' in the weather.

"No, I don't mind the isolation. Simple things we git in Kitwanga. Banking we do in Terrace. You can git most anything exotic there."

That evening the artist talked more about his art-nuko paintings. He wanted to alert people to the nuclear danger. And if the holocaust came, he wanted to leave a record of twentieth-century humanity's self-destruction. In some future age the archaeologists might discover his paintings and learn from them. I could not tell how much of this gloss he believed. He had adopted the role of art-nuko crusader, and had been swept up by his own mythology.

"One stipulation on the bill of sale for all my art-nuko paintings is that in the event of imminent war they must be returned to this bunker forthwith. In the basement I'm going to build a crypt. The paintings will be stored there.''

I asked for a tour of the basement, where he planned to survive the aftermath of the war. We felt our way down the unlit stairs, past his bedroom, and through a dark passageway into the store-room.

''On the shelves will be our dried food and survival gear. In the centre of this room the crate with the paintings will be placed and a concrete crypt will be poured around it. So that it can be opened easily, but still sealed against the weather. Even if the top of the building were to be demolished either by blast or by glaciation or by the ravages of the nuclear winter, this underground room will withstand all that and be here for the archaeologists.

''We've been stockpiling fresh top soil out these windows for the past couple of years. Plans eventually call for greenhouses on the south side. And we could quickly and easily move soil down here for gardening indoors under artificial light. Being this far away from any blast zone, radiation is not much of a threat. The real threat is nuclear winter.''

I asked why he used ''we'' when he spoke of surviving here. Did he have friends who were coming?

''Unlike the right-wing bizzaro survivalists that stock guns more than food, I extend the invitation to survive to just about everybody. I urge people to think about this, especially if they've got children. As nightmarish as it is to contemplate, they've got a responsibility. Do they want their kids to waste away for a couple of weeks in torment and pain?''

He was growing agitated. He had shaved his head, which gave him a ghoulish look in the subterranean dark.

''People say, 'I want to be the first to die in the blast. I want to go painlessly.' But the chances of your going painlessly in a nuclear attack are indeterminable. In fact your chances are probably greater of ending up with a face full of shredded glass, melted eyeballs, and peeling skin. But still alive and having your children clinging to your arms, screaming and crying, and throwing up incessantly. Two weeks of that would be the worst hell I could imagine.

"So, sure, I invite everybody to come out here. I'm so remote that I have no fear of being overloaded with thousands of people a couple days before the bombs go off. I doubt if many people would make it out here at all. But because I am embedded in my species I don't have all the skills, the mechanical and agricultural skills, to survive by myself. My philosophy is the more people who come out here, the better off I'll be. I don't think we'll run out of food because there are too many people. I think we'll be able to grow more because there are enough hands to do it."

The Four Grandfathers

THE NEXT DAY CARL WAVED DOWN THE WESTBOUND train at the flagstop by the bunker.

"What will you do this afternoon?" I asked him.

"I'll have the usual post-guest depression," he replied. "You know—here I am again, all alone. So I'll paint."

At lunch he had choked on a piece of carrot. "Eating alone can be just as lethal as World War III," I had said. But his inner eye was firmly fixed on the big weapons.

We said good-bye in a light drizzle and I began my last cross-country ride. This train ran along the north bank of the Skeena to Prince Rupert; from the map it appeared that we hugged the river closely all the way.

After a cool spring, the late run-off had suddenly flooded the river channel. Large trees, ripped away from the banks upstream, were coursing wildly through the whirlpools and boiling rapids. Above the angry torrent, on the south side, mountains rose into the mist.

I sat alone in the bar and watched the rushing brown water and the high, craggy land. For scenery nothing in the country had equalled this ride. I wondered how a man could concentrate so intensely on armageddon when he surrounded himself with all this natural beauty. And perhaps that was the answer: each thing called up its opposite.

An Indian entered the bar and looked at me. He wore a rich magenta cowboy hat over a wrinkled face. I guessed he might be fifty, but I could have been ten years off either way. He sat down.

"I almost didn't make it at Burns Lake," he began. "I jumped over that creek there and I was running like hell. You could see eight feet between the marks my boots made. The train started to move one half-second after I was on. And here I am." He said his name was Frank.

"Why don't you have a beer with me?" he asked suspiciously after the steward had served him two. I said I had been drinking beer all across Canada and didn't want any more. And besides, it was too early in the day for me.

"Who are you?" he asked.

I told him my name again.

"But what are you really?"

I said I was a writer.

"A writer," he echoed with disbelief. Something malevolent was stirring in his eyes.

"You know what I am?"

I said I didn't.

"I'll tell you. I'm a Indian doctor."

We were watching each other carefully.

"It means I kill people." Into his impassive face crept a hint of triumph. "Yeah. I can kill people when I want to. Not just for anything. For revenge. If someone hurts a person in my family, then I can kill them." His eyes darkened. What I had taken for triumph now looked like fear. There was no one else in the bar area. The steward had closed his canteen door. I felt a strong sense of authenticity from this native, and I felt he was on the edge of threatening me.

"That's the type of guy I am. There's about six of us. Indian doctors." He dropped the subject and said he played the guitar and the fiddle in bars. "And I work skidding logs. I have a Hindu girl in Terrace. Very pretty. So pretty you can't hardly look at her. She's mad at me now." He looked at me suspiciously again.

"I don't trust you," he said. "I see something in your eyes."

"What is it you see?"

"I'll tell you. I see someone else. You're not who you say you are."

I thought: maybe so. Is anyone the man he thinks he is? Perhaps the Indian was making an astute existential observation. But then he blurted out anxiously:

"You're a cop, aren't you?"

I spent a few minutes trying to convince him I was not a Mountie. The steward came out, sold the Indian another two beers, and me one. He seemed a little mollified to see me with a drink in my hand. He raised his glass.

"It don't matter," he said. "You know what I do when I need help? I call to my four grandfathers." The rain had lifted. Here and there the clouds broke and the mountains received washes of sunlight. "You know what are flashbacks? When you see it happen again, something you did, but it happens to someone else. Like if you hurt my family, then something comes back on your wife or your niece." He paused. "Do you know what I am now?"

I said I knew.

"The four grandfathers can make things appear and disappear. They're more powerful than anything. In each direction lives one grandfather. The four corners of Mother Earth."

As we approached Terrace, he said, "You're looking

at someone who's been in the B.C. penitentiary. Fifteen years. I could have been a world champion at rodeo. And I didn't do that murder.''

The conductor leaned into the bar and announced our arrival at Terrace. The Indian stood, put on his magenta hat, and shook my hand.

Prince Rupert

ON THE FINAL STRETCH WE PASSED SHOWERS OF WATER plummeting down from the mountains. "Depending on the time of year," my guidebook said, "you may see 65 waterfalls in this area." I sat by a woman who was going to visit her son, the lighthouse keeper on Lucy Island.

"They have no television, no papers, and very poor radio. They're living in a fool's paradise. But I love to watch the birds and the sea otters when I'm there. Last year I saw a pod of whales."

It was raining again as we pulled into the station. "Three steps and you're in the sea," a man on the train had said, describing Prince Rupert. The tracks came in along the shoreline. Perched on the bluffs above was the town.

I walked up the steep road and checked into a motel with rooms overlooking the sea. While I was changing my clothes the rain stopped abruptly. A still light fixed the sky over the harbour as if a cosmic stagehand had pulled the levers to set a new scene. In this strange hallucinatory light I walked down to the fishing wharfs where I had been told I would find Smile's Cafe, the best fish restaurant in British Columbia. It was closing time, but the waitress agreed to serve me if I would not stay long. Most of the booths were still full—people were eating dessert. An Indian woman I had seen on the train motioned for me to sit down.

"I'm leaving in a minute," she said. "You can have the table." Her name was Sharon. She was a Beaver Indian from Hay River north of Edmonton.

"I know someone here," she explained. "I came to visit him, but he won't be back till tomorrow." Her brown eyes flashed. She had a beautiful angular face.

We made small talk about the long train ride from Edmonton, the wet weather, her young son squirming beside her. I ordered some fish and we sat in silence for a moment.

"Did you ever smell mothballs," she asked suddenly.

I thought about it for a moment. "Yes. Why?"

"How did you manage to pull apart their tiny legs?"

The light was falling as I left Smile's and walked down to the wharf. Fishing boats, some of them with their owners living on board, bobbed alongside the wooden platform. Behind me was the restaurant, built on stilts at the water's edge. A fisherman spoke to me from the deck of his boat.

"Rupert's the only place in Canada where it also rains horizontally." On the boats the men were white. Back up in the twilight streets of the town most of the faces were native.

I remembered a piece from the *Interior News*, the Smithers newspaper someone had left on the train. It was about the Prince Rupert poet, Andrew Wreggit, a writer I had not read. The poet-critic Phyllis Webb had been quoted. "Wreggit shows what it's like to be young in a marginal economy in a marginal culture. . . . Each poem is a drop of blood."

I called the Wreggit listed in the telephone directory. We met the next day over a beer. He was making a living writing scripts for CBC television's popular *Beachcomber* series; and he was working on more poems. Quite a few young people from southern B.C. came up to Prince Rupert, he said. You could be hired here without the work experience you might need in Victoria or Vancouver. He invited me to join his group at the Legion, where they would be playing their weekly darts game late in the afternoon.

On the outside the Legion hall looked as dreary as they do all across Canada, bunker-like bars for old soldiers. But this place overlooked the water and was illuminated by the theatre of changing light on Prince Rupert's waterscape. We sat at a long table, mostly people in their late twenties, drinking beer and taking turns throwing darts at a board.

"There's not a lot to do in Rupert other than darts and softball," the large, sleepy fellow beside me said. "Unless you have money for a boat."

Later that night I read the poet's two little books. They were full of delicately crafted, sad poems. One about the building of an unneeded bridge across a canyon to an Indian village had particular resonance for me. The poem spoke of the ineluctable and unending white incursions into the culture and consciousness of the natives. An engineer is sent to make preparations. He

> does not know why he is there,
> only the bridge in his mind is clear
>
> . . .
>
> He has come because he is the government
> The wires of his thought swing over the current,
> anchor one at a time
> on the other side.

The same kind of mental spanning had, not so long ago, projected rails across Canada and created towns like Prince Rupert. There had been ambitious dreams for this place when the Grand Trunk Pacific opened it transcontinental line in 1914. Prince Rupert was to have been a major Pacific port, like San Francisco, Seattle, and Vancouver. Land prices soared at the first auction of town lots. But the anticipated city did not materialize. Central British Columbia and central Alberta never produced enough shipable commodities to create a second large ocean terminus on the west coast, and Vancouver had the advantage of being closer to Winnipeg. Canada continued to hug its southern border despite the northward push of railway builders, who had imagined the country thickly girded with another population belt at the latitude where only one city, Edmonton, found a way to grow.

The train left Prince Rupert three times a week. I would begin my long ride back east late in the afternoon. Wandering through the hillside town, hewn out of solid rock on Kaien Island, I thought of the great city some people had wanted to see built here. Where would they have put it? The settlement of 14,000 already had its back up against a steep, hard slope; it was a pleasant seaside town, supported by some canneries, a fishing fleet, and the small port. It symbolized the hopes of the railway pioneers, without whose visions these frontier communities would not have been created, but it also symbolized the demise of their dreams. Prince Rupert's destiny was to be a town on the margin of populated Canada, not a Pacific metropolis.

Looking down the hill at the little passenger train waiting in the station, I wondered how many years would pass before it would run only once or twice a week, and then perhaps not at all. In the past twenty years trains had been removed from the schedule in every part of Canada, branch lines ripped up, stations closed and demolished. The remaining passenger routes were probably running out of time.

I had boarded thirty-one trains and followed their thin grey lines across the map looking at the country I called home. There was more to it than I had seen, but what I had seen told me that the Canada I had grown up believing in no longer existed. Now we were deliberating on how to mature beyond our over-confident adolescence, characterized by one prime minister's maxim that the twentieth century belonged to us. So much of our history had been defined by the pioneer values of land development and natural resource extraction, discovery rather than invention, that we were in some ways ill-equipped to face our new age. But Canada remained an experiment, less bound by irrevocable legacies than older societies. We were searching, economically and culturally, for more realistic possibilities than the ones envisaged seventy-five, or even twenty-five, years ago. In older countries the future was inherited, largely predetermined by the past. Here, if we had the will, we could still choose what we would become.

About the Author

Born in Winnipeg, George Galt was raised and educated in Montreal and has lived in France and Greece. A journalist and literary critic, he has been an associate editor at *Saturday Night* magazine in Toronto since 1988.